Distant Love

Distant Love

Personal Life in the Global Age

Ulrich Beck and Elisabeth Beck-Gernsheim

Translated by
Rodney Livingstone

polity

First published in German as *Fernliebe* © Suhrkamp Verlag Berlin 2011

This English edition © Polity Press, 2014

The translation of this work was supported by a grant from the Goethe-Institut which is funded by the German Ministry of Foreign Affairs

Polity Press
65 Bridge Street
Cambridge CB2 1UR, UK

Polity Press
350 Main Street
Malden, MA 02148, USA

All rights reserved. Except for the quotation of short passages for the purpose of criticism and review, no part of this publication may be reproduced, stored in a retrieval system, or transmitted, in any form or by any means, electronic, mechanical, photocopying, recording or otherwise, without the prior permission of the publisher.

ISBN-13: 978-0-7456-6180-3
ISBN-13: 978-0-7456-6181-0 (pb)

A catalogue record for this book is available from the British Library.

Typeset in 10.5 on 12 pt Sabon
by Toppan Best-set Premedia Limited
Printed and bound in Great Britain by Berforts Information Press

The publisher has used its best endeavours to ensure that the URLs for external websites referred to in this book are correct and active at the time of going to press. However, the publisher has no responsibility for the websites and can make no guarantee that a site will remain live or that the content is or will remain appropriate.

Every effort has been made to trace all copyright holders, but if any have been inadvertently overlooked the publisher will be pleased to include any necessary credits in any subsequent reprint or edition.

For further information on Polity, visit our website: www.politybooks.com

Contents

Translator's Note

Translating this book has been a pleasure, partly because of the liveliness and the absorbing interest of the text (some of which at least I hope I have been able to convey) and partly because of the assistance I have received from Ulrich Beck and Elisabeth Beck-Gernsheim, who have been extremely helpful in answering my queries, and, in Elisabeth's case, making suggestions for translating some of the terminology. One of the difficulties in translating a book of this kind has been locating the large number of quotations from English-language sources. Albert Gröber has been indefatigable in tracking these down, and I am extremely grateful to him for coming to my aid so promptly. As always, my wife Krystyna read the translation right through twice and made countless suggestions and improvements.

Rodney Livingstone
Southampton, February 2013

Introduction

In May 2011 the newspapers reported that the boxer Vladimir Klitschko (thirty-five, 6 foot 5 and weighing 242 lbs), originally from Ukraine and now living in Hamburg, had separated from the actress Hayden Panettiere (twenty-one, 5 foot 1 and weighing 110 lbs), who was living in Los Angeles. A newspaper quoted the actress as saying that the reason for the break-up had nothing to do with differences of age or height. 'It really is very, very hard to manage a relationship between two continents.' In an article in the same paper entitled 'Thumbs Down', Ingolf Gillmann criticized the actress for giving her long-distance relationship as the cause of the break-up. 'Dear friends, if you think a long-distance relationship is hard, how are you going to cope with the daily infighting of a close relationship over a period of years?'

A few days before that, a news item in the business section of the major newspapers throughout the world announced that Microsoft had bought Skype, the internet phone provider, for $8.5 billion. 'Microsoft intends to integrate Skype into its existing products . . . With Skype users can make voice calls and video calls to each other via the internet free of charge . . . The service claims to have over 660 million registered users', according to the *Frankfurter Allgemeine Zeitung* of 10 May 2011.

Thus Microsoft appears to believe in the future of love at a distance – at all events this purchase is the most expensive in its entire history. Love at a distance in all its forms is also the subject of this book. In *The Normal Chaos of Love* we showed how individualism, aided by a romanticizing idea of absolute love, has undermined the

traditional forms of living together. The classic family, consisting of
a man, a woman and one or more children, has begun to give way
to a multiplicity of new types of family. Increasingly, the husband is
replaced by the partner of the moment, single mothers and fathers
have become more common, and patchwork families – i.e., new kinds
of extended family – have emerged as the consequence of successive
marriages and divorces. In our new book we open up the horizon to
the *global chaos* of love, with every conceivable kind of relationship
at a distance: mixed-nationality couples, people who migrate for
work or marriage, women who rent out their wombs, and the utterly
normal tragedies of Skype-mediated love relationships.

What we have set out to do is to provide an analysis of the present
state of what we call 'world families', by which we mean love relationships and other forms of relationship between people living in,
or coming from, different countries or continents. Such relationships
may assume many forms and may arise from many different motives.
However, world families in all their varieties share one feature in
common: they are the focal point at which the different aspects of
the globalized world literally become embodied. Global society simultaneously generates contradictory features in world families: unrest,
confusion, surprise, pleasure, joy, breakdowns and hatred. We inhabit
a world in which our loved ones are often far away and those from
whom we are distant may well be those dearest to us.

The crucial point is that world families differ from the normal
single-nation family, which has been the dominant form for so long,
especially in Europe, and which has consisted of people speaking the
same language, having the same nationality, and living in the same
country and in the same locality. But they are also distinct from and
represent something more than the multicultural families that have
become an integral feature of the landscape in such immigration-
friendly parts of the world as the United States and Latin America.
World families form new kinds of combination; they come from near
and far, from equal and unequal societies, and span whole countries
and continents. Whether lovers or relatives in such families like it or
not, they find themselves confronting the world in the interior space
of their own lives. Thus the conflicts between the developed and
developing worlds come to the surface in world families; they acquire
faces and names. Here we find the meeting point of different languages, different pasts and different political and legal systems.

But when we speak of world *families* do we not simply adopt a
concept that has long since been rendered obsolete by the variety of
forms of love and life in Western countries – same-sex couples, single
parents, patchwork families, companions for the current stage of life's

journey and couples living together in separate houses? The Western observer could be forgiven for thinking so. But in non-Western cultures the concept of the 'family' continues to be of central importance. This means that, in what we term 'world families', opposing conceptions of 'family' collide with one another. We find here the flashpoint of religious wars that strike at the very heart of everyday life: these wars turn on the question of what a family is and who belongs to it, the nature of family and what it should be. In short, they strike at the heart of what constitutes a 'good family'.

All universalist social theories of love overlook these religious wars when they speak about the nature of 'intimacy' in 'modern life' in general, as did Anthony Giddens (1992), Eva Illouz (2012) and Niklas Luhmann (1986), and we too were guilty of this in *The Normal Chaos of Love* (1995). They all ignore the fact that what they regard as the universalism of modern love with its various paradoxes of freedom is only one of many possible developments, namely the version that has emerged in the historical, cultural, political and legal context of the West. These religious wars about what constitutes a 'proper family' fundamentally put in question all the unfulfilled promises about making freedom, equality and love compatible with one another.

Moreover, the universalist approach tends to be confined to a narrow range of experience: love between a man and a woman, between one woman and another, between two men – and perhaps also a child. In this book, by contrast, we take a broader view and examine subjects excluded from a national and universalist framework – love that transcends geographical, cultural and political frontiers, marriage-related migration, motherly love at a distance and baby tourism, as well as global patchwork families. In short, we focus on the globalization of love.

It is currently not possible to predict the future development of these chaotic relationships in the age of globalization. This does not mean that we include ourselves in the ranks of the pessimists of distant love, who maintain that we are faced with the prospect of the end of love, and who believe that its numerous shortcomings cannot be made good in principle. We prefer to ask the following question: Could it be that the very things that threaten the world at large will nevertheless register occasional successes in the new forms of love and the family and that we shall master the art of living together by transcending the borders that divide us?

1

Globalization of Love and Intimacy: The Rise of World Families

Art, literature, autobiographical novels and stories have given promi-
nence to a new theme: colourful relationships involving love and
families extending over countries and continents. These new realities
are so widespread and full of surprises that they provide endless
material for novelists and the producers of documentaries. There is
a growing avalanche of books featuring such issues, exploring them
in comic, tragic, ironic or sometimes even shrill tones. They are
stories of love, marriage and parenthood across frontiers and cultural
boundaries; stories about successful or failing relationships; stories
showing how global conflicts come to the surface in the intimacy of
family life. Here are three telling examples.

1   Comedies and Tragedies of Distant Love

Marina Lewycka's novel *A Short History of Tractors in Ukrainian*
deals with tractors only peripherally; it is concerned more fundamentally with an explosion. This explosion is female and enters
Great Britain from Ukraine on a tourist visa with the single-minded
determination to achieve marriage and acquire wealth and a residence permit. 'Two years after my mother died, my father fell in
love with a glamorous blonde Ukrainian divorcée. He was eighty-
four and she was thirty-six. She exploded into our lives like a fluffy
pink grenade, churning up the murky water . . . giving the family
ghosts a kick up the backside' (Lewycka 2005: 1). By dint of her
energetic approach, her tender promises and the assiduous

deployment of her feminine charms, this blonde from Eastern Europe achieves her goal of a 'family passport' – i.e., marriage as the entrance ticket to the well-guarded prosperity club of the Western world.

> She wants to make a new life for herself and her son in the West, a good life, with good job, good money, nice car – absolutely no Lada, no Skoda – good education for her son – must be Oxford Cambridge, nothing less. She is an educated woman, by the way. Has a diploma in pharmacy. She will easily find well-paid work here, once she learns English. In the meantime, he is helping her with her English, and she is cleaning the house and looking after him. She sits on his lap and allows him to fondle her breasts. (Ibid., 2–3)

Betty Mahmoody's book *Not Without My Daughter* (1987) is an autobiographical account based on Mahmoody's experiences when she found herself caught up between Iran and the United States, Islam and the West. The author, an American woman, marries a doctor who has come to the United States from Iran. He decides to return to his native country and tricks his wife and daughter into returning with him, only to detain them there by force. Betty Mahmoody complies on the surface but secretly plans her escape together with her daughter – an enterprise that finally succeeds after eighteen agonizing months and many highly dramatic scenes. The book is a tragedy in which love turns to hatred, with husband and wife at loggerheads and a plot characterized by violence and sacrifice, oppression versus resistance and freedom versus incarceration. It ends happily, however, with mother and daughter escaping from the clutches of sinister forces and returning to their home in America. Mahmoody's tale of women and suffering is a story of the death of a love caught between two worlds from the single perspective of a Western woman, with all her observations, hopes and disillusionments.

Jan Weiler's *Maria, ihm schmeckt's nicht* [Maria, he doesn't like it] (2003) describes scenes from the life of a German-Italian family in a series of anecdotes. The author, whose own life has such a background, regales his public with the comic scenes that can be found in the everyday life of such families from Central Europe. In this instance, the bridegroom comes from mainstream German society – more specifically, the upper middle class – while the bride's father is a guest worker who originally came to Germany from the impoverished Italian south. Once again, the episodes narrated by the author afford us an insight into the contrasting nature of different worlds, though here it takes a comic form. German thoroughness, precision and pedantry clash with Italian temperament, mastery of the art of improvisation and joie de vivre, a clash that provides plenty of surprises, both amusing and less amusing, and possesses a certain rough-and-ready but also warm-hearted charm. In the end, the general message is positive: love is more powerful than the clash of cultures; it builds bridges over chasms.

Different though these three books are from one another, they nevertheless form part of a common narrative. They provide snapshots showing how the world society makes its entry into normal families, how it causes disruption, confusion, surprise, pleasure, joy, break-ups and hatred, and how the storms, crises and thrills of the world become integral components of the lives of ordinary families.

All three books featured prominently on the bestseller lists. They sold millions of copies and were translated into many languages. There are doubtless many reasons for this unexpected success. One is the fact that to some extent they all have biographical foundations, translated into a direct narrative style that connects immediately with readers and grips their attention. Added to that is a potent combination of the erotic and the exotic, and the entire confection is further enhanced by the admixture of comic or threatening scenes. Moreover, subjects of this kind reflect many readers' own experiences, and they can identify with the ups and downs, the pleasures and pains of similar events: my brother-in-law has taken a wife from Thailand; we have just engaged a Polish woman to look after Grandpa; our goddaughter has recently become involved with a theologian from Togo. Where actually is Togo? Does he truly love her or is he just exploiting her in order to gain entry to the developed world?

Connections and questions of this sort are looming ever larger in the everyday experience of the families of the host society. It is through such channels that the economic crises and financial markets of Asia find their way into our own living rooms, alongside the civil wars and political upheavals of Africa and the ideological conflicts and the economic ups and downs of Latin America. The woman from Thailand and the man from Togo are sitting on our sofa; they are present at our birthday celebrations, play football with our son and help to feed Grandpa. Everyone has a daughter-in-law, a son-in-law, a sister, a brother, a male or female cousin, nephews and nieces, grandchildren, etc., who speak our language with a foreign accent, who look different from us and whose names sound strange and almost unpronounceable. Many people may feel relieved to read about scenes that might well come from their own lives and that are made unfamiliar as well as brought sharply into focus by the fictional or dramatic treatment they are given. Confusing events are rendered a little more comprehensible when they are shown to be the experience of many other people. We begin to appreciate that they too have difficulty in coming to terms with the new reality of the family; they too find it tricky dealing with the embarrassing situations and faux pas arising from these encounters between the familiar and the unfamiliar. The popular success of the books referred to above may also be due to the fact that they supply a larger context to the irritations associated with these novel 'diasporic' family networks. They show how one person's fate resembles that of others; they provide orientation and comfort, as well as practical help in the upheavals of the world society that have intruded into the realm of private experience.

The present book, too, is concerned with the turbulences produced by the encounter between proximity and distance. We propose the concept 'world families' as the starting point from which to examine the new realities of the family. Our chief questions are these. How can we describe and systematize developments that have long since become daily experience? How has it come about that love and families have become the point of intersection for global events? What happens when national frontiers and international legal systems, immigration laws and the boundary lines between host societies and minorities, between the developed and the developing world, pass directly through the family? What are the implications for love and intimacy if love becomes love at a distance, long-distance love separated by entire countries and continents?

To ask such questions is to enter *terra incognita*, unexplored territory. There are of course countless studies documenting changes in the family (from unmarried couples living together to the decline in the birth rate). And there are also studies of globalized families both in family research and, above all, in migration research and anthropology. But the crucial difference is that they always confine themselves to one aspect of the realities of the globalized family (mixed-nationality couples or cross-border adoption or long-distance relationships). In contrast, our aim is to examine such phenomena in context. It is for this reason that we have decided on the all-encompassing term 'world families' in order to inquire what it is that ultimately holds together these different forms. We explore their various meanings and commonalities, as well as their differences and incompatibilities. All this is achieved by means of a 'diagnostic theory'.[1]

To anticipate our findings: world families are families in which world conflicts are fought out. Not all families are involved in all conflicts, but all of them are involved in a portion of them. Mixed-nationality couples experience the *tensions* that exist between two countries or between a host society and a minority group. Immigrant families experience the tensions between the developed and the developing world, the global inequalities together with their colonial history, whose after-effects persist in the minds of those living to this day, producing a reluctance to face the truth in some people and rage and despair in others.

We need to forestall a possible misunderstanding. The term 'world families' must not be confused with 'citizens of the world'. The latter expression refers to the caste of the educated upper-middle class, with

[1]We propose a distinction between explanatory and diagnostic theory in times of discontinuous social change. Some writers understand theory as an explanation of observable phenomena that can be perceived as the expression of general, universal 'laws' of social action and social life. They seek answers to the question 'Why?'. This conception of theory goes back to the practice of the 'hard' natural sciences, but it is not the dominant form of explanation. Contributions to social theory as this is widely understood internationally today follow a different pattern. Confronted by the chaos of social events and by phenomena that threaten to overwhelm us, they seek to establish a conceptual framework whereby we can orientate ourselves with the aid of a generalized diagnosis of rapidly changing social conditions. It is precisely for this purpose that we have introduced the term 'world families' in the present book. We are concerned not with a 'diagnosis of the age' in the language of everyday speech, but with generalized, sociological descriptions that are indispensable for a specialized, precise vocabulary – 'multilocal world families', 'multinational world families', 'distant love', 'migrants in search of marriage', 'surrogate mothers', etc. (see pp. 15ff., 65f.; chapter 10) We call this approach 'diagnostic theory'. This historical, inductive form of theory is especially relevant in times of rapid fundamental change in which not just ordinary people but even sociologists are confronted by the enigmas of a newly emergent social reality and find themselves asking where we are, where we come from and where we are headed. These are times in which the question 'Do we still understand the world we are living in?' has assumed greater urgency, both for sociologists and for ordinary people, than the question 'Why is what is happening, happening?'

But the connection between these two questions must be formulated more precisely. In times of discontinuous social change, explanatory theories presuppose diagnostic theories. Only when we have succeeded in describing and understanding the 'inner globalization' of intimacy, love, the family, relations between the sexes, housework, birth, maternity, paternity, etc., within a fully conceptualized theory will we be able once more to raise the question 'Why?'. Only then will it become possible to establish a better modus vivendi with the new discontinuities in the world and the contradictions they engender in people's everyday experience of love and the family.

its knowledge of Chinese literature, French cuisine and African art. In contrast, many of the people who belong to world families in our sense are neither knowledgeable nor open-minded about the world, neither at home on the international stage nor able to speak foreign languages. The breath of the great, wide world has utterly passed them by. Many have never previously left their home village or small town; many are provincial in their outlook and are wary of everything foreign. Some have become members of a world family only as the consequence of violence, civil war or expulsion, or in the hope of escaping from poverty and unemployment at home. Yet others have achieved the same result through dating advertisements on the internet or the accidents of love. In short, external events or actual coercion, rather than enthusiasm or an act of free will, have led many to become part of a global family more or less involuntarily. But, whether voluntarily or not, the different kinds of world family share one common feature: they act as an irritant. They do not fit our preconceived notions of what constitutes a family and is part of its essential nature, everywhere and always. They place a question mark over some of our familiar, supposedly self-evident assumptions about the family.

2   The Landscape of World Families

A change of perspective will give us something of a panoramic view of the range of world families. Following examples taken from literature, we can look at instances taken from reality, a description of the forms of the family as we find them in the social reality of the twenty-first century.

Global Care Chains

Worldwide differences of income make it possible for affluent families to employ home helps, nannies and carers from poorer countries. These poorer countries include the Philippines, a country that could barely survive without the remittances migrants send home to their families. For this reason, emigrating for work receives state support. In the port of Manila, the Philippine capital, for example, women receive training for jobs as servants in global capitalism. Among such women are qualified teachers, bookkeepers and veterinarians. They know how to teach mathematics, produce a balance sheet or cure a sick cow. Now they learn how beds are made in wealthy capitalist countries, in an American hotel, for example, or an Italian household. They learn how a dishwasher works and about the toys with which Canadian or German children pass their time. At the end of six months they will have become 'qualified housekeepers', climb into a plane and hire themselves out in rich industrial nations.

Behind the closed doors of private houses and the family which are supposed to shield people from the turmoil of the world, the separate universes of the global poor and the upwardly mobile middle classes of the world are commingled. Teachers from the Philippines, students from Mexico, translators from Ecuador and lawyers from Ghana make their way to countries where nowadays women are to be found at the head of businesses, universities and political parties. However, the goal of such women migrants is to undertake work that has been regarded as women's work for centuries: they clean, cook, and look after children and the frail elderly members of foreign families.

By now, women, who commonly are in the minority in the job market the world over, amount to over half the total number of migrants. They represent the 'female face of globalization' (Hochschild 2000). Nowhere can this be seen more clearly than in the Philippines, a country that exports workers as other countries export coffee or cocoa, a country where thirty years ago women formed 12 per cent of emigrants, while today they are 70 per cent.

This has now become a worldwide pattern characteristic of our age: the greater the success women enjoy in the world of work, the more help they need in the home. This help is no longer provided, as in earlier ages, by slaves or servants but by the (shadow) global economy for cheap labour in a radically unequal world.

This creates a growing interweaving of destinies and situations that ignores frontiers and covers entire continents. The wives of the successful middle class, ground down by the persistent demands of their career and family, urgently seek relief, so that they inevitably have recourse to the services of the 'female global others'. Women on the other side of the world are in urgent need of money with which to feed their families. And a well-qualified Filipina teacher working here as a global nanny earns several times what she might expect from regular work as a teacher in the Philippines – if she could indeed find a job.

One consequence is that love and care become 'commodities', exported, imported and delegated to others by indigenous women. We may say then that globalized work in the family constitutes the 'gold of the poor', a further 'resource' that can be exploited by the rich. The poor also benefit financially from these transactions, though admittedly they earn only a fraction of what the 'local', 'normal' workers would receive. Nevertheless, the great wide world is alluring, an imagined consumer paradise (Ehrenreich and Hochschild 2003; Hochschild 2003).

Global Inequality Becomes Personal

Debates about immigration are premised for the most part on a clear line of demarcation between legal inhabitants and illegal immigrants, between those who are officially registered and visible and those who live in the shadows. People who think in the categories of the law make a clear distinction between legal and illegal. Many transnational families are a mixture of legal citizens and their illegal relatives whose lives are determined above all by the fear of discovery. One example is the Palacio family. Estrellita's mother is heavily pregnant. She has crossed the Mexican frontier in order to secure for her daughter the privilege of a birth in the United States and hence of American nationality. Estrellita's mother's brother-in-law is what the Americans call an 'undocumented worker'. The tightening of the laws on immigration in the United States has driven a wedge between members of the family. While Estrellita's status becomes more privileged, her mother's brother-in-law's fear of discovery intensifies. Among the seven siblings of the Palacio family, their marriage partners and their children, we find American citizens by birth, naturalized immigrants, people with limited rights of residence and undocumented immigrants.

Even this brief portrait affords us a glimpse of a 'melting-pot family' of a new kind. It is not merely multinational (and perhaps multi-religious); it is also 'multi-(il)legal'.

The Brave New World of Globalized Pregnancy and Birth

A married couple from Germany waited two years for the arrival of their twins, who had been born to an Indian surrogate mother. The German authorities refused to issue passports to the children, who had been born in India, because surrogacy is forbidden under German law. The authorities in India – where surrogate motherhood is permitted – treated the children as German because the parents were German nationals. Accordingly, they refused to issue Indian travel documents for the twins. Their father, an art historian, fought a desperate battle in both the German and the Indian courts to be allowed to bring his stateless children to Germany. He was finally successful. The Indian authorities issued passports after all, and the twins were then given

visas with which to enter Germany ('exceptionally' and 'for humanitarian reasons', according to the German Foreign Office). The parents
could now adopt their 'own children' in Germany by way of an
international legal process.

Here we see that families are not simply condemned to being
steamrollered by globalization. They have long since become agents.
With the aid of the new options made available by reproductive
medicine, birth and parenthood can be separated and 'offshored', like
jobs. The scope for action created by medical technology makes it
possible to separate conception, pregnancy and parenthood and to
reorganize them across national frontiers. What used to be called
simply 'motherhood' can now be broken down into such categories
as 'egg donor', 'surrogate mother' and 'carer'. The attempt to combine
these different forms of motherhood into a coherent legal form frequently turns into an obstacle race between the different and even
conflicting provisions of national jurisdictions.

Grandparental Love at Distance

Alex has just turned three; he is full of curiosity and energy. He
loves muesli and chips and, even more, he loves his cars. He was
given a new one yesterday, a big red bus, and this morning he was
in a hurry to show it to his grandparents. They love their grandson
more than anything in the world. They see him every day. Every day
there is a quarter of an hour, and sometimes even half an hour, of
'Grandma and Grandpa time', a fixed ritual which is staunchly maintained and respected. It is time reserved exclusively for Alex and his
grandparents.

A perfectly normal happy family? Yes and no. Those involved live
hundreds of miles apart, the grandparents in Thessaloniki and Alex
in Cambridge, England. Skyping brings Grandma and Grandpa into
the nursery and transports Alex to Thessaloniki, while all of them
remain where they are – love at a great distance as love of one's
nearest and dearest, defying all distances and frontiers.

3   World Families Turn Established Notions
Upside Down

The pages of an atlas, with its black demarcation lines separating the
differently coloured countries, are still symbolic of the mental and
geographical maps that most people carry around in their heads and

that provide them with their picture of the world. The globe divides up into separate nation-states, and this encourages the expectation that every human being belongs in one place and one place alone for a specific period of time. This implies an unambiguous correlation between a person's identity and a specific location, and anything that deviates from this encounters mistrust and resistance.

It is true that everywhere in the world the majority of families live their lives in accordance with this homogeneous model of the family domiciled in the country to which it belongs by right – mother, father and school-age children dwell in one and the same household and locality, have one and the same citizenship and one and the same national origin, and speak one and the same mother tongue. This is a combination that common sense regards as both necessary and natural. But our present-day experience fits this model less and less well. More and more women, men and families have broken with what seemed hitherto to be a law of nature and live – partly by choice, partly by force of circumstances – in families that include strangers and distances.

Thus the point of entry for an assessment of the new landscapes of love and the family involves the following insight. We have to recognize that, for more and more people, three existential bonds that had always belonged together in the past – the bonds of place, country and family – have now begun to float free of one another and become separate elements. The belief that by their very nature families belong to a particular territory is overwhelmed by an active process of globalization both from below and from within. Just as there are transnational firms and transnational states (such as the EU), so too we are now witnessing the birth of transnational families. And this gives rise to a new set of questions. Do world families constitute a counterweight to global capitalism, opposing it by means of cross-frontier networks of mutual assistance? Do families have a future as a lived global politics? How can the disagreements that separate nations from one another be bridged, silenced, exposed, resolved, endured and perhaps even transformed into an opportunity to liberate people from the narrow-mindedness of national origin?

When people spoke of family in the past, what they chiefly meant was the innermost core of the family – i.e., father, mother and child – and this was always associated with the more or less explicit expectation of spatial closeness and living together. This rule did not preclude temporary periods of separation and, as with other rules, there were exceptions (seafaring families, for example). Fundamentally, however, it remained true that a family involved a direct face-to-face relationship, which implied physical presence. A mere glance at history and the history of concepts suffices to demonstrate the truth of this.

For all the changes that the concept has undergone over the centuries, one characteristic remained, and that was the link to a particular place. Originally, indeed, the link to a particular place was the defining attribute of a family. In ancient Rome the word *familia* did not refer primarily to people who were related by marriage or descent. It included all those who formed part of a man's property and who belonged to his household in the wider sense: wife, children, slaves, manumitted slaves and livestock. Only gradually, with the onset of modernity, did a narrower conception of family come to prevail, one that ultimately referred exclusively to 'persons related to one another and living under the same roof' (Mitterauer and Sieder 1980: 19f.). And, despite all the changes in society to have emerged in the course of recent decades, a common location continues to be crucial. According to a widely held definition, still influential to this day, the standard North American family consists of a heterosexual husband, a heterosexual wife and their biological children, all living together under one roof. Moreover, the husband is generally the primary breadwinner (Harris 2008: 1408). Every pillar of this definition of the normal family has been undermined by actual developments: the heterosexuality of the married couple, biological parenthood, to say nothing of the male breadwinner. But the essential feature – that families have to live together under one roof, this premise of a single location, a face-to-face relationship and direct interaction – has never been seriously questioned.

The roof metaphor includes nationality. In all the talk about 'love', 'marriage' and 'the' family, it is generally held to be self-evident that the people connected in this way belong to the same nation, speak the same mother tongue, possess the same citizenship and enjoy the same civil rights.

But what if the shared household or the shared roof has ceased to exist, and what if there are no times or only rare occasions of shared togetherness? Can we then still speak of family, or does it mean that the family no longer exists – or even that there is a family of a new kind? What if there is no longer any such thing as a shared household but only several households spread over several countries? What if the family now includes people of different nationalities who originate from different continents? But if a roof, a locality, a household and a nationality can no longer be numbered among the basic premises of a family, can we still speak of family at all? How are we to live the paradox of a 'global intimacy'?

4　Towards a Definition of 'World Families'

Up to now we have spoken of 'world families' (or 'families at a distance', or 'global families') and differentiated them from 'one-nation families' (or 'close-knit families', or 'local families'). But what are 'world families' actually? How can they be defined? How can we place them in the centre of a new diagnostic theory and of an empirical study capable of inquiring into the globalized landscapes of intimacy, love, parenthood and divorce, etc.?

World families are families that live together across (national, religious, cultural or ethnic, etc.) frontiers. They are families that stick together even though they consist of elements that conventionally do *not* belong together. The glue provided by pre-existing traditions is replaced by *active trust*. Such families show that they can succeed even though received wisdom says they are doomed to failure; the 'alien other' becomes the nearest and dearest.

Two basic types may be distinguished. By love at a distance and world families we understand, in the first instance, couples or families that remain together despite living in different countries or continents. They are 'multi-local world families', sharing the same culture of origin (language, nationality or religion). An example would be the married woman with children who emigrates from the Philippines to take up domestic work in Los Angeles in order to support her family back home (see chapter 6). By love at a distance and world families we understand, second, couples or families who live in the same place but whose members come from different countries or continents and whose conception of love and the family is essentially determined by their country of origin. To illustrate this we might think of a family in which the husband is American and the wife Chinese and who are living with their children in London (multinational or multi-continental world families). What do these two types of world family have in common? They are the site at which the differences in the globalized world literally become embodied. Whether the lovers or the family members like it or not, they find themselves confronted by the world at the heart of their own lives.[2]

---

[2]To explain some of the dimensions of the world in world families, we could point to the global other as part of our lives; to cross-border communication; to global inequalities acquiring names and faces; to people caught up between different national legal systems; to the religious war in search of 'the good family' – see chapter 10; on the current debate in the social sciences about love and intimacy in modernity, see our distinction between nation-based, universalist and cosmopolitan approaches on pp. 65f., as well as our Introduction.

This definition is straightforward and immediately comprehensible, but on closer inspection it turns out to have one defect: it does not go far enough. It is unable to grasp world families in all their diversity. We can readily think of instances that do not fit our definition or do so only at a stretch. To take but one example, how are we supposed to think of the second or third generations of immigrants from other countries or continents once they have established families with partners from the host society?

Our beautifully straightforward definition has evidently reached its limits here. We therefore propose the following addition: whether such families can be numbered among the 'world families' depends on whether *'lasting existential relationships with the "other" culture of origin'* are actively being maintained *'across national frontiers or continents'*. This would be the situation where grandparents in Istanbul see their grandchildren in Ulm every day – via Skype – and tell each other stories. Where there is a close, regular, emotionally important link between the cultures, it appears meaningful to speak of world families.

And where will Susan and Liz fit in, two sisters from an Anglo-Pakistani family? Their father, a Pakistani, returned to his homeland shortly after the birth of the younger daughter and has since disappeared. The two girls were born in Lancaster and live there with their mother; they have never been to Pakistan and have no contact with their father's family. But whereas Susan, with her light hair and freckles, takes after her mother in looks, Liz strongly resembles her father, has a darker skin and black hair. She is constantly being asked where she comes from as well as being abused as a 'Paki'. The two girls live in the same place, Lancaster, speak the local dialect, go to the same church – they both belong to the Church of England – and do not know anyone in distant Pakistan. And yet there is a crucial difference between the two girls. Susan, who can hardly be distinguished from other girls in the majority population, seldom thinks about the Pakistani side of her family. Liz, on the other hand, is constantly reminded of it, feels like an outsider and as if she were not fully accepted. In the light of this brief biographical information, we would say that Susan belongs in the main to a close-knit family (a one-nation family, local family). Liz, on the other hand, is tied to the same country against her will because the majority population turn her into a 'Pakistani'. Thanks to the accidents of biology or genetics, combined with the stereotypes and prejudices of the society she lives in, she has in a sense become part of a world family.

Such examples make it clear that our beautiful, straightforward definition may indeed capture some essential features of the architecture of world families. But in many instances it does not suffice for a confident attribution. Reality is far more varied, richer and more perplexing than is suggested by such box-ticking expressions as 'geographically separate' or 'common culture of origin'.

Furthermore, on closer inspection it becomes evident that world family and one-nation family are not absolute antitheses but the two ends of a continuum that contains many intermediate, subsidiary and mixed forms. This blurred picture is not the product of an imprecise analysis; it is rather an essential feature of reality.

Looked at in sociological terms, world family and one-nation family are ideal types. The kinds of family we encounter in the real world, however, are frequently not so clear-cut and cannot always be assigned to one category or the other. They are fuzzy at the edges, they form transitional stages, become transformed and find themselves in constant flux. Sometimes they fit better in one box than another, depending on people's life history, a particular biographical phase, external contingencies and, not least (as we shall see in subsequent chapters) social circumstances: government, politics, the legal system, stereotypes of foreigners, etc., etc. This means that the logic of such family constellations is defined in terms of *more or less* rather than either/or: some are world families for the most part; others are predominantly one-nation families. To sum it up in a different metaphor: there is no such thing as a little bit pregnant, but a little bit of a world family is perfectly possible.

Thus our answer to the question 'What are world families?' is really straightforward. But it becomes complicated, protracted, detailed and ambiguous when we apply the definition in an attempt to explore the new landscapes of distant love.

It may be objected that the concept of 'families' in 'world families' ignores the diversity of forms of the family that have long since been acknowledged in the field of culturally homogeneous life forms and were a focus of our own study in *The Normal Chaos of Love* (1995). Is it not anachronistic to speak of world families? Would it not be essential to speak instead of world companions of the moment, world extended families, world post-divorce parenthood, world single parents, etc.?

But this is the point. If we take what is broadly speaking the non-Western point of view, world families are in fact *families* in the traditional sense, far more so than in the Western usage. A concept of world families that resists the culturally homogeneous understanding of family and society must not simply acquiesce in this tension between East and West; it must give it expression. This explains why this question of contextual plurality implicit in the concept of world families finds itself caught up in the trench warfare that rages about the true meaning of the 'good family'. The contextual nature of world families can be expressed in the following paradox. If we wish to avoid anachronism, we must construct a concept of world families that appears anachronistic from the vantage point of Western observers. (It should be noted, incidentally, that we consciously use 'world families' in the plural because it has become customary for sociologists to use the term to include unmarried couples, post-marriage couples, homosexual and heterosexual couples, motherhood, fatherhood, etc.)

At this point, at the latest, we have to decide to whom we are referring when we speak of 'we'. We writers? We sociologists? We Germans? We, the inhabitants of the First World? We members of the human race? The fact that we can ask such questions points to the possibility that the seemingly harmless word 'we' has a fatal propensity to obscure world conflicts and to make us forget the particular nature of our own situation. This problem becomes especially acute when we are dealing with world families and the misunderstandings simmering in them. We, the authors, are keenly aware of this 'we-trap', and are simultaneously conscious that we too have stumbled into it.

Our understanding of culture shifts in the course of the transition from one-nation families to world families. It is self-contradictory to speak of a 'culture' of world families, since we cannot conceive of a unified 'world-family culture'. 'World family' is the opposite of a vision of relatively separate cultural worlds in which people live side by side on the model of territories separately administered or governed.

World families do not enter one culture when they leave another; you cannot simply move backwards and forwards between cultures or say with precision at any given moment which culture you belong to and which culture you are heading for. The concept 'world families' becomes meaningful only as the negation of this idea of cultures as natural unities that you cannot choose and to which you have been assigned by fate.

This notion of 'culture' also repudiates the idea of culture as being tied into an ethnic or national totality as the natural condition of Being-in-the-world, while all other conditions – finding oneself between cultures or stemming from different cultures and being subject to different national allegiances – are felt to be 'abnormal', 'hybrid' and even 'dangerous'. Assumptions such as these on the part of an essentially homogeneous and circumscribed 'culture' are quite literally blood-stained; they are the product of cultural crusades, forced assimilation and power-led nation-building.

If it makes sense to embark on the voyage of discovery to the unexplored landscapes of the forms of love and life of world families to which we invite our readers, it does so only as the negation of such ideas of cultural homogeneity, multiculturalism and multi-communitarianism. For all these concepts represent the negation of the both/and nature of the forms of love and life which this book sets out to illuminate.

2

Two Countries, One Couple: Tales of Mutual Understanding and Misunderstanding

Andrea comes from Flensburg, her husband Latif from Iran; Patricia is an African American and lives with Frank, a white man; Rachel, who is Jewish, is in love with Murat, a Muslim. Couples like these whose love crosses national frontiers or ethnic, cultural or religious boundaries used also to exist in former times. They were rare exceptions then but have become far more common over recent decades – in Asia (Shim and Han 2010), the United States (Lee and Edmonston 2005), Europe (Lucassen and Laarman 2009), and not least Germany (Nottmeyer 2009). There are now a growing number of couples who clearly differ from each other in respect of nationality, skin colour, religion or citizenship.

Many factors have contributed to this fundamental transformation of love and the family, or, to put it more romantically, to this mutual opening of hearts. In the first place, quite prosaically, social and political conditions have changed. Increasing social mobility now characterizes many countries. More specifically, the legal barriers that once ruled out such 'mixed' unions have been dismantled. In many of the US states, for example, laws barring marriages between blacks and whites lasted well into the twentieth century. The position is similar in South Africa, where marriages across the colour line – i.e., between people of different colours – remained difficult until the end of Apartheid in 1994.

These legal impediments have now been done away with, not everywhere, but in large parts of the world. This situation has been accelerated by the globalization process and the geographical mobility accompanying it. As a consequence of migration, flight and expulsion, as well as the international division of labour and the cross-border expansion of industry and mass tourism, the number of people who have abandoned their homeland and their culture of origin has been on the increase. Such people cross borders or the boundaries of particular groups for a longer or shorter period of time. They may be born in one place and grow up in another, and live and work, love and marry in a third. Whether it is a matter of French students who go to Germany for work experience or of Swiss tourists who go to Kenya on holiday, encounters between people of differing origins, whether social, geographical or ethnic, are becoming increasingly common. One consequence is the rapid growth in the number of mixed marriages. 'Opportunity makes lovers.' But this should be rewritten now and for the future: 'it's the internet that makes lovers.'

Following globalization, the outstanding feature of online dating lies in the infinite number of possible partners to be evaluated 'rationally' according to pragmatic criteria. The internet is bringing about a change in the social quality of love relationships. It uncouples intimacy and bodies, intimacy and the individual human being. This gives shape to a paradox: it creates a space for *global* intimacy, *anonymous* intimacy. To what extent does the experience of virtual love contribute to the intensification of intimacy or the release from inhibitions? Or does intimacy now assume different forms?

1 Do 'Mixed Relationships' Differ from Others?

In politics, the media and the public sphere generally, the new realities and opportunities for love encounter a diversity of reactions. Some people reject them and do whatever they can to attack them as a betrayal of their own (German, Hungarian or Polish) identity, as an offence against race and blood. Others welcome them as the bearers of hope for a new tolerance and understanding, as harbingers of a better, more colourful and peaceful world.

We do not intend to discuss these or other judgements in these pages. Instead, we shall inquire into the nature of such unions to see whether they share noteworthy features. Our starting point is straightforward: how far and in what way do such mixed unions differ from relationships where both partners come from the same country, speak the same language and have the same citizenship?

The question of the degree to which mixed-nationality or intercultural couples differ from partners from the same or similar backgrounds seems harmless enough but can appear suspect or provoke hostile reactions, depending on context. A cautious approach is recommended in order to keep misunderstandings within bounds.

The first truth is as follows: *the* mixed-nationality couple does not exist any more than does *the* foreigner. In ordinary life there is a vast difference if a German who was born in Upper Bavaria marries an Austrian woman from Salzburg or a woman from Kenya. In the former case, there is hardly any indication that we are dealing with a mixed-nationality couple, whereas in the latter it is obvious that the Bavarian has married a 'foreigner'. The prejudices and resistances such couples encounter differ radically in the two cases. They are all the more significant the more obvious it is that the foreign partner is visibly and audibly 'foreign'.

What does the concept 'foreigner' mean here? Georg Simmel's famous definition of the stranger as a person who 'comes today and stays tomorrow' points to the difficulty of distinguishing between 'us' and 'others' (Simmel 1908: 509). In other words, the stranger is not someone who belongs to the unknown world out there, but a person whose simple presence puts in question the natives' seemingly 'natural' beliefs about who belongs and where the frontiers lie. It is this feature that defines mixed-nationality couples and marriages. The strangers who 'come today and stay tomorrow' – in other words, who both belong and do not belong because they contradict the self-definition of the majority – live and love in our midst.

The Ethnic Trap

Many politically committed people accept the principle that distinguishing between mixed couples and other couples is both wrong and dangerous. Anyone who adopts this distinction has to use passports or origins as distinguishing features. Doing this means labelling mixed couples as special cases, 'different' and deviant – a form of racism, whether conscious or not. That is the objection to such a procedure. Many social scientists argue along the same lines. From their point of view, ethnic origins are given too much weight in many studies (Sökefeld 2004). It follows that such authors object to any tendency towards 'ethnic reductionism' and propose instead that, when we look at immigrants from India (or Turkey or Poland), we cannot explain their overall behaviour in terms of their 'Indianness' ('Turkishness' or 'Polishness'); we cannot explain it as the consequence of the alleged dominance of an ethnic identity (Baumann 1996: 1). For, if we do, they warn us, we will end up falling into the ethnic trap; we shall simply repeat the current clichés and simplified stereotypes to the effect that, e.g., Turks are traditionalist. That gives us licence to dramatize the differences between Turkey and other countries while allowing us at the same time to obscure the multiplicity of tensions and conflicts within Turkish society – as if doctors, lawyers and civil servants in Istanbul lived and thought much like Eastern Anatolian peasants. Such scholars go on to argue that, if we are to avoid the pitfall of ethnic determinism, we must place individuals at the centre of attention. If we transfer this maxim to the analysis of mixed marriages, we shall have to focus entirely on the participants and their relationship instead of being fixated on their ethnic roots – or, more precisely, the differences between the partners' origins.

In other words, we must take care when examining attempts to ascribe great importance to the culture of origin in mixed relationships. Such views are also voiced by many men and women who live in such relationships. In response to questioning by social scientists, they emphasize over and over again that they are individuals, have individual characteristics and are not merely the products of their origins. They claim that they remain together because they understand each other and not because their partner has a different nationality or skin colour. They protest against the overemphasis on the *exotic* and the assumption that they think of their partner exclusively as a member of a distant, alien group. They are equally opposed to people *dramatizing* their relationships and to the half-curious, half-mistrustful and inquiring glances with which the world around them responds to their liaison. Distancing themselves from that, their credo runs: we are nothing special; we are just like other couples. We have feelings, wishes and hopes; we quarrel from time to time. We are no different from other couples in that respect. We may consider as representative a study of mixed-race couples in the United States: 'We're no different than anybody else. We have the same concerns for a family, the kids . . . my house, my dog, my job, my daily life concerns' (interviewee in Rosenblatt, Karis and Powell 1995: 24). 'A relationship is a relationship is a relationship. You find common ground with another person and you make compromises and you develop a trust, an understanding, hopefully love, and you live like everybody else' (ibid.: 26).

Individual or culture of origin? Does this mean that the latter is irrelevant to relationships? This is how we might interpret the statements of men and women who find themselves in such mixed relationships. But that is not the whole story. The study cited here (and the picture is similar in countless other studies and reports) also reveals the problematic obverse of the desire for parity (as expressed in the statement 'we are all human'). We learn of events and experiences that run counter to the picture presented above, events that are not merely coincidental because they differ, or are perceived differently, from those experienced by ordinary couples. Many people have the feeling that they are constantly being scrutinized or are regarded with amazement – particularly when the difference of origins is striking. For example, one woman observed of her own black-and-white family: 'The thing is that we are always in a goldfish bowl . . . Society thinks they have a right to comment on us, to us, about us, as if by right. Or there is an expectation that we will confess our innermost fears for all to consume' (interviewee in Alibhai-Brown 2001: 85).

Such statements reflect the way people are compartmentalized into groups with particular characteristics – and the provocation that results when they fail to stick to these 'natural' limits and disrupt the 'natural' order of things simply by being together. They then become the objects of other people's looks and of general curiosity. It should be noted that this otherness of other people is just as dependent on the self-image and self-understanding of the couple as of the picture of outsiders formed by the powerful 'natives'.

In what follows, when we describe such typical experiences, this does not mean that they are unique and entirely alien to mononational and monocultural families. Such situations doubtless arise in ordinary relationships from time to time. The crucial distinction, however, is that they are far more frequent and bruising in mixed relationships. They take on a dramatic, explosive quality of their own. They also form a red thread that colours the entire lives of mixed couples.

2   Lives in Transition

The Burden of Memory

Anyone who arrives in Germany as an immigrant has many experiences behind him, often painful ones – experiences that are for the most part remote and alien to those who have spent their lives in the secure prosperity of Germany. They include leaving behind your native country, leaving behind the people there, the language, the landscape, the aromas and the sounds. Leaving behind also perhaps hunger and poverty, perhaps political upheavals, flight and expulsion, right down to massive threats and even the direct use of force – the baggage of memory that the immigrant carries around with him contains many things. He can endure all that because it is his life's history; he cannot dispose of it like a tiresome burden. He carries it around with him into his new life – and his new love.

His partner from his new country may not always appreciate why he sometimes overreacts, recoils, and becomes withdrawn or sentimental at moments that seem trivial or harmless to her. What's the matter with him? Why is he suddenly making a fuss? In her autobiographical novel, Lena Gorelik, who had come to Germany from Russia when she was still a young girl, describes a scene that is relevant to the baggage of memories. It concerns two young women with different backgrounds. For the girl who was born in Germany and had grown up there, shopping and trying on clothes was a recognized leisure activity. For the girl who had come to Germany from Russia, shopping brought back memories of being forced to spend hours in queues. She tries to explain this to her German friend:

> I have spent so much time standing in queues that it will do me for the rest of my life . . . Shopping was terrible. 'We have run out of bread', my mother would say, and I would pretend not to hear her. I'm ready to do whatever she wants, but please, please, don't make me go shopping. 'So will you just run along and join the queue?' my mother would say, as if she had not even noticed my sudden silence. So I run along. Buying bread is not so easy, nor is buying anything, for that matter. The first couple of supermarkets I come to won't have any bread; the shelves will be empty for the most part, the only things that will be left are matches and soap; for some unknown reason sufficient quantities of matches and soap were always available in Russia. If I'm in luck the third supermarket would have bread, but you couldn't be sure. I would just have to join the queue and hope the bread won't run out. You could tell from a long way off whether the shelves weren't empty, or at least one shelf. There would be a huge, noisy crowd standing in front of it. Tired-looking people carrying a lot of bags wait impatiently, perhaps quarrelling in advance, though they don't even know what goods might be there for them to buy. (Gorelik 2004: 48–50)

If things are going badly it is at moments like these that cracks appear in a relationship, maybe even open conflict. This is because each partner feels alone and misunderstood. When things are going well, one person talks and the other listens, and this can form the foundation of a new, shared world. The indigenous partner obtains a glimpse of life on another continent. A window opens out onto his or her partner's native country, its history and present situation, people and landscapes there. Distant love, then, means travelling in one's mind to faraway places while sitting at home in one's living room. Life in a mixed-nationality, intercultural relationship can be an education in knowledge of the world.

Moreover, the foreign continent need not be all that remote geographically. Sometimes it can be found in one's own home town. In the case of partners with the same citizenship but different ethnic backgrounds, the partner who comes from the majority population may well have very little idea about life on the other side of the ethnic divide. If you belong to the club, you do not even see those who are forced to remain outside. People whose skins are white do not even notice the privileges that automatically go along with that – and the fate of those with skins of a different colour. If a white man is married to a black woman, and if the relationship between the two is governed by mutual respect and trust, the white man will over a period of years receive lessons in a very special kind of ethnography: a native land that goes beyond tourist prospectuses and nostalgic idealization; a native land as a place where minorities are exposed to everyday acts of exclusion and discrimination.

An example of such ethnography can be found in the writing of Jane Lazarre, a white American married to a black. In her *Memoir of a White Mother of Black Sons*, she describes how her relationship with her husband and sons changed her view of American society: 'This is the story of a change in a white person's vision through self-discovery to conscience. It is the story of the education of an American woman' (Lazarre 1996: xxi).

> I am hearing a story about common, everyday racism from one of my sons. It is a prototypical story of young Black maleness in an American city, 1990s. Khary's [the son's] friend has rung the bell one night and is waiting for him to come downstairs. The friend, also Black and nineteen years old, drives the family car, a Toyota. We live on a racially mixed street in a racially mixed neighborhood, yet when Khary comes downstairs, he finds three cops surrounding his friend who is spread-eagled on the front of the car, being searched. Suspecting he had stolen the car, the cops approached him while he was standing against it, and when he objected, turned him around roughly and began their search. I am outraged and shout: 'But this is unbelievable!' 'Unbelievable?' my son says angrily. 'Unbelievable, Mom? It happens to me all the time. If I'm not searched I'm still stopped and questioned, whenever I'm driving a decent-looking car. (Ibid.: 32f.)

Shifting Power Relations

Mixed-nationality unions mean not only that life histories have diverged in the past, but that such divergences may well persist in the present. This applies particularly when love has led the 'foreign' partner to leave his or her own homeland and migrate to a foreign country. There will be moments – or even perhaps months and years – when such people feel lonely and miss their natural, familiar environment. They will often feel insecure, dependent and inferior, and they may well lose confidence and a sense of identity. At home they may have been doctors, engineers or teachers, with a good income and a secure position. Such people were respected citizens in their own right, members of their home town and their country. And now? They have lost status, are compelled to take language lessons, beg for a residence permit and fight to have their educational qualifications recognized. And if such recognition is not forthcoming, which is mainly the case, they are forced to make do with inferior positions or are condemned to unemployment. Where this happens, there is a shift in the balance of power between the partners that is independent of their personal qualities, skills and achievements. It is normally the 'indigenous' partners who emerge the clear winners. They do not undergo such dislocations and the continuity of their lives remains undisturbed. This is because they know the language and are conversant with the ways of dealing with the manifold difficulties of everyday life. They retain their own social circle, their family and friends. And we should not forget that, because they have the right of residence, they can follow their own professions and thus have an independent income of their own. At the same time, the native partner acquires greater responsibility and additional obligations. Because he is the one who knows his way around, he has to assume the leadership role, in dealing with the authorities, for example. The longer this situation lasts, the more he feels it – consciously or unconsciously – to be an imposition, time-consuming and unjust.

The fundamental insight is that the change in geographical location may well lead to a shift in the internal workings of the relationship. As Irene Hardach-Pinke writes in her study of German–Japanese relationships, 'The partner who was previously a foreigner now turns into a cultural expert, while the partner who was previously at home now turns into a disorientated foreigner' (Hardach-Pinke 1988: 149). In the new environment the partner may lose some of his or her former charisma. A competent, independent native becomes a clumsy, dependent foreigner; the exotic, fascinating foreigner becomes a run-of-the-mill native, an ordinary person. One of the people interviewed in the study, a Japanese man with a German wife, describes such a transformation as well as his own disillusionment: 'When I married Marion, I felt that she was a highly independent woman. At that time she was always on the move, travelling all over Europe. If she had been as dependent on me then as she has since become I would never have married her!' (ibid.: 146).

This may be an extreme case, but it is symptomatic. We see again and again how, when a person moves to a different country in order to be with another person, significant adaptations are required from both partners. The balance of power in the relationship has to be renegotiated and a new equilibrium established. In the absence of this, the relationship will be put under severe strain. If it does work, however, new horizons and prospects will open up to the benefit of both partners. Changing one's world can lead to success or failure, the beginning of the end or the start of a new beginning.

Prejudices and Barriers

In Germany in the nineteenth century, if a 'Catholic' man wished to marry a 'Protestant' woman (or vice versa), this was regarded as a mixed marriage and was wrong for that reason. Such marriages could divide families; they were transgressions, rebellions against the imperatives of faith – a sacrilege. Catholic priests and Protestant parsons alike composed diatribes against them, complete with prophetic warnings that God would assuredly punish all sinners, who would be struck down by all manner of evils, from illness and disease in the case of the man right down to the premature death of a child; their houses would burn down and floods would destroy their fields (Beck 2010: 57–9).

Such dramas have long since been relegated to the past, at least in Western countries. As secularization has advanced, religious affiliations have declined in significance, in politics as well as in the world of work and private life. This applies with particular force to marriage. In marriage, happiness in this world has assumed priority for most people, both adults and children. Whether one's son-in-law is a Catholic or a Protestant has largely ceased to be an issue that provokes dissension between the generations.

The situation is different if one's daughter's choice has fallen upon a foreigner, especially a foreigner from a non-Western background or one with a different colour skin, let alone of Muslim faith. Even today, such features would be all too likely to provoke disapproval in the minds of many families in the majority population. The prejudice and opposition that such unions encounter on all sides constitute a classic theme in the literature on mixed marriages (Sollors 1997). And, even today, as many reports show, we can see that they are capable of triggering very 'mixed feelings' (Alibhai-Brown 2001). Following the murders perpetrated by the National Socialists, any open expression of racist attitudes became taboo in Western countries. But in recent years, faced with the sustained inflows of immigrants and the processes of globalization, a demarcation line has become established – in politics, the media and ordinary life – a line based on questions of ethnic origins. It is the distinction between 'us' and 'others', one's own country and strangers, foreigners – in short, people who simply do not belong here (Beck-Gernsheim 2007b). The idea of a colour-blind society indifferent to questions of ethnic origins has now receded into the remote distance (Williams 1997). The tendency to think in terms of polar opposites can remain dormant over long periods of time before it finally breaks through. It may be triggered, for example, by the question of the future of one's own daughter (and the grandchildren she may be expected to produce). Is it not the parents' duty to issue a solemn warning and make absolutely clear to her what she can expect if she goes ahead and marries an Arab (or a Turk or a black)?

If all else fails, you can escape from parental objections by breaking off all contact. But in some countries – above all in Germany – mixed-nationality/intercultural couples may find themselves confronted by more testing obstacles. The enemy here goes by such names as officialdom, authorities, regulations and administration. The obstacles put in one's path by bureaucracy are legendary, even among the members of the majority population, who relish the opportunity to regale one another with amusing stories of obstructive officials. Yet they have very little idea of the powers available to bureaucracy when dealing with 'aliens'. Such people are forced to submit to endless scrutiny, searches and inspections so as to forestall possible threats. These efforts are further intensified when it comes to marriage and the family, which are the special responsibility of the state. In Germany you have to produce all sorts of papers for this – documents, stamps, certificates, written endorsements and translations. Such investigations may well serve to reassure the native population. But they inevitably lead to a clash between alien worlds. In the well-ordered, air-conditioned offices of German public servants it is hard to conceive what life is like in regions submerged in civil war, poverty and chaos, regions from which people can barely escape with their lives, where a public infrastructure can barely be said to exist, and where there is no functioning registration system in place. How is a German official supposed to deal with all this? How should he judge conditions in such faraway places? All that the media provide him with are pictures of poverty and destitution displaying the gulf between Germany and other countries. This makes mixed couples appear abnormal, suspect even. Is the non-German partner just in search of a visa, a new passport, a residence permit? Are we just looking at a sham marriage?

In the light of these circumstances, anyone who perseveres with a proposed marriage must be prepared to navigate an obstacle course: countless visits to the authorities, costly phone calls to embassies, petitions to consulates, the translation of documents, etc. Marriages may be made in heaven, but mixed-nationality unions have to make their way through the limbo of officialdom.

Couples of different religions who live in Israel or Lebanon are exposed to even stricter constraints. Neither country recognizes civil marriage and no clergyman will marry couples of different religious persuasion. In other words, marriage in their own country is impossible for such couples.

Ways out can be found in the age of globalization. 'Marriage tourism' is now an option. Whereas enormous efforts might be needed in one's own country, simpler solutions may well be on offer abroad, provided one can find a pathway through the transnational jungle of legal clauses and regulations. It is no accident that the wave of marriage tourism in recent years has seen the rise of agencies specializing in gratifying the hopes and wishes of mixed-nationality/intercultural couples. The difference is striking. Whereas traditional organizers seek to provide a suitable (romantic or exotic) ambience for weddings, internet agents use a much more down-to-earth approach: they speak of 'supranational cooperation' or 'solutions free from red tape'. One agency promises 'weddings faster than in Las Vegas'; another requires 'a minimum of paperwork' and claims to be able to help 'hopeless cases', boasting that its services are 'ideal for multinational couples'.

For this to function, the agencies concerned must satisfy two conditions. On the one hand, they need the relevant legal expertise and must be able to apply it across national frontiers. They have to know which states (federal territories, regions or districts) take a more relaxed view of the rules governing weddings, or at least are willing to stretch a point in applying them. On the other hand, they need practical experience of particular places and particular staff. At which local districts or register offices are the staff prepared to interpret the rules more leniently or even occasionally to turn a blind eye to defective documentation?

Evidently, both conditions are satisfied adequately, since the system does function. Couples from Germany travel to Denmark; American couples fly out from the USA to the Caribbean and couples from Israel and Lebanon to nearby Cyprus. To gain an idea of the overall picture, surveys suggest that at present around 6,000 couples from Germany get married in Denmark each year and around 1,500 couples from Israel get married in Cyprus (Bozic 2009; Manetsch

2008). The geographical destinations may vary but the life projects associated with them are similar. In either case, the point of the journey is to exploit legal and procedural loopholes in order to arrive in the safe haven of marriage and thus accomplish what other couples achieve as a matter of course.

Subject to Suspicion

To sum up our inquiry thus far: interviews and accounts given by intercultural couples reveal two characteristic elements. On the one hand, they all insist that they are nothing out of the ordinary; on the other hand, their experience tells them that they are in fact different. Many of their statements oscillate between the two. How can that be? How can we explain this paradox? This question has been addressed by the study of interracial black–white marriages referred to above. Rosenblatt, Karis and Powell make a closer examination of the statement 'We're no different than anybody else', and they provide two interpretations. We might call the first the 'habituation effect'. According to this idea, most people regard their own life as normal – regardless of how extraordinary it may look to outsiders – because they have grown used to it and have developed ways of coping with whatever difficulties it poses. In this context, their claim to ordinariness takes the form of such statements as 'We have found ways of dealing with our differences', 'We shall manage alright' (Rosenblatt, Karis and Powell 1995: 37). Together with the force of habit, there is a further interpretation, namely the attempt to break free of the role of the stranger who represents a threat to normality. In this sense the statement 'We are no different than anybody else' is also a statement *in opposition to* the prejudice and hostility of a society that views mixed relationships with a blend of fear, curiosity and rejection. It means: leave us in peace, we belong together whether you like it or not. We are not performing animals in a circus; we don't want to be stared at all the time. And, above all: we are not exotic creatures; we are fed up with being regarded as a problem (ibid.: 36f.). The young woman who feels as if she is living in a gold-fish bowl (see p. 24 above) describes her situation in this way: 'We have no personal lives, no private lives. . . . That is why so many of us are defensive' (Alibhai-Brown 2001: 85).

Looked at in this way, the statement 'We're no different than anybody else' represents a kind of defence against the critical gaze of people around such couples. It can be explained by the internal dynamic at work. But, as Rosenblatt, Karis and Powell show, such a strategy does not come without cost. For it obscures or ignores situations in which mixed-nationality or intercultural couples are in fact forced to confront challenges. The fact that we fail to perceive cultural differences does not mean that they do not exist. On the contrary, it is then that they often develop an especially insidious effect, a subterranean energy.

> The partners bring different values, standards, practices, expectations and experiences to family rituals, the expression of emotion, the management of money, purchasing, dealing with illness, matters of etiquette, dealing with police, teachers, physicians, and other authorities. Cultural differences are likely to challenge any couple relationship. Perhaps the challenges are greater in couples who deny the differences by thinking of themselves as an ordinary couple.

For this reason, the authors come to the following conclusion:

> We do not want to diminish the claims of ordinariness. The couples had good reason to claim that they were like most couples in their everyday life. But we also do not want to diminish the duality of their ordinariness. Even if one argues that many same-race couples experience difficulties like those the couples who were interviewed experienced with family opposition, cultural differences, hostile neighbours and so on, there is a set of experiences shared by many of the couples interviewed that are unlikely to be part of the experience of same-race couples. (Rosenblatt, Karis and Powell 1995: 38f.)

So are cross-cultural couples different from others? It is obvious that they are frequently exposed to different experiences. This includes primarily their dealings with culturally specific signals, since these generate exceptional force in the case of mixed marriages.

3   Decoding Intercultural Differences

In the rapidly growing recent literature dealing with intercultural communication or intercultural understanding (Heringer 2007; Maletzke 1996; Oksaar 1996), one theme stands out strongly: it is the question of the rules governing communication, both verbal and non-verbal, and, above all, the ways in which these rules differ in different cultures. To mention just a few examples: When should we speak, what should we talk about, when should we remain silent and for how long? Is it alright to make eye contact? How loudly may we talk and is it acceptable to display emotion? What form of words shows that we are being polite? What compliments are expected and what presents should we bring and on which occasions? And who should pay these compliments or bring these presents and to whom? And, conversely, which compliments or presents may cause misunderstandings and embarrassment, or even offence?

Vasco Esteves is a Portuguese married to a German woman. When he describes his first impressions of Germany, you can still hear the shudder in his voice:

> I noticed that Germans never looked me in the eye, except of course when they had to speak to me! I noticed this especially in public. In the street, for example, everyone walks past everyone else just as if he were the only person in the world! Even on public transport you can sit or stand opposite someone for an entire journey without exchanging glances with anyone even once. . . . I must admit also that I had difficulties speaking to people in Germany at first. I couldn't talk properly to my Portuguese friends in cafés because everyone around us was so silent – even though the cafés were full of grannies. The same goes for the tram. I always felt I might be irritating someone when I spoke in public (or were *they* irritating *me*?). The explanation turned out to be quite straightforward. What people objected to was not speaking as such but simply people whose voices were too loud! To be sure, it is equally improper to speak in public to someone you don't know unless there is a very good reason to do so. A straightforward question such as 'Are you going to Frankfurt too?' is likely to produce the response, 'What gives you that idea?' or – in the best case, a succinct 'No, I get out at the next stop.' People clearly do not realize (or refuse to admit that it is reasonable) that a general question of this sort is simply intended to begin a friendly conversation or to show interest in another person. . . . It took me quite a while to realize that, by initiating a conversation or talking too loudly, we (Southerners, North Americans and all other extraverts on the planet) are just intruding into the *private lives* of ordinary Germans and thus restricting their individual freedom! By the time I realized this I must have given offence thousands of times and presumably caused irreparable damage! (Esteves 1993: 183–5)

For the most part we are unaware of such culturally prescribed rules, but it is evident that, the more they diverge, the more they will give rise to misunderstandings, irritations or embarrassing situations. This can be seen in business relations as well and may even lead to deals breaking down (e.g., Thomas 1999). It also applies in private life, in relations between men and women, both on falling in love and later on in married life.

In such situations it can be very helpful to recognize that the signals sent out by other people may be culturally specific and that they must be 'decoded' culturally. This can forestall the conflicts that arise from misunderstanding their spontaneous utterances or reactions. When a couple from the same background say things like 'You're crazy' or 'I can't stand you', they understand what is meant because they are familiar with the same associations or images and share the same horizon of meaning. In mixed relationships, however, the ability to decipher or 'decode' statements may be wanting. Words uttered in anger may then be taken literally – and indeed too literally.

A woman from Northern Europe marries a man from the South, but disagreements soon emerge. In the course of a violent quarrel, he shouts at her in his mother tongue and she, enraged and hurt, at once packs her bags and returns to her parents' house. The woman came from Lübeck and was called Tony Buddenbrook. She felt she had been insulted by her husband, Alois Permaneder, a man from the depths of Bavaria. In a moment of anger, he had shouted, 'Go to the devil, you filthy slut!' (Mann 1930: 389). To be sure, what he had said to her in his Bavarian dialect was hardly a term of endearment, but it was by no means the appalling slur on her character that it had seemed to her.

As may readily be imagined, this process of cultural decoding is not always straightforward. And it does not become any easier if rage, heightened emotions and disillusionment are involved and the rules of reason have been set aside. Dealing with such situations calls for practice and patience – to say nothing of love, trust and the belief in one's partner and one's relationship. The fact that such difficulties are not insuperable has been demonstrated by all couples who have succeeded in living together and staying together despite national or cultural differences. We may surmise that, with time, they become experienced in detecting and interpreting such culturally determined signals and in reacting to them appropriately. They become everyday experts in a noble art, that of cross-cultural dialogue.

A Common Misunderstanding

Whenever such differences and the explosive force which they are capable of generating are discussed in seminars or lectures, objections are frequently encountered from the ranks of the home participants. Someone will object that they are familiar with similar misunderstandings, that their German partner frequently reacts in just the same – strange, incomprehensible – way, and that what we are seeing here are not national differences but differences between the sexes. And, indeed, men and women do often have different communication patterns and ways of talking, and these frequently lead to misunderstandings, accusations and recriminations. This criticism is therefore quite legitimate and could even be extended to include references to the fact that a common culture contains a diversity of groups with their own ways of interacting, ways of talking, and rules governing forms of closeness or the distances to be maintained. Examples are the relations between blacks and whites in the USA or between East and West Germans in Germany.

Group distinctions of all kinds flow into everyday modes of behaviour. But it is a mistake to play one group off against another, as if the existence of significant distinctions between men and women rendered differences of culture and nationality otiose. The opposite is the case. Where there are differences of nationality, they may well overlap with other differences and intensify them, thus making it even harder to disentangle the root causes of misunderstandings. Christine Miyaguchi is an American woman married to a Japanese. She is very aware of the scope for misunderstandings:

> All husbands and wives quarrel from time to time. Some of these quarrels are minor skirmishes; others assume the dimensions of a fully fledged war. There are days when each partner would prefer to withdraw into a demilitarized zone and send out emissaries to conduct peace negotiations. And everyone knows how tangled communication between married partners can become sometimes – it's as if they spoke different languages. But that is as nothing compared to the confusion when they come from two different cultures and really do speak different languages! (Miyaguchi 1993: 172)

Love and Food

If only it were a matter of the diversity of communication styles and linguistic forms! In that event how straightforward, how monotonous, life in cross-cultural relationships would be. But in addition we must often take account of people's culturally diverse habits, expectations and values in other spheres. Let us take the relatively simple example of eating and drinking and whatever is connected with it. We may refer once more to Tony Buddenbrook, who in her letters home describes the curious eating habits that prevail in Bavaria:

> I enjoy drinking the beer – I drink a good deal, the more so as the water is not very good. But I cannot quite get used to the food. There are too few vegetables and too much flour, for instance in the sauces, which are pathetic. They have no idea of a proper joint of veal, for the butchers cut everything very badly. And I miss the fish. It is quite mad to be eating so much cucumber and potato salad with the beer – my tummy rebels audibly. (Mann 1930: 307)

A little later on, finding herself married to a Bavarian, she tries to win him over to the food from her home region. 'Yesterday we had sorrel with currants, but I wish I hadn't, for Permaneder objected so much to the sorrel – he picked the currants out with a fork – that he would not speak to me the whole afternoon, but just growled' (ibid.: 360). As we know, the marriage did not last long. The distance separating Tony's Lübeck refinement from Alois Permaneder's Bavarian coarseness was not confined just to culinary matters.

Fortunately, such differences of temperament are not always insuperable. For many cross-cultural couples, food and drink is a large subject, a setting for prolonged adaptation and hidden traps for the unwary. Food is not simply a matter of nourishment but involves such things as spices (why is everything so hot, why is it so bland and tasteless?). Food also means coping with the requisite implements (do you eat with chopsticks, cutlery or your fingers?). It also entails basic rules of politeness (when to eat up everything and when to leave something on the plate; when to accept a second helping and when to say 'No thank you'; which is the right way to behave?). Food is also associated with various taboos (no pork for practising Jews; no beef stew for Hindus). Food raises questions about deep-rooted notions of health, our bodies, nature (this is healthy, that is easily digestible), as well as deep-rooted dislikes and anxieties (my stomach turns at the thought of it). A Swiss woman married to a Ghanaian has written about divergent eating customs:

> At the beginning of our marriage my husband always thought it amusing when I laid the table nicely, especially if there were visitors, and when I put out different foods for the different courses: hors d'oeuvres, salad, main course, dessert, and so on. He thought this was my personal romantic streak, a kind of whim of mine . . . In Ghana the cooked food is presented in little bowls and people eat when they are ready. It is normal for one to three people to share the contents of a bowl. People eat in the inner courtyard, sitting on low stools. No one uses a table. There is no talking during the meal; food is there to fill your stomach with; it is not a social occasion . . . I have learned to understand, although not really to have become reconciled to the idea that a man can come to the table and just start eating while I am still in the kitchen, or that he should leave the table when he is finished. Eating habits are still something of a bone of contention in our family, even today. (Knecht Oti-Amoako 1995: 11)

Where expectations diverge so widely, food ceases to mean just food. It also means: What do you think of my memories, my traditions, or everything that is familiar to me and I am used to? Do you insist on having everything your own way or will you respect my customs and my preferences? Are you adventurous or are you stubborn and hostile to anything new? Do you like learning about the world I come from or do you reject whatever forms part of my background? Will you just hold back or will you come to meet me halfway? Are you prepared to join in our experiment in living together?

4 Rediscovering the Roots

Even couples who over the years have proved themselves to be adepts of the art of intercultural dialogue may find themselves surprised on occasion by the differences in their own lives and backgrounds. These elements of surprise can be found scattered throughout texts and studies dealing with intercultural relationships. Having repeatedly come across similar stories in the relevant literature, we decided to refer to the basic pattern as instances of 'reverting to the biographical past'. Here are some examples.

Ken and Jenny have been married for a number of years, but, although his family is Jewish and hers Methodist, they have never quarrelled about religious matters. At Christmas they have always gone to stay with friends or with Jenny's mother, but after their daughter was born they decided that for the first time they would spend Christmas together at home. And that's when it happened. When Jenny said how lovely it would be if they had their own Christmas tree for once, Ken responded with some irritation. He replied gruffly that he had imagined that they would celebrate Hanukkah – even though he had not given Hanukkah a thought since leaving his parents' house years before (Mayer 1985: 142). Similar stories can be found in a study of mixed couples in France. We learn of an Armenian who is married to a Frenchwoman and has lived in France for forty years. He suddenly wants to discover his roots and goes back to Armenia. Having returned from there to France, he feels the need increasingly to listen to Armenian music. The Frenchwoman is herself of Muslim origin but had converted to Roman Catholicism many years previously. To her husband's surprise, she suddenly begins to visit her original family more frequently and ends up keeping the fasting requirements of Ramadan (Barbara 1989: 55).

Provocative Choices

How do people arrive at such biographical relapses? The person who is involved in them – much to the surprise of his or her partner – is for the most part surprised too. Nothing in their lives up to then pointed to such an outcome. If anything, the opposite was the case. Many people who enter into a marriage across national or cultural boundaries have no powerful ties to their culture of origin, or, if they have, they have become estranged from it early on, rebelling against their parents' values and outlook (see, e.g., Barbara 1989; Elschenbroich 1988; Hecht-El Minshawi 1990, 1992; Katz 1996; Khatib-Chahidi, Hill and Paton 1998; Schneider 1989). Elschenbroich, for example, writes as follows about mixed marriages between Germans and foreigners:

> In the dynamics of the parent–child relationship, the choice of partner is a challenge to the parents: 'I am not the person you imagine I am or want to have!' . . . The choice of a foreign, perhaps even exotic partner is an attempt to get rid of the German or the 'bourgeois' aspect of one's character. (Elschenbroich 1988: 365)

And then, after a few years, but sometimes only after a great many years, comes the regression to the biographical past. One partner begins to take seriously something that was of little importance to him or her hitherto. And the other partner is taken by surprise. Again and again we learn about such 'elements of surprise' (Mayer 1985: 145). They seem baffling, and the other partner is disconcerted (Schneider 1989: 7, 57). Finding himself taken aback in this way, a non-Jewish man asks his Jewish wife, 'If Judaism means so much to you, then why did you not just marry a Jew?' And this question, or questions like it, recurs with many couples (ibid.: 81). Elschenbroich's study shows how the German men and women who had begun by vehemently repudiating conformism and German narrow-mindedness later develop a strong identification with their own origins. In their relationships with their foreign partners they feel themselves to be 'more German than ever before', and they discover, often for the first time, just how deeply their roots are embedded in the value system of their country of origin (Elschenbroich 1988: 368).

If circumstances are unfavourable, such regressions generate their own dynamic. It is easy to picture how the misunderstandings build up. Anyone who experiences his or her partner's reversion to the past will begin by feeling confused by the partner's unaccustomed behaviour. This confusion may then turn into a genuine sense of insecurity. He or she will feel put out, injured, rejected and even threatened by the sudden change in a person who now appears as a stranger. This gives rise to a vicious circle of mutual recriminations.

The Family Life Cycle and Intercultural Relationships

When such reversions to the biographical past occur in the lives of many mixed couples, what triggers them is never purely personal; it is never the product of one's partner's sudden outburst of irrationality. On the contrary, there must be a more universal basic pattern underlying the particular constellation of mixed-nationality/intercultural relations. The American sociologist Egon Mayer has provided an explanatory framework that demonstrates the different phases characteristic of relationships between couples. If we follow this model, the reversion to the past ceases to appear as a blow coming from outside. Rather, it looks more like an event arising from, and explicable by, the internal development of the phases of the relationship.

At the very start of the relationship, in the initial *Sturm und Drang* of first love, the lovers see nothing but themselves. The world outside recedes, the past is unimportant, only the present matters. At this stage, the lovers feel full of a strength that carries all before it, and they rise up against conventions, barriers and rules. They regard all such things as superfluous ballast. They set out to discover the world anew and indeed to make it new. Love is a 'revolution for two' (Alberoni 1983).

But revolutions are tiring. They cannot be sustained for a lifetime. The lovers gradually begin to develop habits, to find their own rules and rituals, which relieve them of the burden of constantly having to invent something new. This is the point at which they come into contact with cultural traditions, including the traditions contained in their own origins. They are then forced to decide what matters to them, what they want and what they do not want. As they deepen their relationship and initiate the dialogue of mutual revelation, mutual self-disclosure and acceptance, the lovers encounter the past – their own past and that of their partner. The deepest internal strata that lovers reveal to each other are embedded in the framework of their respective cultures, heritages, origins. As Mayer says, there is no such thing as a 'culture-free inner self', a culture-free identity (Mayer 1985: 68–73).

If the relationship grows stronger, the partners will regularly arrive at points at which they come face to face with their own history. According to Mayer, this is a consequence of the specific nature of the family. Because the family life cycle has its own rhythms, a typical sequence of events, phases, highpoints and crises – the celebrations and holidays in the course of the year, with the marriage ceremony, births and child-rearing – it contains many moments that trigger memories, evoke traditions or remind people of their family origins. It is true enough that many traditions that had earlier been rejected continue to be rejected, as angrily and fiercely as ever. But there are points in time that sometimes stimulate a new response, triggered perhaps by one or the other significant event, or by this or that turning point in one's life, and suddenly you find yourself thinking of the past with a new warmth or even yearning. You may even want to incorporate bits and pieces of the past into your current life. It is through such devious routes as these that people may suddenly experience these reversions to an earlier biographical stage – if indeed they do experience them (see Mayer 1985: 144f.).

Typical Triggers

So much for Mayer's explanation. If we consider other relevant studies, we come across much material that supports his findings. For example, although these reversions to the past often strike those affected as disconcerting and even inexplicable, they reveal typical patterns and triggering factors to the outside observer. They are often associated with biographical phases, with family rites of passage of the kind depicted by Mayer. A classical triggering factor is the arrival of children (see, e.g., Barbara 1989: 107ff.; Katz 1996: 164f., 174; Pandey 1988: 135ff.).

Contemplating the future of one's children inevitably reminds people of their own childhood and leads to a confrontation with their own past, the process of socialization they experienced, and their own values and wishes – in short, with their own identity. Regardless of the issue at hand, whether considering the style of education, the names given to one's children, questions of religion, language, the stories they are told or the songs with which they grow up, a parent is inevitably confronted by such questions as: What aspects of my own childhood matter to me? What should I pass on to my children? What should they learn to preserve? In other words, if they acquire none of these things, will I become a stranger in my own family? Does that mean that my contribution, my history will be utterly forgotten?

Running Away and Looking Back

From our own perspective, it makes sense to take up Mayer's argument, build on it and strengthen it. Our suggestion, which is basically quite simple, is that, whereas Mayer focuses on the different phases in the life of a couple or on the family cycle, we can focus instead on the phases in the life of an individual – in other words, the individual's progress from growing up to adulthood and growing old. The author of a study of intercultural marriages observes that 'Home is a great place to run away from as long as you can go back once in a while' (Romano 1988: 114). We all know that youth is the time for running away, just as it is the time for searching around for other people, finding them and establishing ties. It is not by chance, then, that for some people choosing a partner is associated with running away – in the sense of establishing a relationship with an 'other' (a foreigner, a black, a Jew, or even an other of the same sex – anyone in fact who would be an 'other' in their parents' eyes). The point is a demonstration, a provocation, an act of will that signals rebellion. 'Love' and 'asserting one's independence' – two powerful motives at the same time. What a thrill!

Until the day comes when the young become older. As the years pass, the majority lose their youthful passion and calm down. Their gaze ceases to be directed exclusively towards the future; they now look back to the past as well, pondering the lives they have lived hitherto. Many now question things previously taken for granted, and by the same token they find that many things acquire a positive gloss in retrospect, or even come to be viewed sentimentally because images of love, closeness and warmth are easily associated with childhood. With such subtle changes in feeling, the desire grows to revive traditions, celebrations and customs from one's family of origin. Such a turnabout may come as a surprise to outsiders and appear utterly inexplicable. But, as Immanuel Kant ([1784] 1991) remarked, human beings are made of 'crooked timber'; their emotional lives are not as one-dimensional as is often imagined, but rather multi-layered, complex and ambivalent. And this is true not least of a person's relationship to his or her own past. That relationship is frequently at odds with itself, or, as Werner Sollors describes it, 'The melodrama of different generations obscures the tension in human desire between the wish to escape ancestors and the yearning to fulfil their legacy' (Sollors 1986: 221).

Now it may be objected that, over the course of years, changes may occur in the thinking and attitudes even in the case of couples of the same nationality, religion or culture. There may well be a shift from running away to a subsequent rapprochement. The crucial distinction, however, is that, where a couple come from different backgrounds, the 'memory chest' of each is filled with different contents. And in later life, when people come to root around in their memory chest, retrieve bits and pieces and consider them anew, and when they take the decision symbolically to put this or that part on show in the living-room display cabinet, their partner who lives in the same house may well be taken aback. That is the essence of the surprise element that we called the reversion to the biographical past.

If a couple have succeeded in building up enough points in common over the years and have enough shared memories in the memory chest, and if each individual has enough flexibility, imagination and curiosity, unexpected changes of this kind can act as a stimulus for the other partner. In that event the reversion to the past can mark a new beginning for both of them.

Adventures

When two people of different origins fall in love and set out on a life together, it is a challenge, a daring exploit, an adventure. From the point of view of the lovers it is an encounter of two people in love, a case of two hearts beating as one. But in mixed relationships it is also an encounter of two worlds. People who by origin are worlds apart from each other take the decision to set up house together, share bed and board, in good times and in bad, until death do them part. What a decision, what a grand design! It is unsurprising that such an encounter of disparate worlds may sometimes end in disaster. On the other hand, a meeting of two worlds can also bring new insights. Those involved then begin to see their own familiar world through fresh eyes, and blank spots start to appear on the map of their home territory. And, as they find themselves drawn into their partner's world, they begin to discover its specificities, values, rituals, customs and expectations. Anyone who joins forces with a partner from a different background necessarily finds him- or herself in receipt of a lesson about a hitherto unknown part of the world.

A basic feature of mixed marriages is the simultaneous presence of the near and the far, the familiar and the strange. 'She is the closest of distant women' – this was how a man in a mixed marriage described his partner (Barbara 1989: 193). Anyone who hopes to eliminate such differences once and for all is doomed to failure. The better course of action is to accept that they exist and to acknowledge and accommodate them; the motto is that they should 'learn to live with their differences' (Schneider 1989: 1, 248). In many situations, despite everything a couple may have in common, it is possible to build bridges only with superhuman efforts (and even then it does not always work). Some things remain barred forever while others can be communicated verbally, with the aid of a sense of humour and the strength of a shared intimacy.

Mixed-nationality or intercultural couples find themselves confronted more frequently than others by unexpected questions and decisions. Depending on circumstances, this can lead to overloading and the collapse of the relationship. On the other hand, it creates the opportunity for greater frankness in everyday life and the capacity to venture on new beginnings. If the relationship prospers, something of the initial adventurousness remains alive, together with the optimism and the readiness to try out something new and to experiment. Where this is the case, mixed-nationality marriages remain especially fresh and alive, perhaps to a greater degree than others (Elschenbroich 1988: 366). As an American woman married to a Swiss put it, such a marriage produces 'the worst possible surprises, but also the most beautiful experiences. Basically, it means that what you expect to happen never does, while what does happen is something you never dreamt of in your wildest dreams' (Bonney 1993: 105).

3

Love Has Two Enemies: Distance and Closeness

'Geography spells the ruination of love', Erich Kästner wrote as early as 1931 (1990: 60). Was he on the mark with his pessimistic diagnosis? How much distance can love survive? How much distance does love need? How does love at a distance transform the 'nature' of love, its form, its luminosity and its fascination? Is love at a distance a diluted love, a remnant? Does it symbolize the end of love? Does love at a distance kill off nearby love or does it fan the flames? All these questions have many answers. One is as follows.

If the bold lovers of yesteryear regarded themselves as having broken free from the earthly shackles of class and status (as we see from the testimony of novels, plays and the letters of romantic love), new and different hopes inspire the lovers of our own day. Today they want liberation from the bonds of a shared locality, a shared language and a shared citizenship. Looked at in this light, distant love may be thought of as an intensified form of romanticism, one that acts even more radically in stripping away social and cultural bonds, dispensing even with geographical proximity and national and ethnic identity.

Regarded historically, there is nothing new in this. Both the European nobility and the wealthy bourgeoisie practised early forms of 'distant love', whereas now, at the start of the twenty-first century, 'world families' are being reinvented in a more democratic and popular form. While the nuclear family based on the nation-state was supposed to last for ever, it endured in reality no more than a few decades – until the late 1960s, when student unrest and the women's movement started up in the industrialized countries of the West.

These movements not only called into question the existence of the nuclear family; they also cast doubt on the inequality between men and women embedded in it and deemed natural (Beck and Beck-Gernsheim 1995). Today, at the beginning of the twenty-first century, the retreat from the normal family continues but with an added dimension. The nation-state, which now routinely intervenes in the private space of the individual, finds itself opposed by love and its call for freedom. 'Love your enemies' – this venerable biblical injunction now gains a new meaning. It has been secularized, and its reach has been extended into the realm of the personal and the private, not to say the erotic and the sexual.

In the present chapter we shall explore what happens to love when it becomes distant love, when it is brave and courageous enough – perhaps even over-exuberant and rash enough – not to be deterred by national boundaries and vast distances. In the process we make a distinction between two forms of distant love. On the one hand, there is the love that is defined by the geographical distance between the lovers; on the other hand, it is the cultural distance between the lovers that is foregrounded.

1   The Social Anatomy of Distant Love

From Local Neighbourhood to Internet Dating

Distant love is defined by geographical distance; the lovers live many miles apart, in different countries or even on different continents.

It is a mark of partner choice today that the range of possibilities has expanded enormously. To exaggerate only slightly, we may say that the world of limited choices for lovers has been transformed into a world of boundless opportunities. First, boundaries within society have become increasingly porous and social controls have become far weaker. In former times, the family unit regulated the choice of partner and ensured that lovers were directed down the right paths, appropriate to their financial and social status. Nowadays, the family unit – where it still exists – has lost a major part of its influence. The chaperone, who once acted as the guardian of both propriety and status, has entirely disappeared. The process of getting to know suitable partners has now done away with all the rules governing membership of the so-called better class of people; the invitation lists of the upper classes have ceased to be dominated exclusively by questions of lineage. Places with a far greater social mix have now come into being for people to make one another's acquaintance. They include the world of work, associations, fitness clubs, and so on.

In the same way, the handicaps of geography are losing their potency. In earlier times, mountains and ravines could make communications difficult between one village and the next, and life was lived mainly within a circumscribed neighbourhood. Now, however, the life world has become much larger. Mobility between two places, or even between two countries, has long since become an integral part of our daily lives – whether for language courses, business trips or holidays. The space for meeting new people has expanded commensurately – and with it the opportunities for potential romantic encounters.

Added to this is the new virtual space, the internet, a space for meeting new people, which is developing at an explosive rate. Its search engines bring a worldwide supply of new and constantly renewed opportunities directly into everyone's homes or onto their laptops. With the internet the temptations on offer are infinite. A paradise of unlimited possibilities opens up before us. The search engine is 'cause, instrument and result all in one – a self-expanding search process' (Hillenkamp 2009: 126).

Optimization is the watchword of these searchers' search. The greater the choice, the stronger the temptation. Who knows – perhaps the next click of the mouse will lead to the ideal candidate. So keep on clicking! We need to find the best available person – who, however, will never be found. ' "I have to keep on looking to see what new, pretty, interesting woman will turn up next. You can look every day. What will life have in store for me today?" That is the credo of the romantic of maximum possibility and the realist of the virtual world. "I love you" means "I shall delete my mailbox for you" ' (Moreno 2010: 85). A promise that, like so much to do with love, is easy to make but hard to keep.

Where do lovers find each other? 'Above all, at work, then in their circle of friends, and after that on the internet. The internet is in third place, before the club, the disco, the holiday or the café. A recent study shows that, for 30- to 50-year-olds, a third of all contacts that lead to a firm relationship begin on the internet. And the trend is upwards' (Moreno 2010: 85).

Love used to be and still always is something *imagined*. As we all know, it takes place largely in the mind. What is special about love on the internet is that it takes place *only* in the mind. The internet changes the overall nature of love. First, it makes it possible for lovers to love without being physically present, and, second, it ensures the anonymity of the contact between them. Third, it unleashes the imagination, and, fourth, the optimization rule prevails: if you are committing yourself for life, look to see if you can discover someone better.

The absence of the body and the anonymity guaranteed by dating on the internet tend to accentuate the romantic nature of the search, but can also encourage searchers to cast off their inhibitions.

> It is well known how the search for partners on the internet organizes and presents an infinite range of possible partners. The dating agencies no longer provide the searcher with two or three possible partners; nowadays they offer them a few hundred thousand, a few million. People are informed how many hundred thousand or million people are *online now* and can be contacted *immediately*, how many *contacts per hour* there are, and how many thousand photos have been put online during the past hour . . . The search for partners on the internet liberates from all time and space everything that takes place in the town and after dark. All of this can be done outside the towns and at any time. The liquidation of space that can be observed in the town has now been extended to the countryside. Going beyond the limits of the night, a characteristic feature of nightlife, is done even more systematically. People now see even more other people, and they do so faster . . . The internet implants in people's minds the idea of unlimited possibilities. Even those who do not go onto the internet in search of partners for the purpose of sex or to share their lives still experience their world as the world of the internet. They know what the possibilities are. They know what other people do. They have the same imagination. (Hillenkamp 2009: 123ff.)

Love Without Sex

The growth of opportunities to meet new people is not the only novel factor. A further difference is that, with love at a distance, the scope for yearning also changes, namely what love means for the experience of yearning, what it can and cannot achieve in connection with the sensuality of love, the relationship between love, sexuality and intimacy, and the relationship between love and everyday living, love and work.[3]

To experience love at a geographical distance means believing that an intense intimacy and emotional life is possible even though over extended periods of time sex is *something that can only be talked*

---

[3] All this is *terra incognita*! Apart from the first autobiographical reports (such as those by Freymeyer and Otzelberger 2000; Brunold, Hart and Hörst 1999), nothing has been written on this subject; what follows is therefore a sketch of our impressions, which stand in need of confirmation or otherwise by empirical research.

about. Love as transmitted via the media, telephone and internet must necessarily sacrifice much of sensuality. It must dispense with hands, skin and lips touching, with true eye contact and with the ecstasy of orgasm induced by contact with a lover. What remains is the sensuality of the voice, of language, of narrative and listening, of seeing and gazing. Love in the presence of the beloved can be silent, while love at a geographical distance must be kept alive and maintain its fascination simply with language and with looking. That is its opportunity but also its frailty. The one-dimensionality of the means at its disposal can mean that it will have no more than a short life, a swift death.

In a culture like that of the West, where direct physical contact and the ability of people to touch each other constitute an essential part of the experience of love, love at a geographical distance is scarcely sustainable in the long run. The 'pure' location of distant love is the sound of the voice, the narrative that is familiar with the other person's interior landscape and is able to respond to it – the narrative, in other words, that has mastered the art of intimacy. By intimacy we mean the ability to make the other person feel close despite the actual distance. 'Art' here is art in the highest sense. If it is to thrive, this intimacy calls for the exchange of self-portraits in narrative form, in which the two people concerned are present in a quite natural, everyday way. Thus distant relationships are able to break through what would be loud silences in nearby relationships. If the couple have times that are reserved exclusively for a mutual unburdening, this can even lead to a special closeness and intensity. Because their conversation is less exposed to distractions, it can concentrate entirely on speaking or looking, and this creates an opening for broaching essential questions of the relationship between two people.

All this notwithstanding, there is something monastic – monkish and nun-like – about love separated by geographical distances. It remains abstract because it is confined to email and Facebook, texting and Skype. In its pure form, distant love is scarcely liveable for non-monks and non-nuns. Normal people need oases of direct love from time to time, a sensuality comprehending all the senses, a love to the point of fulfilment. And for the other times they need the rituals and symbols that remind them of their moments of togetherness, and enable them to rediscover them, preserve them and reinforce them. Intimacy at a distance may sound romantic, but it is a form of romanticism that draws nourishment from the sober virtues of regularity, reliability and long-term planning. Intimacy at a distance depends on firm arrangements if the inner bond is to be sustained (e.g., Skyping every evening, meeting every six months). And this intimacy may always break down, as Erich Kästner notes in his customarily laconic way:

> When two people are never together, except for two days and one night in every month, their friendship is bound to be undermined, and when that state of affairs goes on for years, as it has done with us, the whole relationship breaks down. That has little to do with the inherent quality of the two persons, the process is inevitable . . . Of course we became alienated. Neither knew what friendships the other made. We didn't notice how we were changing or why we were changing. Letters are no good. And then we met, kissed, went to the theatre, asked for the latest news, spent the night together and separated again. Four weeks later, the same routine was repeated. Mental proximity and then love by the calendar, with your watch in your hand. It was hopeless. She in Hamburg, I in Berlin – geography spells the ruination of love. (Kästner 1990: 60)

But can we not argue with equal justice that geography enables love to blossom? A dialectics of distant love and nearby love prompts the question: How much nearness and how much distance can love survive?

Love Without Living Together

There are plenty of people to preach to you about both distant love and nearby love. Some recommend distant love as therapy for disappointments in nearby love. Others praise love from nearby as therapy for disappointments in distant love.

What is indisputable is that distant love has its advantages, particularly when the couple can adapt it to their own needs and desires. Many people even say that proximity is a myth. They say that the nearby love for which distant lovers yearn is stifling amid the daily routine. Too much closeness destroys love. Distant love keeps it youthful. It releases lovers from the need, the exorbitant need, always to have to keep on declaring one's love. It makes the impossible possible; it reconciles disagreements; it permits both closeness and distance, a life of one's own and a life together.

Such diagnoses doubtless contain a kernel of truth. Distant love is based not just on the separation of love and sexuality but on the divide between love and ordinary life. Distant love is like sex without having to launder the bedclothes, like eating without the washing up, like mountain hiking without sweat and aching bones. Who would object to that?

Nevertheless, distant love is no recipe for everlasting happiness; it is no holiday on the Isle of the Blessed while all around the majority of couples wither away in a life of routine. For we must not overlook the risks of a life removed from the vicissitudes of ordinary existence. I am thinking here, for example, of the danger of presenting an improved version of oneself in the course of exchanging signs of mutual affection. Or the other danger of idealizing one's partner, ascribing to him or her perfections that will not stand up in the harsh light of reality. Considered in this light, love at a distance means learning how to rhapsodize. Distant love is the love of the Sunday self for the other person's Sunday self, purified of the mundane realities of ordinary life. It is a love in which you do not have to reach an understanding about household routines or the horrors of imminent family visits. But because you experience only aspects of your partner's life, and because you know about much in his or her life only through his or her narratives – in short, because many potential crisis zones are concealed by distance – the relationship lacks the connection to ordinary reality. This allows the imagination to run riot.

> Relationships at a distance can be deceptive. It is easy to idealize your partner simply because you do not see important aspects of his personality. Or you are tempted to belittle him and project your own disappointments onto him. If I am having a bad time, he should have a bad time too or else he won't love me. One often fails to notice how one's partner develops. Or one has ceased to be the person one's partner still imagines. (Freymeyer and Otzelberger 2000: 161)

The reality check approaches when the distant lovers' great dream comes true: when one day they are together again and become a couple of nearby lovers. That is when they take leave of leave-taking. It is at this point that many people uncover hitherto unsuspected aspects of the beloved because they had been mercifully concealed by distance. In that situation distant love may become a wish-fulfilment once again. And 'If only you were here', the cry of distant lovers, turns into that other cry, 'If only you were there'.

Motherly Love from Afar

The bond between mother and child is another relationship that crosses national frontiers, and even continents, with increasing frequency. Mothers from Asia or Eastern Europe emigrate to North America or Western Europe so as to find employment as maids all

work. They are often illegal immigrants, often badly trє.
almost always poorly paid. Many are employed in a worlԝ
industry, the nanny industry. They function as 'substitute mothers' ᵢ.
the families of strangers, looking after the children, feeding them,
washing them, putting them to bed and playing with them. At the
same time, they are 'distant mothers' to their own children whom
they have left behind in their native land, more or less adequately
cared for by an aunt or a grandma, but sometimes left to their own
devices. Distant love here refers to the dilemma of a mother who
abandons her own child out of love for it in order to earn money
abroad so as to pay for its food, healthcare and education. Thus
distant love also refers to the situation of the children who have been
left behind and who yearn for closeness, human warmth and security,
and who miss their mother.

The costs incurred by this sort of distant love sometimes come to
light when the separation which may have lasted several years is over,
when the mothers have had their children restored to them and they
are on the point of realizing their life's dream: nearby love. Conflicts
frequently escalate between people who have been reunited but who
then become estranged.

Los Angeles, for example, is a city inhabited by many women who
have migrated there from Latin America and who have brought their
children to be with them after some time has elapsed. A counselling
service has been set up in one of the schools to lend support to families of this sort. The counsellors find that the children frequently
unleash a torrent of abuse against their mothers: 'I know you don't
love me. That is why you abandoned me!' The children tell how they
kept on praying that their mothers would be captured on the American frontier and sent back home. And they call on their mothers to
admit the error of their ways and to ask forgiveness for having abandoned them.

For their part, the mothers talk about how they have suffered from
the separation. They have won through and survived only thanks to
their love for their children. They have earned their money through
hard work so that their children should have a better future. Now
they want to be respected for the sacrifices they have made. They are
convinced that they have acted rightly and that the separation was
justified because it has paved the way for greater security for their
children.

The children insist, however, that they would rather have gone
hungry and stayed with their mother than have had enough to eat
but be separated from her. 'I didn't want money. I wanted you there.'

They tell their mothers they would never treat their children in the same way when it is their turn to have children. They would never leave their own children in order to look after those of other people (Nazario 2007: 245f.).

A counselling service is not the sort of place attended by people who have their own lives well in hand; it is a service for those who are no longer able to cope. Other reports make it clear that plenty of families survive years of separation without any dramatic ill-effects. Once they are older, many children recognize what their mothers have done for them and the opportunities they have created for them. But, even as young adults, they say they would never consider the option of such a separation for themselves (Parreñas 2003: 51).

Distant Love and the Labour Market

Why do a growing number of people allow their lives to be shaped by the various patterns of distant love? Why do they acquiesce in the endless recurrence of leave-takings alternating with spells of living alone? They do so because, in the first place, this form of life has its advantages if conditions are favourable. In the second place, this way of life is often not chosen voluntarily but is the consequence of exter-nal constraints – such as a job, for which mobility and flexibility are the prime prerequisites of success. As far back as the 1970s, Arlie Russell Hochschild described the demands placed on young aspiring scholars: 'Take your best job offer and go there no matter what your family or social situation. Publish your first book with a well-known publisher, and cross the land to a slightly better position, if it comes up' (Hochschild 1975: 49).

These demands have not diminished since that time. And they remain especially potent throughout the economy as well as in many other spheres of activity. Many people say that distant lovers are love nomads, love monads who always have everything they need with them on their laptop: their mobile office and their virtual love.

Looked at from this perspective, distant love is what remains when work and career overwhelm everything else, sweeping away the fron-tiers protecting private life. In this sense, distant love is love in a suitcase – a handy parcel that, like the electric toothbrush in one's culture case, can be easily packaged and plugged in anywhere – there, it's working, and my teeth are white and shiny. Becoming 'one's own entrepreneur' and plugging and unplugging one's electric toothbrush-love are things that go together admirably.

Children no longer have any place in such a society. The 'we' of distant love can be summed up in the formula: self-love *à deux* plus career as a hobby, but without children. This 'we' does not acknowledge the existence of the following generation, and in that sense it has no future. It is the residual 'we' of the radically individualized society.

Those who forego the pleasure of having children are only being consistent if they renounce nearby love. In that event, they will be at liberty to seize global market opportunities for jobs wherever and whenever they present themselves. In an age of global labour markets, distant love is the basic form of love. Taken to their logical conclusion, global capitalism and distant love are two sides of the same coin.

It follows that there is an elective affinity between capital, which overrides frontiers and the controls of the nation-state, and distant love, which breaks free from the framework of the normal family (with its shared household and the same citizenship). The fact that distant love breaks with the conventions of the normal family is not just an act of provocation. Rather, it adjusts to the demands of globalized capital, which itself penetrates the realms of intimacy and sexuality, transforming them into spheres compatible with the market. Thus the separation of love from sexuality, everyday life and parenthood cannot simply be consigned – as it is by Niklas Luhmann's theory – to the communication code of love (Luhmann 1986). It must also be viewed as reflecting the correspondence between changes in the forms of love and the dynamics of the world market as it tightens its grip on both external and internal reality. Distant love is the flexible love of 'flexible human beings' (Sennett 1998); it is the template in which labour market flexibility has become the principle informing the identity and organization of one's own life. If in future a working life involves five job changes, that means ten profound changes for a working couple. What marriage, what family can survive that? The way out points clearly to distant love with no children.

2 Lost in Translation

World families occur in two different forms. What is typical of the first form is, as we have said, geographical distance – in other words, the fact that couples and other members of the family may live in different places or even different countries. The second group is characterized by cultural distance. Here, members of the family live in the same house or as part of the same household but stem from highly diverse cultural (ethnic, national) backgrounds and have had very different experience and expectations, not least as regards personal relationships and their view of the connection between love, marriage and happiness.

The Many Meanings of Love

Many people argue that love is universal. People have always and everywhere fallen in love. Songs about all-consuming love are sung in every language. The art of love and its power have enabled it to conquer people's hearts despite all obstacles and to overcome the barriers of property, religion and nationality, of age and sex.

This idea is captivating but false. Following the creation of Eve from Adam's rib, mankind became dependent on sex for its continuation. Love stories are at the root of the sagas of antiquity. Epics, plays, poems and novels explore love and the relationships of couples in every conceivable variation. But the meanings of sexuality, love and marriage, and the forms in which they are practised, are by no means identical everywhere in the world. It is true enough that there are enough overlapping meanings in the world's languages to enable people all over the world to grasp the word 'love' and the values ascribed to it. But we may not infer from this (as do the exponents of the doctrine of love as a universal) that, when people use the word 'love', it will lead them to the same values and practices. To take a current controversial issue as an example, consider the question of arranged marriages. Some people talk of 'arranged marriages' and regard them as part of parents' concern for their children, while others regard them as 'forced marriages', the ruthless pursuit of parental interests, and indeed as criminal acts. Such attitudes cannot easily be reconciled. The gulf between them affords us a glimpse into the jungle of rival perspectives that opens up when we attempt to define what is meant by 'love', 'sexuality' and 'marriage' in particular contexts, and to uncover the commandments and prohibitions contained in them.

'Love' is an 'open-textured' concept – that is to say, when two people from different cultural backgrounds discuss it, with a complete understanding of what is at issue, they can nearly come to blows about whether or not a particular behaviour can satisfy the exalted requirements of the term. We can only guess at the consequences for world families. Conflicting attitudes constantly come to the surface. And participants in such debates are constantly forced to seek ways of bridging their differences.

Homosexual and Heterosexual Couples

Even in the internal Western discourse on love, the conflict of meanings is intense, with regard to both heterosexual and homosexual couples, and to their models and practices of love and intimacy. Heterosexual and homosexual intimacy and sexuality alike are saturated with sexual stereotypes and patriarchal forms of domination that are in glaring conflict with the supposed autonomy of individuals. In this respect, according to prevailing opinion, inequality is less marked in the case of homosexual couples than with heterosexuals. And, in fact, studies of same-sex couples show both partners seeking new forms of intimacy and striving to soften the hierarchical nature of both their work and their lives (Dürnberger 2011; Kurdek 2007). However, a number of studies show that people's imagination and energy are directed more towards exploring the experience of intimacy than towards efforts to maximize equality between the partners (Connell 1995; Morgan 1996).

At the same time, empirical studies allow us to sketch a picture containing unexpected nuances and subtle distinctions. According to them, men and women can seek and find greater equality in intimacy even in heterosexual relationships in which the old patriarchal sexual stereotypes persist more stubbornly in actual life patterns (Connell 1995; Hey 1997; Jamieson 1999; Morgan 1996).

> The couples have applied reflexive awareness of the malleability of the world and themselves to creating a framework of rules. The dialogue that they engage in, reworking what is fair and what is not, is a practical as well as political, sociological and philosophical piece of personal engagement. Any consequent politicization and personal empowerment has stemmed not only from a preoccupation with their own relationship but a more general engagement with the world. While starting from their own situation, their rules of fairness seek universal principles and are not tied to or derived from knowledge of each other's unique qualities. (Jamieson 1999: 486)

It is doubtless rash to relate such findings to distant love and world families, and yet the similarity is striking. In love relationships social distinctions are not abrogated; on the contrary, sexuality, love and the family provide the locus in which disagreements resulting from pre-set conditions are negotiated. The universalism of love, or, more precisely, the promise of universalism, bewitches us, deadens our senses, seduces us and smuggles the world's conflicts into the beds and hearts of lovers. Delusion is the prerequisite of delight. But even where social expectations are unthinkingly introduced into relationships, new resolutions can arise. People who fall in love across the boundaries of inequality frequently succeed in discovering their own forms of intimacy and sexuality. This may well enable them to withstand tensions between the worlds embedded in the family and to negotiate compromises.

Marriage Polish Style Versus Marriage American Style

Eva Hoffmann, who as a young girl emigrated from Poland to the United States with her parents, gave the book she wrote about her life the title *Lost in Translation*. In its description of scenes from her life, the book shows how all translations convey no more than an approximation of the original meaning, because words are embedded in experiences, values and horizons of meaning that bear the imprint of a particular cultural background and are lost in the process of translation. One scene begins with an interior monologue during a car journey. 'We're driving, my Texan and I, in his clunky Chevrolet from Houston to Austin, where we'll visit some friends. The highway is nearly empty and very hot.' She describes how she had forgotten the landscape of her childhood of which she is reminded by the sight of the Texan landscape. 'Otherwise, there's nothing but us and the speed of the car and the endlessly receding horizon' (Hoffmann 1989: 198). In order to open herself up to the freedom that America offered her, she had to learn how to forget the aromas and the natural flora of her youth in Poland. But the memories that come flooding back cause her to panic. There follows an internal debate:

> Should you marry him? The question comes in English.
> Yes.
> Should you marry him? The question echoes in Polish.
> No.
> But I love him; I'm in love with him.
> Really? Really? Do you love him as you understand love? As you loved Marek?
> Forget Marek. He is another person. He's handsome and kind and good.
> You don't feel creaturely warmth. You're imagining him. You're imagining your emotions. You're forcing it.
> So you're going to keep me from marrying him? You realize this is an important decision.
> Yes, that's why you must listen to me.
> Why should I listen to you? You don't necessarily know the truth about me just because you speak in that language. Just because you seem to come from deeper within. (Ibid.: 199)

For Eva Hoffmann the question 'Marriage: yes or no?' yields not one answer but two, one in Polish, the other in American. In her mind's eye she sees the Poland of her childhood, a world in which marriage meant a lifelong commitment, without exception and with no escape, until death do them part. Mindful of this lifelong commitment, her Polish voice says No. But another voice, the voice of her new American home, now makes itself heard. Here in America, it whispers, marriage is not necessarily a commitment for life. Should it turn out to have been a mistake, it is open to correction. There can be a divorce and a second try. Hence the American voice advises: Go on, try it out. Say Yes!

Here we see the world's disagreements embodied in one and the same person. A conflict between the old native country and the new one. It is a conflict between two worlds and two worldviews.

Pushy Men Versus Easy Girls

The same is true of sexuality, the amalgam of love and pleasure. Sexuality does not simply abide by the laws of nature and hormones; it is determined essentially by cultural rules. The more these rules originate in different worlds, the more easily they give rise to misunderstandings, embarrassments and irritations – and these may even reach boiling point. An episode narrated by Watzlawick in a textbook of social psychology illustrates the difficulty. It focuses on the period during the Second World War when American troops were stationed in Britain (see Watzlawick, Beavin and Jackson 1972). As may easily be supposed, it was not long before the first love relationships developed between American men and English women. Soon afterwards, stories started to do the rounds according to which such encounters took a surprising turn and went well beyond the bounds of propriety. There grew up a 'male' and a 'female' version of what happened next. Many of the Americans boasted of their conquests: English women were easy game! At the same time, English women told one another that the Americans were real devils when it came to sex. They couldn't wait to go all the way! Who was too forward for whom in this situation? Was it the men or the women who failed to abide by the rules of propriety?

Watzlawick and his colleagues offer an interpretation that foregrounds cultural differences of sexuality and love. According to their analysis, the approach of the sexes to each other – from the first introduction right up to intercourse – follows the rules of an invisible protocol that is pre-defined socially and of which the individuals concerned are mainly unaware. More specifically, this protocol contains rules governing the temporal sequence of the steps involved in the growing acquaintance. The crucial point is that different rules obtain in the USA and Britain. It is perfectly true, according to Watzlawick, that in both countries there are around thirty steps to be taken. But in America you can kiss sooner (say, after point 5 of the scale of steps – i.e., passionate hand-holding). That would seem 'cheeky' to the English women because their own internalized protocol states that kissing (to say nothing of tongue-kissing) can take place only after step 25 – that is to say, after the various adventures with creeping fingertips, on the inside of the thigh, for example.

If the American soldier, with his list of things to be ticked in his head, moves on to the kissing stage, say after point 5 (brushing her nipples with his fingertips), the Englishwoman thinks she has been out-manoeuvred because, on her internal checklist, a tongue kiss comes just before actual penetration. As the recipient of an unexpected kiss, the Englishwoman has only the choice of breaking off the romantic encounter immediately (which would mean that all her efforts at lovemaking had gone for nothing) or else giving a green light for the final act, in which the curtain would fall, as would everything else that had served as a defence (Watzlawick, Beavin and Jackson 1972: 20).

In other words, two culturally based misunderstandings in a sexual encounter lead to the climax.

3   Love, Marriage and Happiness: Multiplied, Divided, Inverted and Recombined

Should marriage be based on love? Is it profoundly immoral or even barbaric if two people marry without being in love? Or is love a highly unreliable companion, far too ephemeral as an experience on which to found a family? Is our aim to find happiness in marriage, or would we be better advised to look for it elsewhere? Is love the most beautiful of all feelings, or is it dangerous because it bewitches the senses and confuses our minds?

Different epochs, cultures and nations have produced very different answers to these questions. We shall select four from the cornucopia of relevant models in the present and the past and sketch them briefly. They can be presented roughly in historical sequence as far as their beginning and dominant phase are concerned. But it would be a gross error to suppose that they will disappear completely as new models or patterns of life come to the fore. They continue to exert an influence to a greater or lesser degree, partly covert and partly overt. This applies especially beyond the Central European or Western space. At the opening of the twenty-first century, what we see is not the victory of a single model but the coexistence and rivalry of various models, which have resulted in the emergence of a number of hybrid forms.

Marriage, Children, Maybe Love

In pre-modern Europe the entity known nowadays as the 'family', and studied as such, included, in addition to members of the extended family, maids and servants, etc. The wishes of the individual were subordinated to the needs of the community. Needless to say, passions and even sexuality were not unknown both alongside marriage and before it, but, in the list of what counted in marriage, affection, love and feelings did not occupy centre stage. What was of primary importance was a union that obeyed the rules of property ownership and status.

In other words, people made matches for good or ill, got on with their work, and produced and brought up children. People did not expect to enjoy their 'individual happiness'. The search for happiness was an alien concept. You accepted your fortune or misfortune as it came – in the spirit of resignation to God's will. This does not mean that people were unhappy. To infer that would be to apply the yardstick of contemporary Western society to pre-modern conditions of love and life.

The morality of those days was not concerned with sexuality as a source of pleasure; sexuality was directed at the procreation of children, the maintenance of dynasties and families. Lust, to say nothing of the art of sexuality, was condemned by theologians as sickness and sin. The monks, made intimately conversant with the thrills of love through the confessions of their sinful sheep, developed into the pioneers of a black art of eroticism with its prohibitions: he who burns with excessive ardour for his own wife acts disgracefully. Untrammelled love, the passion that lovers feel beyond the bounds of wedlock, is altogether too great. 'A rational man shall love his wife prudently and not passionately; he shall tame his desires and not allow himself to be inveigled into intercourse' (St Jerome, cited in Flandrin 1984: 155). Even the sagacious Michel de Montaigne wrote in his essay 'Of Moderation': 'Marriage is a solemn and sacred tie', in which sexual desire is unseemly, unless 'the pleasure we extract from it' is 'a sober and serious delight', tempered by a certain kind of strictness; 'it should be a sort of discreet and conscientious pleasure' (Montaigne 1908).

If in the course of time no affection arose, but on the contrary mutual dislike increased by the day, the married couple were nevertheless indissolubly bound together until death. Divorce was scarcely an option. With the passage of time the anxieties and hopes of parenthood, the shared labours in house and home, the survival of sickness and other crises might even foster the growth of a kind of love and intimacy. This is demonstrated by statements in which married couples testify to their mutual affection.

What then is the secret of a happy marriage? One possible answer is that, if you have no expectations of happiness in marriage, you are unlikely to be disappointed.

Love, Marriage, Children

Nowadays, the 1950s and 1960s are regarded as the Golden Age of marriage and the family. In the normal (Western) family, a man and a woman decide to get married out of mutual love; both partners are of the same nationality and the wife bears her husband's name. This marriage is supposed to represent a community of feeling and should at least begin as such. And it should last a lifetime. If all goes well, if life takes its predicted course, it all begins with a romantic encounter, two hearts beating as one. This is followed by announcing publicly the happy choice of partner and the wedding, and after this comes the lengthy middle phase devoted essentially to bringing up the children. It can be summed up in the formula: love, marriage, baby carriage.

During this period the influence of religion, convention and tradition was still pervasive, especially in private life. Life was regulated by strict standards of custom and propriety; every infringement was to be condemned. Divorce was possible, but its cost was a major deterrent. Since divorce entailed a lifelong stain, a permanent damage to one's reputation, it was resorted to only in extreme cases – for example, when the marriage escalated into a lifelong feud. The majority still preferred to make some sort of accommodation – either resigning themselves to accepting the situation or acquiescing in overt or clandestine affairs.

Love, Marriage, Maybe Children, Maybe Divorce

By the end of the 1960s the power of the old (family) values had started to wane. A succession of other socially accepted patterns of life began to appear alongside the normal family. Following the massive criticism of the institutions of marriage and the family by the student movement and the women's movement, there was a rise in the numbers of couples living together without marriage. This kind of relationship was highly charged emotionally and associated with loftier expectations. Many people adopted the motto 'live life to the full without regard to the conventions' – and this goes for love relationships as well. The freedom to love, the I and the Thou that becomes We, that creates itself as We – this We should become a small infinity for lovers (Beck and Beck-Gernsheim 1995).

In this model the stability of partnerships and family is based on the shaky foundations of the sentiments of love. In the beginning was the Big Bang of romantic love: the emergence and consolidation of the fleeting experience of love between two free individuals for the formation of partnerships, relationships for the purpose of weddings, marriage and parenthood on the basis of personal choice, guided by sexual attraction in a space full of the promise of unlimited possibilities.

Since this love knows no bounds, when it wanes, the foundations of marriage and partnership will have vanished. If the promises of individualized love fail to materialize, those involved will simply be left with an experiment that failed, for whatever reason. This means that it is permissible, even rational, to break it off. A love whose legitimacy was grounded in itself has divorce as its corollary. Thus divorce gradually becomes normal, since every failed attempt to achieve a happy marriage can be followed by a further attempt. Individualized love not only presents people with ever new opportunities for happiness, it also gives them new forms of unhappiness – and the two are indissolubly linked. This is the normal chaos of divorce (Beck and Beck-Gernsheim 1995).

Love and Many 'Maybes'

Today, at the beginning of the twenty-first century, the model of individualized love has become universal. Wherever it assumes a radical form, everything is related to 'me' – and that includes the 'us'. It is an 'us' that is one thing above all else, namely a space for self-presentation and self-dramatization. Literature provides succinct illustrations of this development. Earlier on, breaking away from the family, escaping from its grasp, its constraints, was a dominant theme. Nowadays, in contrast, more recent literature focuses on the futility of the desire for a happiness that knows no bounds. Lifestyles in the age of a radical individualization are presented either with sober detachment or else with irony or even satire.

If we follow these accounts we see both men and women caught up in the infinite loop of an unquenchable desire for happiness (Hillenkamp 2009; Strauss 1976). There has also been a transformation in the horizons of love. To put it bluntly, everything revolves around sex, around love, around children, around supporting them, and around the acquisition and maintenance of wealth. But the primary concern is how the person with whom I am living, or whom I am marrying, enriches and glorifies me and succeeds in disclosing my self to me.

The characters portrayed here as the protagonists of an increasingly intensified process of individualization are not concerned primarily with the relationship or the marriage (though that is a concern). People dress individually. People create themselves individually. The worldwide cosmetics, hairdressing and face-lifting industries produce individual self-dramatizations on a conveyor belt. But the decisive factor that identifies me for all the world to see is my choice of partner – for the time being (Gilbert 2010).

No matter whether the partner is rich or poor, Catholic, Muslim or atheist, one thing can be predicted with some certainty: he or she will have at his or her disposal a stock of complex, internalized stories about the miracles of their love and marriage or the wounds inflicted by their separation, stories that can be produced at the drop of a hat, and told and retold. And it is even possible to predict the structure of these marriage narratives that explain to the world how I have become what I am now.

Their first characteristic is that they tell the story of two people (and not their parents or relatives, friends, etc.). Before they first met, these two individuals were engaged on a solitary journey through a life full of temptations and mishaps. The screenplay of this individualized odyssey is a saga full of ironic twists and turns, surprises and contradictions.

The transition from love to partnership or marriage (and, later on, from marriage to divorce) is treated as an epic journey through a golden haze (or else as tragedy). If you ask a modern Western woman how she met her husband or partner, when, where and how she fell in love with him, she responds with a complex and deeply felt personal narrative that she has carefully constructed, memorized and saved for reproducing on suitable occasions in order to be able to collect the interest due to her in recognition of her original selfhood (the currency of prestige of the age of the sovereign self). It might be fruitful to collate these marital narratives of How-I-became-what-I-am-today and compare them as typical narratives of men and women or else as instances of sexual stereotypes.

Doubts ('She wasn't really my type'); strokes of luck ('In my narrow student lodgings where we discussed our seminar projects there was really room for only two pieces of furniture, a chair and a bed'); resistance and other obstacles ('My father turned off the flow of money so as to put an end to our relationship, although its only effect was to bring us closer together') – these tropes are the core of the narrative structure.

In the same way, the end of the narrative is worth analysing. *Before* the divorce the story would end with redemption ('Today I cannot imagine what life would be like without him/her'). *After* the divorce, the doubts that were always there in the background make their appearance ('Why did I always repress my early doubts and refuse to take seriously the many signs of his/her infidelity?').

And, predictably, the fact that the narrator is not just the victim but also the author of his or her own love story is an integral part of the model of a radically individualized love. He or she ascribes to him- or herself a key role in the unfolding of the story, arising from his or her own decisions (or failures to decide) and actions (or failure to act). But there are limits; the separation, the divorce, is of course the other person's fault!

This means that, at the start of the twenty-first century, love is treated as an absolute in the radically intensified Western model, and the contradictions between individualization, happiness, freedom and love form the indispensable precondition of everything: partnership, marriage, parenthood, the shared household and the shared finances. But also of separation and divorce. And the second marriage.

A fixed sequence? Such a thing no longer exists. Instead, we see a series of phases, of biographical stages and transitions. At family parties the husband meets the former husband, the third wife of my first husband turns up too; my children start quarrelling with your children and our children. Marriage and divorce are both revelations of one's own self.

Pragmatic Marriage

The biography of the American journalist Elizabeth Gilbert resembles in many respects the lives of many individualized women in the West: success in their careers, but a troubled personal life and a failed marriage. Before embarking on a new marriage she would like to discover the secret of a successful marriage and undertakes to research the matter. In the course of her studies she comes across the Hmong people, an ethnic group originally from South-East Asia, who fought on the American side in the Vietnam War and suffered great losses.

Many of the survivors migrated to the United States, where they soon stood out because of the strength of their group identity as well as their uncompromising resistance to the blessings of modern life (Fadiman 1997).

Elizabeth Gilbert's chief interlocutor from among the Hmong was an old woman, a grandmother, a key figure in the Hmong's network of families and relations. The conversation ran into difficulties when Gilbert asked the woman to tell her story of her marriage – in the hope that she would hear some anecdotes about how she came to love her husband.

'What did you think of your husband, the first time you ever met him?

Her entire wrinkled face arranged itself into a look of puzzlement. Assuming that she had misunderstood the question, I tried again:

'When did you realize that your husband might be somebody you wanted to marry?'

Again, my question was met with what appeared to be polite bafflement.

'Did you know he was special right away?' I tried once more. 'Or did you learn to like him over time?'

Now some of the women in the room had started giggling nervously, the way you might giggle around a slightly crazy person – which was, apparently, what I had just become in their eyes.

I backed up and tried a different tack: 'I mean, when did you first meet your husband?'

The grandmother sorted through her memory a bit on that one, but couldn't come up with a definitive answer aside from 'long ago'. It really didn't seem to be an important question for her.

'Okay, *where* did you first meet your husband?' I asked, trying to simplify the matter as much as possible.

Again, the very shape of my curiosity seemed a mystery to the grandmother . . . Anyway, she said, it is not an important question as to whether or not she knew him when she was a young girl. After all, as she concluded to the delight of the other women in the room, she certainly knows him now.

'But when did you fall in love with him?' I finally asked, point-blank.

The instant Mai translated this question, all the women in the room, except the grandmother, who was too polite, laughed aloud – a spontaneous outburst of mirth. . . .

I persisted, following up their peals of laughter with a question that struck them as even more ridiculous:

'And what do you believe is the secret to a happy marriage?'

Now they really did lose it. Even the grandmother was openly howling with laughter. . . . All I could understand was that these

Hmong ladies and I were clearly speaking an entirely different language. (Gilbert 2010: 33–5)

What we in the West have become accustomed to thinking of as a 'family' has become so minute that it would have to be examined under an electron microscope in order to be seen at all. Our 'family' consists of small groups of people who live their lives in large, thinly populated buildings in accordance with the unwritten laws of 'one's own life' and 'one's own space'. The opposite situation obtains among the Hmong. If the Hmong family is anything, it is definitely not the framework of life, love and the family in which people worship day after day at the altar of individual decision-making and in which they seek out mutual emotional support if they are afflicted by the punishment of divorce.

A Clash of Love Cultures

World families often consist of a patchwork of the different models. One and the same family may well contain, e.g., a secular daughter, a strict fundamentalist father, a half-secularized, half-religious mother, and a fundamentalist son who was born in the West but who holds anti-Western views. In other words, a family of this kind embodies the contradictions between old and new models of love, sexuality, marriage and the family in ways that may coexist but which may well lead to conflict within it. We can see here in exemplary fashion how world families may represent a microcosm of divergent but interconnected lives in which pre-modernity and the first and second modernities jostle for supremacy (Beck and Grande 2010). We may distinguish three basic positions in the current sociological debates. Love and intimacy in the modern world may be seen as 'characteristic of the nation-state', as 'universalist' or as 'cosmopolitan' (see also the Introduction). In the context of the nation-state, the core of the family is a secular version of the Holy Trinity: one household, one nationality and one identity. But lovers and the family have long since made their escape from this model and have been trying out a kind of solidarity between strangers. The universalist approach is akin to this. It combines the great transformations of love and intimacy with the development of European modernity, or, more precisely, with the historical emergence of the conflict between freedom, equality and love (Beck and Beck-Gernsheim 1995; Giddens 1992; Illouz 2012; Luhmann 1986, *inter alia*). In this instance the particular nature of the European tradition is misinterpreted as the universal route to the paradoxes of the freedoms of modern love (an error that also disfigured our earlier diagnosis of the 'normal chaos of love').

The cosmopolitan approach, however, which we sketch in the present book, shows how in world families the European, and more generally the Western, model of love and the culture of love and the family derived from other world regions are partly woven together and partly subsist in a state of conflict. Looked at in this way, world families combine elements of tradition and modernity, proximity and distance, the familiar and the foreign, similarity and difference – combinations that bridge different epochs, countries and continents and reflect the turbulences of the globalized world in the intimate realm of private life.

4

Cosmopolitan Communities of Fate

Whether we are discussing mixed-nationality couples, distant love, immigrant domestic workers or baby tourism – the patterns of love and types of families that we have brought together under the heading 'world families' – one thing is clear. They can be understood only from a cosmopolitan point of view, not from a national or universalist perspective. At the same time, it is no less true that profound changes of the kind that we have identified in relations between the sexes can also be detected in a different form in other aspects of society. This explains why the transformations we can see in relationships between couples or within families do not seem exceptionally odd or exotic; they fit in with a larger process of development, a basic tendency of modernity in the early twenty-first century. At the present time, we are witnessing not only the emergence of world families but also the increasing overlap between the world religions, the growth in risks across the world, etc., all of which take place against the background of a world market that increasingly invades every facet of life. Hitherto our world was defined essentially by the nation-state, a form of society that permeated politics, the economy and everyday life. That world is now in the process of being transformed into one in which nation-states are changed from within and the contours of a world risk society become more and more visible.

We describe this process as one of cosmopolitanization. This means more than merely globalization or growing transnationalism. It is more than the quantitative increase in the interconnections between countries and continents. Cosmopolitanization refers to a state of interdependence between individuals, groups and countries that is not just economic and political but also ethical, transcending national, ethnic, religious and political boundaries and power relations. These mutual dependencies form a kind of cross-border community or even numbers of such communities, each with a common destiny (Beck 2006; Beck and Grande 2010).

Regardless of national frontiers and geographical distances, these cross-border communities are to be found in a vast variety of forms and locations – whether as love (see world families) or as economic rivalry on the world market (high-wage economies versus low-wage economies), or again as threats to mankind (climate change, nuclear power, etc.). Cosmopolitanization as a cross-border community with a common destiny means that the 'global other' has become a part of our own lives. The inhabitant of the Brazilian rainforest, the peasant in Eastern Anatolia, the financial adviser in London or Manhattan may never meet, but they are connected with one another. This allows us to infer the supreme imperative of cosmopolitanization: whether or not we like people whose skins are a different colour or who belong to a different nationality or religion, whether we find their customs congenial or strange, or whether we regard them as enemies, we are nevertheless obliged to coexist with these distant and/ or alien and sometimes even hostile others; we must reach understandings with them and work with them because there is no other way for us to survive. The days of autonomy, of national self-sufficiency, of splendid isolation are gone for ever.

The idea that cosmopolitanization imposes a kind cross-border community can be seen with especial clarity in the increasingly globalized medical industry. The growth of medical transplants has led to the emergence of a shadow industry which supplies the world market with fresh body parts. But what have fresh kidneys got to do with cosmopolitanization?

1   Fresh Kidneys, or Global Inequality Embodied

Our world is characterized by radical social inequality (Beck and Poferl 2010). At the lower end of the global hierarchy, countless human beings are caught up in a vicious circle of hunger, poverty and debt. Driven by sheer need, many people are forced to take desperate steps. They sell a kidney, a portion of their liver, a lung, an eye or even a testicle. This leads to the emergence of a community of a very special kind: the destiny of inhabitants of affluent regions (with its complement of patients waiting for organs) is coupled with that of the inhabitants of regions living in poverty (whose body is their only source of capital). Both groups are concerned with existential matters in the most literal sense, with life and survival.

An empirical case study undertaken by the anthropologist Nancy Scheper-Hughes (2005) has shown how the outcasts of the world, the economically and politically expropriated – refugees, the homeless, street children, undocumented migrants, prisoners, ageing prostitutes, cigarette smugglers and thieves – hand over parts of their bodies to transplant doctors. The doctors insert these organs into the sick bodies of others, literally incorporating them into people who belong to a social stratum with enough money to pay for the organs of the global poor. The outcome is a modern form of symbiosis in which medical technology is able to fuse two bodies, transcending distances and frontiers in the process.

In the body landscapes of individuals, continents, 'races', classes, nations and religions all merge. Muslim kidneys purify Christian blood. White racists breathe with the aid of black lungs. A blonde manager gazes at the world through the eye of an African street urchin. A Catholic bishop survives thanks to the liver taken from a prostitute in a Brazilian favela. The bodies of the rich are ingeniously transformed into patchwork creations while those of the poor are converted into one-eyed or one-kidneyed spare-part stores which come in handy for mutilations of many kinds. And, needless to say, all this takes place quite without compulsion, 'voluntarily', as the recipients of the organ commodities – namely, the wealthy sick – like to emphasize (while the payments they make to the people mutilated in the process are reinterpreted as contributions to humanitarian aid). In this way the piecemeal sale of their organs becomes a form of life insurance for the poor, one in which they sacrifice a part of their current existence in order to be able to survive. The net result of the global spread of transplant medicine is the 'biopolitical citizen' – a white, male body, fit or fat, in Hong Kong or Manhattan, furnished with an Indian kidney or a Muslim eye.

This radically unequal cosmopolitanization of bodies takes place silently, without any personal interaction between donors and recipients. Kidney donors and recipients are mediated via the world market but remain anonymous to each other. Nevertheless, their relationship is existential, vital for the survival of both, albeit in different ways. The henceforth indissoluble union with the distant, alien other – which is what we call cosmopolitanization – makes no assumptions about personal acquaintance, personal contact or any mutual knowledge. In short, cosmopolitanization in this sense may include dialogue with the other, direct communication (in the case of mixed-nationality marriages), but it can also occur as a speech-free, contact-free union (as in the case of kidney transplants).

In this latter example, we discern the lineaments of the human condition at the start of the twenty-first century. The contrasts between national and international, inside and outside, 'us' versus 'the others', are all overwhelmed by the advance of modernity and have become anachronistic. They evaporate and melt into new forms.[4] 'Fresh kidneys', transplanted from one body to another, from the globalized South to the globalized North, are by no means exceptional. They are symptomatic of a widespread development. Love, parenthood, the family, the household, careers, work, the labour market – the institutions and entire aspects of life of disparate worlds find themselves joined together and transformed in their innermost being. The weaving together of these disparate worlds can be seen on supermarket shelves, in the labels of the different foods, on restaurant menus (if you pay, you can eat the food of the entire globe); it permeates art, the sciences, the world religions and bursts in upon us in the form of global risks, such as climate change or the world financial crisis.

In the German debates, some dismiss globalization as a current fad; others raise it to the status of a new destiny for mankind. But both extremes imply that it is all happening 'somewhere out there'. It is generally supposed that nation-states continue on their way unperturbed. Cosmopolitanization, however, shifts these interconnections between the world's regions so that they become manifest somewhere beneath the level of the nation-state. Distinctions between 'national' and 'international' are blunted if more and more people work in a cosmopolitan way, make love in a cosmopolitan way, marry in a cosmopolitan way, live, travel, go shopping and cook in a cosmopolitan way. Such distinctions lose their edge if the inner identity and political loyalty of more and more people pertain not to a single state, a single country or native land, but to two or even three at the same time; if more and more children are born to mixed-nationality families, grow up with several languages, pass their childhood partly in one country, partly in another, or even in the virtual space of television and the internet. Whoever makes so bold as to proclaim that multiculturalism is dead is blind to the reality. What we are witnessing is the death not of multiculturalism but of the

---

[4]This is precisely what is meant by 'reflexive modernization'. The side effects of radical modernization undermine the institutional, legal, political, moral and social foundations and dichotomies of the first modernization – i.e., the modernity of the nation-state (see Beck 1996; Beck, Bonß and Lau 2003).

monoculturalism of the nation-state. The growing integration of different worlds is now irreversible, and the changes it introduces into the nation-states are fundamental.

2 The Power of Capital

The dismantling of national trade barriers that followed rapidly upon the collapse of the Soviet Union and the end of the East–West conflict has led to a redistribution of power between nation-states, on the one hand, and worldwide economic agents, on the other. Companies are the gainers in this process because (like world families) they can cut the umbilical cord binding them to a single place or a single nation-state (Beck 2005). Several factors have contributed to this change. First, new communication technologies and frontiers open to capital and information flows enable jobs to be exported to wherever wages, safety regulations, welfare contributions, etc., are lowest.

Second, modern information technologies make it possible to create social proximity even where geographical distances are great, and hence to build cooperation between the different branches of a company in whatever countries they are located. By setting up transnational forms of organization, companies are able to take on workers in distant countries and continents, combining the strengths of one location with those of another in a different country.

Third, transnational concerns have the power to play off countries and production sites against one another by luring them into a global competition for the lowest wages, the lowest tax rates and the best infrastructure. In the same way, they can 'punish' countries that are thought to be too expensive or hostile to investment by closing down plants and moving production facilities elsewhere.

Fourth, and last, transnational businesses can manage their assets so that they invest, produce, pay tax and have their home base in different localities and in this way construct an impenetrable jungle out of the different strands of the production process. They can thus exploit the benefits and disadvantages of different locations – a game that can be highly profitable for people able to manoeuvre between different national jurisdictions.

This is how economic interests succeed in throwing off the shackles of the nation-state and democratic controls. This process leads to a separation of politics and actual control, a process fraught with consequences (Bauman 2010: 203).

In earlier phases, the nation-state had succeeded in developing political and administrative mechanisms that could tame industrial capitalism and ensure that the social and cultural wounds it inflicted on society were kept within bounds. Since this was achieved within the framework of the nation-state, a kind of marriage between politics and power came into being. This marriage has evidently come to an end. Power, transformed and diffused, has been partly moved to cyberspace, to the markets and to mobile capital, and partly shifted onto the shoulders of individuals who have to bear the risks on their own. At the present time, there is no institution in sight that could control and tame the power of capital as the nation-state had done previously, even though there are a number of experimental, perhaps even embryonic, seats of government beyond the nation-state. Examples are the meetings and pronouncements of the G20 or G8 states.

3 Outsourcing Jobs

The power accruing to capital has set in motion a profound change in the labour market, without public endorsement or any democratic procedure, without consulting those affected or giving them the right to express an opinion. Tectonic shifts are taking place in the labour market – from North to South, from West to East – and these shifts threaten the livelihoods of millions of people. They find themselves confronted with an entirely new historical event. In affluent countries workers are becoming replaceable; they can be made redundant and replaced by workers in poor, low-wage countries.

In the age of the first modernity, when nation-states were powerful and sovereign, national frontiers acted as a bulwark against international competition between workers. Today, when the second modernity holds sway, a capitalist economy specializing in outsourcing generates an increasingly intense competition between native and foreign labour – Korean factory workers against Japanese factory workers, Polish craftsmen against British craftsmen, and so forth. In this context, existential interdependence means that the unknown other becomes the internal economic enemy of the inhabitants of affluent countries because he threatens their jobs, their wages and their prosperity.

What we are witnessing is an involuntary process of cosmopolitanization. It overrides national frontiers and bypasses the sovereign claims of nation-states. Its political implications are huge. As a consequence of competition among employees on a global scale, feelings of resentment in prosperous regions towards the 'others' are on the increase. Xenophobia is spreading. This example shows us how subverting national frontiers leads to a new hardening of attitudes towards outsiders.

Even if people's life worlds have ceased to be small-scale, isolated and provincial but are increasingly sucked into the maelstrom of global events, it does not follow that their horizons are expanding and that they are becoming more open-minded and sophisticated. The cosmopolitanization of life situations and life worlds does not necessarily lead to cosmopolitan attitudes. In other words, it is one thing to be affected by global processes; to become more open-minded and more sensitive to global events is quite another.

4 Competing World Religions

For centuries the universalist claims of the three great monotheistic religions were civilized and tamed by territorial frontiers. The greater the flow of migrants, the more populations become mixed and diverse, the more information flows swell with the arrival of the new media, then the more directly the different religions impinge on one another. Jews, Christians and Muslims all pray in the same place (Beck 2010; Bauman 2009). As the many millions of believers scatter throughout the globe, their gods, who alone can bring them salvation, go with them. They, the rulers of the world who tolerate no other gods beside them, are forced to dwell in close proximity to one another. It is only now, when all attempts to shield religions from one another have failed, that we perceive the explosive force that arises from this simultaneous confluence of geographical proximity and social distance.

The juxtaposition of the world's religions and their interaction produce a multi-monotheistic entanglement in which the one and only God of other religions, the universalist aspirations of the different faiths, are brought into direct contact with one another. The potential for conflict and perhaps even violence is self-evident.

5 Climate Change: A Threat to Humanity

Traditionally, the climate and the weather were instances of nature in itself, a category on its own, uninfluenced by society and culture. Different regions, different countries, had their own climate. Lemon trees flourish in Italy; in England it rains; it freezes at the North Pole; while Germany has the changing seasons – spring, summer, autumn and winter.

Now, at the beginning of the twenty-first century, we are experiencing the 'end of nature', the post-climate era. Climate change unites nature and society. The weather is local and regional while simultaneously the climate is global, or, more exactly, cosmopolitan – that is to say, it determines the local weather. The destiny of human beings in far-distant regions is linked to ours and ours to theirs. Climate change is calculated in global climate models since it is no respecter of national frontiers. Our lives and the survival of all are interconnected. Whoever uses an electric toothbrush in Germany will bear his share of the responsibility, or even guilt, if natural disasters occur on the other side of the planet, in Japan or Australia.

6   Risk Communities as Imagined Communities

Twenty-five years ago – in response to the Chernobyl nuclear disaster – an explanation was offered for the fact that the great risks of the present day are associated with the emergence of global communities with a common destiny.

> There has certainly been no shortage of historical catastrophes in this century: two world wars, Auschwitz, Nagasaki, then Harrisburg and Bhopal, and now Chernobyl. This calls for caution in choosing our words and brings our view of distinctive historical characteristics into sharper focus. All the suffering, deprivation and violence inflicted on man by man had previously only been known under the category of the 'others' – Jews, blacks, women, asylum seekers, dissidents, communists, etc. There were fences, camps, urban districts and military blocs on the one hand and one's own four walls on the other hand – real and symbolic boundaries behind which those seemingly not affected could withdraw. All of this both continues to exist and yet has ceased to exist since Chernobyl. It is the *end of the 'others'*, the end of all our sophisticated distancing manoeuvres, something that atomic contamination has brought home to us. *Deprivation can be isolated, but this is no longer the case with the dangers of the nuclear age.* That is where its new cultural and political strength lies. Its power is the power of danger, which nullifies all the protected zones and differentiations of the Modern Age. (Beck 1986: 7)

Modern societies, Western and non-Western, rich and poor alike, find themselves confronted by historically new, global risks (climate change, financial crisis, terrorism, etc.). These confrontations assume different forms in different societies, but all of them force everyone to confront the 'cosmopolitan imperative': cooperate or be doomed!

Only common action gives hope of salvation! The great global crises – environmental, technological and economic – generate decision sequences that will transform the political dynamics of nation-states. A historically new kind of community with a shared destiny, uniting the global North and the global South, is in the process of being born. This has nothing to do with cosmopolitanism; it is not a call for a 'world without frontiers'. On the contrary, it is registering an empirical fact: the great risks of today are forcibly bringing about the creation of a worldwide community because the survival of all depends on whether they are capable of common action.

The initiative of groups in civil society, individual states and global cities can bring about the creation of 'risk societies' that are based on the awareness of a shared responsibility and on the knowledge both that great threats cannot be contained geographically and that they produce consequences whose dire effects will persist into the distant future.

This makes it clear that cosmopolitanization can be arrived at by two different routes. On the one hand, individuals, groups and associations can actively open up their hearts and minds to alien worlds, customs and precepts of faith (of which world families provide numerous examples). On the other hand, without playing an active part, individuals can simply let themselves be swept along by the tide of global events. However, even if all human beings are sitting in the same boat, the shared community of modernity, this does not mean that they are all equal or that they enjoy equal rights. On the contrary, the fragility of the boat – to extend the metaphor – represents a threat to all, and this looming destiny makes everyone conscious of the world's inequalities, even the affluent secluded in their gated communities. The universal nature of the threat and the existential entanglement of rich and poor are but two sides of the same coin.

7 The Cosmopolitanization of Everyday Life

Cosmopolitanism is concerned with values, cosmopolitanization with facts. Cosmopolitanism in the philosophical sense, from Immanuel Kant to Jürgen Habermas, is a global political project, whether from above (governments and international organizations) or from below (the actors of civil society). Cosmopolitanization, on the other hand, acts from below and from within, in everyday life, and is often involuntary and unnoticed. Cosmopolitanization extends from the upper reaches of politics and society down to the everyday lives of families, conditions in the job market and individual lives and bodies – even if, at the same time, people continue to wave national flags, appeal to the traditional values of the dominant national culture and proclaim the death of multiculturalism.

Cosmopolitanization points to the erosion of the definitive frontiers that once separated markets, states, civilizations, cultures, life worlds and human beings. It refers also to the concomitant existential, global entanglements and confrontations, but by the same token it includes too the encounters with other people in one's own life. The same thing holds good for distant love and world families, as well as the job market, religion and major threats, etc. Only by taking the parallel presence of such facts into account will we be able to grasp the scope of the changes taking place today in love and the family.

5

Intimate Migrations: Women Marrying for a Better Life

Increasing numbers of people venture into patterns of love and life that transcend geographical and national boundaries and so create world families. But why do they do this and by what means does it all take place?

People do not just wake up one morning to discover that their relationships have changed overnight and they are now part of distant families and world families. On the contrary, the transformation takes place silently, by stealth, and in part, at least, as the consequence of individual decisions (such as marriage or migration). But aren't we told every day that ancient walls and barriers are still being built and reinforced? Isn't the spectre of a fundamentalist Islam haunting Europe? And now, to our surprise, we are supposed to believe the opposite message, that individuals from disparate worlds with different passports and no language in common are getting married – despite all the obstacles that officials can strew in their path. How can that be possible? Are we supposed to believe that the wave of marriages and cohabitations with foreigners and people from distant parts is a kind of drunken frenzy? Is it just a euphoric lapse triggered by trips abroad or clicking on the internet that blinds people to the rampant conflicts in the world?

No. We are talking here about universal and individual constraints, seductions and impulses. What appears to the individuals concerned, from below, from the grassroots, as a unique, incomparable event, looks to the observer from above, from a bird's-eye view, like something akin to incipient epoch-making changes in the world as a whole. In a world in which the close connection between love, place, passport and nation begins to crumble, disparate worlds start to mix and merge everywhere, and the marriage contract acquires (perhaps without wishing to) at the micro-level the function that state treaties possess on the macro-level. A personal peace treaty is concluded between alien and distant countries and states as a foundation on which to experience a relationship, to bring children into the world and to establish a family.

Let us begin with the view from below, the perspective of people who migrate in order to marry. It is not always chance, nor is it always the power of romantic love, that brings mixed-nationality couples together. Such unions may very well start with a purposeful search, a hope for life in a new country and for a better life. Sometimes the process begins with a marriage agency, the personal advertisements in a newspaper, a commercial or state-organized marriage tour, or an internet forum. In short, many mixed-nationality unions begin not with love but with the hope of emigrating in order to escape from poverty and the dire prospects in one's homeland. The drama of 'emigrating in order to marry' follows the instruction manual that tells you how to cock a snook at the massive preponderance of global inequality. Popular language has developed graphic and derisive labels with which to describe these procedures: from 'mail-order brides' via 'visa wives' to 'imported husbands'.

Together with flows of capital and information, immigrants have become the signature of the age, and, among the various movements of people, migration for marriage plays a prominent part. It is to be found in countless places, in numerous versions, along routes that are specific to particular countries and genders – for example, from Russia to Germany, from the Indian subcontinent to Great Britain, and from China to South Korea.

At the present time, the number of such marriages is not only growing, it has increasingly come to attract the attention of the public. Such marriages have become a focus of politics and media interest. They are discussed among social scientists and writers and on talk shows. In such debates, migration for marriage has acquired an aura of the dubious or even the disreputable. It seems to be attractive and offensive in equal measure, a mixture of passion and calculation, desire and subterfuge. In politics and the media such marriages are often criminalized; they are suspected of being sham marriages. Feminists frequently see them as part of the worldwide exploitation of women and refer to them as instances of male violence (or, more precisely, as part of the pattern in which the dominant Western man exploits the helpless foreign woman). Ordinary citizens commonly regard such marriages as alien and even barbaric because they signal the precedence given to instrumental motives – an offence against the ideal of love prevalent in Western society, a breach of a cultural taboo. We see here the hint of a 'feminist nationalism'. All of a sudden, conservatives discover the rights of 'our' – German, French, Western – women to mobilize opinion against the invasion of 'foreign brides' and erect new barriers against them.

'Marriages between unequal worlds' reflect personal motives that contain a witches' brew of global power relations, ideological boundary disputes, emancipation hopes and family realities. This combination finds itself on a permanent war footing with the bureaucratic and legal either/or of the nation-state. We explore the nature of this jungle in three stages.

1   We lift the veil on the secret of the link between marriage and migration. Why does this curious, paradoxical union of two different aspects of life come into being at all, and why is it doing so at this moment in time? What drives men and women to embark on a twofold new beginning? Why do they try to start a new life in an unknown world and why is that decision crowned with the further decision to begin a life of two worlds as a couple?
2   The great theme of migrating for marriage begins with the small print – i.e., with the pragmatic question of how to discover two different worlds that wish to unite through marriage.
3   Finally, we shall turn our attention to the murky circumstances that have converted the term 'marriage migration' into a battle cry. What is so offensive about it? Why does the mere idea make people feel uncomfortable? What is the source of the wish to exclude people who have entered a society through marriage, a wish that has come to the surface in the public image of immigrant marriages and has turned them into something of a political football? How are these images created and who creates them? And, last but not least, where are these myths produced, where are these legends created that do so much to obscure the realities of the world we live in?

1   Dreams of Migration Versus Barriers to Migration

Hopeful Would-be Migrants

The process described in the union between marriage and migration points to something more than an event affecting two individuals. It

involves this, of course, but also something else. The term points to
the gulf between rich countries and poor regions, the effects of migration policies, the flows of information and images and the fact of
tourism, as well as the growing aspirations to equality of people in
non-Western countries. Migrating in order to marry amounts to an
individualized group event in which hopes collide head-on with
resistances.

This has at least one consequence. The gaze that focuses only on
'our' situation – i.e., on the impact on Western countries, misses the
point. Marriages resulting from migration involve the marriage of
different worlds, and such a marriage can be understood only if the
fusion of disparate horizons moves into the centre of attention. In
other words, marriages resulting from migration are multi-
perspectival. They are events that unite the countries of origin with
the host countries; they arise from the everyday encounters and problems between both sets of countries and reinforce that process of
interaction.

The term 'migration for marriage' reminds us of the term 'globalization as destiny'. Looked at in this context, women who migrate to
marry (and it is mainly women who do this) appear as *victims* in an
as yet undefined space. To be sure, both words – 'migration' and
'marriage – presuppose a certain minimum of activity on their part.

If such activities suggest that the countries of origin and destination are existentially intertwined, we begin to see how perspectives
and standards, life plans and practices, do not just relate to one's
immediate environment but are also incrementally affected by influences coming from the world as a whole. Migrating for marriage
takes place in the cleft between growing poverty and growing prosperity, and also in the understanding of the standards of equality and
fairness that are being exported from the Western democracies into
the furthest corners of the world. It gives rise to a range of feelings,
to hope and despair, expectations and disappointments. And, not
least, it produces the confidence that, in the light of the rhetoric of
equality current in affluent countries, crossing borders in order to
better oneself can lay claim to a certain legitimacy. The erection of
fences and highly modern fortifications with which the prosperous
democracies of the West surround themselves amounts to a mockery
of their own protestations of equality. Building such walls has ceased
to appear to be their 'natural right'; it looks rather like the strategy
adopted by the haves to prevent the have-nots of this world from
sharing in their prosperity.

Migrating to marry is not a movement that is set in train God
knows where in the depths of poor countries and then unexpectedly

lands on the doorsteps of Western families. Its dynamic is the expression of a movement that begins largely in the West, inspired by two factors: the search for lifelong partners and the proclamation and growing acceptance of universal human rights. Looked at in this way, migrating to marry also arises from the West's confrontation with its own contradictions.

The sheer extent of global inequality is a familiar fact and has been confirmed by many academic studies (see the summary in Beck and Poferl 2010). While one part of mankind lives in peace and relative affluence, the other part – the majority – lives in politically and economically unstable regions, in conditions of poverty and wretchedness, persecution and the lack of rights. At the same time, these antithetical worlds are increasingly integrated, not just in economic terms but also through their politics, their legal systems, their education systems, and not least in the cultural sphere. By exporting the images and promises of Western ways of life, the media create new reference points and standards of comparison in non-Western nations, and thus modify the expectations, hopes and aspirations that leave their mark on everyday life. And this applies with particular force to the impoverished regions of the world. As has been widely documented, the products of the mass media have proliferated in recent decades and have become increasingly more accessible. Film and television, video and the internet – all these media transmit information, both accurate and less so. They also tell stories, some true and others less true. In either case, they produce messages, inducements and promises that stimulate people's imaginations. The anthropologist Arjun Appadurai (1991) has drawn particular attention to this. According to Appadurai, the impact of the media has increased enormously. They spread to distant lands and continents, and their influence is not confined to the major cities but extends also to the remotest villages.

To repeat, images transmitted in this way do not always do justice to reality; they convey fictions and myths. But nowadays such images influence the life projects of more and more people in more and more places. 'More and more persons throughout the world see their lives through the prisms of the possible lives offered by mass media in all their forms. That is, fantasy is now a social practice; it enters, in a host of ways, into the fabrication of social lives for many people in many societies' (Appadurai 1991: 53–4). Instead of resigning themselves to the life assigned to them by fate, more and more people are finding ways to conceive of other worlds and compare them with their own. In consequence, their lives are no longer determined solely by the immediate realities but increasingly by global scenarios as presented and suggested by the media as more or less readily attainable, either directly or indirectly. Sonia Nazario has shown in her documentation of the experiences of Latin-American domestic workers who have immigrated to the United States just how migration dreams are formed and how they turn into life goals. A central figure of her report is Lourdes, a woman from the slums of Honduras, whose dreams were shaped early on by the glittering world of North America as conveyed through images on television:

> Lourdes knows of only one place that offers hope. As a seven-year-old child, delivering tortillas her mother made to wealthy homes, she glimpsed this place on other people's television screens. The flickering images were a far cry from Lourdes's childhood home: a two-room shack made of wooden slats, its flimsy tin roof weighted down with rocks, the only bathroom a clump of bushes outside. On television, she saw New York City's spectacular skyline, Las Vegas's shimmering lights, Disneyland's magic castle. (Nazario 2007: 4)

Worldwide tourism has similar effects, as has been shown, e.g., by Scott Lash and John Urry (2002). For what the natives see are infinite numbers of tourists, idling their time away for weeks on end, while consuming and shopping on a grand scale – here too we see images of affluence.

The question inexorably provoked by the new conditions of worldwide networking is obvious: why live here oppressed and in poverty if elsewhere there are people who can eat their fill, who own a house and a car, and who can visit a doctor when they fall sick? Why go on suffering here? Why not make the effort to go there?

Restrictive Migration Laws

Such hopes of migration are not easily satisfied. Ever since poverty and unemployment started to increase even in the developed world, many countries have drastically reduced the number of people immigrating in search of work. But such measures have only a limited effect. In many poor regions of the world hopes of being able to migrate continue to thrive despite the growing obstacles. As studies have shown, many would-be migrants do not readily give up; instead they look for ways out, loopholes in the regulations, so as to obtain entry to places where they can hope to make a better life for themselves. As the American sociologist Caroline H. Bledsoe has written: 'As states respond, attempting to impose clarity that will in turn allow them to impose restrictions, the results will inevitably have yet more loopholes and ambiguous meanings that people at the margins in turn may try to press' (Bledsoe 2004: 97). As a result, highly ingenious cat-and-mouse games spring up between the immigration authorities and would-be immigrants (Palriwala and Uberoi 2008: 46), and which side wins out depends on the local and national conditions in particular situations.

2 Border Artists

In this situation the conditions of entry to Western countries acquire crucial importance. Because the life project of migration essentially depends on them, they become the yardstick by which people elsewhere in the world seek to orientate themselves – not as a template they simply adopt, but as a model they actively help to shape by discovering and taking advantage of the precedents it sets. Many would-be immigrants become 'acrobats in the manipulation of boundaries', showing themselves to be adept, ingenious and flexible in the process (Beck 2006: 103–5). What they do is to translate regulations into strategies for action; they strive to adapt their personal characteristics, distinguishing features and circumstances, so as to make them correspond as closely as possible to 'passport requirements'. And they make the necessary changes quite literally, so as to seize the window of opportunity in the competition to gain entry to the country they have chosen (Bledsoe 2004).

One way forward is through education. A case study by Annett Fleischer (2007) shows how a particular kind of socialization emerged in Cameroon, with 'education as a motive for emigration', or, more precisely, an education as preparation for university study in Germany (in Cameroon, Germany is the country they yearn to be in because historical links are still important).[5] The older members of the entire immediate family choose, from among the growing sons and daughters, nephews and nieces, the person who is especially intelligent, socially adroit and linguistically talented. He – or she – becomes the hope of the entire family, the person for whose benefit all available resources are mobilized. Everyone contributes to the support of this one person to finance language courses, further education, visas and the cost of travel. In this way the chosen candidate is systematically groomed to satisfy the requirements of German officials. The family treat the entire venture as an investment in the future. In Cameroon,

---

[5] Cameroon was at one time a German colony. Because of this historical connection, in the late twentieth century both the German Federal Republic and the German Democratic Republic offered scholarship programmes for students from the country.

as in many other countries, migration is both a family and a community project, and it is organized in accordance with fixed rules of a reciprocal system of exchange, which is based on trust. Thus whoever succeeds in getting to Germany with the aid of the extended family will be expected to provide services in return – remittances, consumer goods, or help for additional members of the family to migrate to Germany.

In other regions of Africa hopes focus on sports training. If one of the sons displays athletic ability and dexterity with a ball, families pool their resources to build on his abilities by providing him with training in the hope of attracting the attention of a professional talent spotter who could arrange for him to be discovered by one of the international clubs – and with it gain admission to the ranks of potential football millionaires (Walt 2008).

But these are exceptions, special cases that presuppose historical links or unusual talents. The normal situation is that those willing to migrate have three options: illegal entry (highly risky), asylum application (very unpromising) and the right to bring family members into the country.

Different countries have different laws regarding the right to bring in family members; they are sometimes strict and sometimes more generous, but they are basically similar (Kofman 2004). Anyone legally resident in the United States, the European Union, Canada or Australia can bring in close family members living elsewhere. As a rule, these family members include parents, children and marriage partners. Since there is a huge tension between the hopes of migration and the obstacles in the way of migration, and bringing in other family members is the option offering the easiest route to immigration, marriage has acquired a historically new significance for the younger generation of would-be migrants – those who have not yet started a family of their own. In these circumstances, marriage becomes an open sesame and a springboard to the developed world. The tension between the hopes of migration and the obstacles in its path is the stuff from which new preferences in the choice of marriage partner are born. It is the stuff of new dreams which spread throughout the world; they are dreams of marriage which permits entry into one of the affluent nations (as a new family member).

The methods for finding a suitable partner for such a marriage vary, depending on local conditions and personal circumstances. We should like to elaborate on two dominant approaches. The first is a basic option, open to everyone; the second is a special option, which is tied to specific conditions and is available only to particular groups. (We are looking at a hypothetical contrast here – that is to say, one with obscure points and diffuse edges, so that the forms described here do not represent absolute opposites; the reality contains transitional and hybrid forms.)

3 Commercial Matchmaking

How do people from the poorer regions of the world go about finding a man or woman from the wealthier countries who might be willing to marry them? The answer is that, as demand has grown, a market has come into being to meet it. The age of globalization and global capitalism is also the age in which a world marriage market has come into existence, with a broad range of commercial options and opportunities which set out to satisfy the needs of aspiring migrants. The international matchmaking industry – an industry whose origins go back to the 1980s and that has expanded strongly since the mid-1990s (Lu 2008: 133) – includes both marriage agencies and professional or semi-professional individuals. The forms of broking extend from the internet, newspaper advertisements and organized travel for people in search of marriage partners, right down to sex tourism. In Russia alone there are now almost 1,000 agencies offering the relevant services. And in Russia there are now anything between 10,000 and 15,000 women annually who leave the country to get married (UNFPA 2006).

Which of the above methods is chosen depends on the legal, economic and cultural context – whether in the country of origin or in the target country – just as much as on the personal assumptions, characteristics or preferences of the would-be migrants themselves. In what follows, we give examples of three geographically and culturally very different approaches to the transnational, commercially mediated search for partners.

Farmer Seeks Wife

The few farmers still surviving in the highly industrialized countries often live in very straitened circumstances (low income, an uncertain future, long working hours and poor working conditions). Because they have had enough of this sort of life, many women who have grown up in the countryside move to the towns. The men who remain, confronted with a massive dearth of women, often find themselves living on their own. Some seek happiness by resorting to the organized methods of seeking a partner; increasingly they go beyond the frontiers of their own country because this offers them far superior opportunities – with women who dream of life in the West and who are willing to take their chances with the difficulties and obstacles in their path. Many forms of organization have sprung up to bring these two groups of people together – from the activities of commercial matchmakers down to trips to meet potential brides organized by various local authorities.

Take South Korea as an example. In the last two decades the country has enjoyed a tremendous economic boom, accompanied by globalization in many spheres of activity. At the same time, its traditions, with their emphasis on family roots and origins, are still powerful, and ethnic homogeneity is an essential cornerstone of national identity. In this cultural context mixed-nationality marriages inevitably encounter hostility and appear as disruptive influences, because they signify a transgression against group boundaries and a close relationship to 'others'.

Notwithstanding such barriers, the number of mixed-nationality marriages has been growing steadily for the past few years, and in fact the increase is not inconsiderable. In 1990 only 1.2 per cent of all marriages included one foreign partner, whereas in 2008 the proportion of such marriages had risen to 11 per cent (Shim and Han 2010: 241f.). If we look more closely at the demographic data we see that this growth was triggered by one particular group (ibid.: 246). This group was that of the South Korean farmers, who had resolved on taking a wife from Vietnam, India or another Asian country, thus contributing to the boom in mixed-nationality marriages. And so in South Korea, as elsewhere, it is among the rural population of all places where mixed-nationality alliances take place – in other words, the very places where attachment to the soil, love of one's homeland, and traditional values take precedence over open-mindedness towards 'others'. However, if in future the number of mixed-nationality marriages rapidly increases, it will ultimately also be as the product of massive publicity campaigns.

> In South Korea, billboards advertising marriages to foreigners dot the countryside, and fliers are scattered on the Seoul subway. Many rural governments, faced with declining populations, subsidize the marriage tours, which typically cost $10,000. The business began in the late 1990s by matching South Korean farmers or the physically disabled mostly to ethnic Koreans in China. . . . But by 2003, the majority of customers were urban bachelors, and the foreign brides came from a host of countries. The Consumer Protection Board can only estimate that there are 2,000 to 3,000 such agencies. (Onishi 2007)

Wedding Advertisements and the Internet

In India too, at the beginning of the twenty-first century, marriages are often arranged by parents, frequently with the assistance of the entire clan. Admittedly, the criteria governing the search for a suitable mate are often determined by aspects of modernity, and indeed globalization. This is made clear in a case study which describes the process of matchmaking among Tamil Brahmins, a group that (in Western terms) belongs to the Indian upper-middle class (Kalpagam 2008). The plans, hopes and ambitions of the Tamil Brahmins are directed at a single goal: migration to North America. Success in making the leap to the USA or Canada has become the paramount life project, the yardstick of prestige and the ultimate status symbol.

Cultural desirability is not the least among the factors taken into consideration in the evaluation and selection of marriage candidates. Right at the top of the wish-list of desirable sons-in-law we find young men of Brahmin origin living in the USA or Canada. The forms of the search are gradually modified and optimized so as to ensure as wide a choice as possible. Whereas in earlier times the dominant role was played by contacts in one's immediate social circle, other mediating institutions now gain in importance, since they can enable those in search of marriage partners to cast their net more widely. One example is the so-called advertisement route.

> Diasporic alliances in the 1960s and 1970s, like alliances with partners in India, were largely settled through personal kin and friendship networks. As local alliances became increasingly difficult to settle in this way, personal networks were complemented through impersonal networks, especially matrimonial advertisements. . . . And as more women came to be employed, even the marriageable girl herself would go to the newspaper office to place the advertisement . . . Today internet advertising has added a new dimension to the business of identifying compatible partners. (Kalpagam 2008: 100)

In the case of such Indian–American alliances with what is known as an America *varan* – i.e., a prospective marriage alliance with Indians in the USA – a particular hierarchy has been developed:

> In the scale of symbolic capital, America *varan* alliances are exceptionally prestigious. . . . The prestige of an America *varan* itself varies depending on whether the boy possesses a Green Card or an H-1 visa; whether the boy went to the US/Canada for higher studies and then settled there; or whether he went there for employment. In case of

emigration for employment, there is a distinction between employment for a short-term job contract . . . and a more enduring job contract with prospects of permanent relocation. The America *varan* alliance with Green Card-holding boys ranks as the most prestigious match. (Ibid.: 101)

Chain Migration

As many studies have shown, migration often takes place as part of a chain. What this means is that, if a few men or women belonging to one ethnic group have succeeded in making the leap to the West and have settled in one place, they are soon followed by other people from their home village or town. This is because the leap required to settle in a new country is made easier by the fact that people can look to the pioneer generation that preceded them to provide them with information and help.

The same pattern holds good for those who emigrate in order to marry. Sometimes, women immigrants who have come to the West in order to marry are instrumental in finding jobs for other women from their home region. This helps them to take the first steps to establish themselves in their new country – and many of the latecomers meet and then marry Westerners (Jensen 2008). Sometimes, the pioneer immigrants themselves become active as marriage brokers, keeping an eye out in their new environment for potential partners for members of their own family or other women from their village (Lu 2008: 132f.). Such activities often start with their being asked by a cousin or niece interested in emigration to find them a possible husband. Alternatively, a Western man wants a non-Western wife and asks the pioneer immigrant whether she can help (Lauser 2004: 124f.). Such searches may sometimes be performed out of friendship, without payment; in other cases, the intermediary expects remuneration.

4   Matchmaking Via Transnational Family Networks

So much for the basic option of transnational matchmaking, an option that is available to all would-be migrants. Over and above this, there is a special option available only to world families who can satisfy two conditions. The first is that the families must have members already settled in the global West; the second is that transnational family relations should play a crucial role in the social lives of these groups.

The regions in which both conditions can be satisfied are chiefly the countries actively seeking immigrant workers. As is well known, in the second half of the twentieth century many Western industrial countries hired foreigners to fill gaps in their own workforce. Many immigrant workers never returned home but settled in their new country instead. This is why, in the countries from which workers were recruited, there are many families today with an uncle or brother, a sister or niece living abroad – not just in the towns but also and especially in the countryside.

At the same time, world families in non-Western societies – especially in the countries from which workers were recruited – continue to be strongly influenced by notions of collective responsibility. That is to say, solidarity, respect and obedience continue to govern the family unit despite its being widely dispersed, and mutual assistance is a natural expectation and a duty even beyond frontiers and across continents. People help one another out building houses, in business and in the search for a job. And they are especially helpful when it comes to emigration. In many cases, emigrating is not an individual action at all but, rather, a family enterprise (e.g., Pries 1996; Shaw 2001). The same thing is true of marriages. Marriage is the alliance not so much of two individuals, but of two family groups, which explains why the search for a suitable partner and the final selection falls principally to the parents – although the sons and daughters normally have a say in the choice and family networks are also involved.

This means that people living in a country from which migrants have once been recruited have the advantage. Instead of being forced to rely on commercial methods of finding a marriage partner who would make suitable 'immigrant material', they can make use of family networks and appeal to family loyalty. 'Young men pin their hopes of social advancement on going to England and marrying a relative there' (Shaw 2004: 279; see also Bledsoe 2004: 104). Young men – and also women – from other countries cherish similar hopes. The same message resonates from Turkey to Morocco: 'Marrying the daughter of an immigrant is the best way to secure legal entry to the Netherlands or another Western country' (Böcker 1994: 97).

Relatives who have arrived in the West may have additional reasons of their own for looking to their former homeland for a son-in-law or daughter-in-law so as to maintain their links there (Beck-Gernsheim 2008). And even where this is not the case, relatives in the country of origin can work to strengthen family ties by exerting social pressure (Ballard 1990: 243; Shaw 2001: 326; Shaw 2004: 281; Straßburger 1999a: 157f.). This is where the concept of honour, one of the bedrocks of social order and social cohesion, assumes crucial importance. Anyone who fails to uphold the obligations of loyalty threatens the family's reputation and honour. Thus, if migrants fail to acquiesce in the marriage requests from the country of origin, their relations can accuse them of flouting basic moral principles, with consequent damage to their honour, their reputation and their entire position in society. One example can be found in the Mirpuris, Muslim immigrants of Pakistani origin in Great Britain. Roger Ballard gives a vivid description of the mixture of free choice and external pressure underlying marriages with partners from their land of origin.

As soon as the question arises of marrying their sons and daughters, the Mirpuris who have siblings in Britain – and that is the majority – remind their relatives of their family obligations and of their common cultural tradition. This tradition includes the idea that marriage partners should be found chiefly from among the circle of close relatives (cousins should marry each other). This explains why the nephews and nieces who are growing up in Britain should be the leading marriage candidates for the offspring of the siblings who have stayed behind in Pakistan. A further factor is the firm belief of the Mirpuris who have remained in Pakistan that the relatives who have moved to Britain enjoy an agreeable life there, and this reinforces the sense that this places them in the debt of those who have remained at home. Whoever has enjoyed good fortune and success should do what he can to help less fortunate family members – that is the rule. The Mirpuris in Britain find it almost impossible to resist the massive pressure of such expectations. Not only do they continue to feel beholden to their geographically distant relatives, they also know what to expect if they are rash enough to spurn offers of marriage from back home. Their relatives would regard such a rejection as an affront, a snub and a profound insult – and would react correspondingly by telling everyone about it and denouncing the failure of the migrants to behave in an honourable fashion. To avoid such a fate, the Mirpuris who have settled in Britain are prepared for the most part to accede to their relatives' marriage proposals (Ballard 1990: 243; Shaw 2001: 326; Shaw 2004: 281).

In the light of these conditions, it is unsurprising that transnational marriages between the new country and the old are widespread. The comparative data all reveal a similar pattern: whether it is a matter of Turks in Germany, Pakistanis in Britain or Moroccans in France – many immigrants, even those of the second and third generation, find a partner from their home country. Here are three examples.

- A study of immigrant marriages in Belgium based on information from the Belgian census of 1991 shows that around 70 per
  cent married someone who came to Belgium from Turkey for
  the wedding. Among the Moroccan migrants, a good 50 per
  cent married someone who arrived in Belgium from Morocco
  for that express purpose (Lievens 1999).
- A study by Gaby Straßburger, who examined 29,000 marriages
  of Turkish immigrants in Germany in 1996, found that over 60
  per cent married someone who was previously living in Turkey
  (Straßburger 1999a: 148).
- The data held by the Dutch Central Statistical Office for the
  years 1999–2001 show that almost two-thirds of the Turks and
  Moroccans resident in the Netherlands found marriage partners
  who immigrated to the Netherlands after their marriage. This
  applies to both men and women. The figures for the second
  generation are somewhat lower, but still reach levels of between
  50 and 60 per cent (Bijl et al. 2005: 4).

Whether we are considering the basic option or the special option
makes little difference: both methods of finding a marriage partner
reveal the same trend. A new criterion for deciding on a marriage is
becoming established in the age of immigration and globalization.
The growing tendency for people in the former Eastern bloc and the
developing world is to ask whether the young man or woman is likely
to open the door to migration. In this process the geographical distance between the country of origin and the host country is no irrel-
evance; on the contrary, it acts as a covert marriage broker and
witness in these unions.

5 Tragic Stories: Migrants as Victims

People from countries with marriage-seeking immigrants tend to see
this form of migration in a positive light. It is a passage to hope
(UNFPA 2006).

The situation is very different in the destination countries of would-
be marriage migrants. In those countries, migrating in search of marriage has a dubious reputation. It is regarded as indecent and offensive
and is viewed with distrust and suspicion. It is associated for the most
part with tragic stories, stories of deceit and disillusionment. It takes
many forms, but again and again it ends up with a single message:
what began as a project full of hope usually ends badly.

We can distinguish between two different kinds of tragedy. In the first, more common kind, women who migrate in order to marry appear as victims; in the second, relatively rare kind, they appear as the perpetrators.

From Hope to Despair

Women who migrate in order to marry are generally portrayed as victims in sociological studies and popular publications, as well as in reports in the media and fiction (Beck-Gernsheim 2007a; Beck and Beck-Gernsheim 2010). They are victims of forced marriages, of the slave trade and, above all, of men who take advantage of their plight – the insecurity of their status, their imperfect command of the language, their defective knowledge of their new country. Such men are commonly lacking in feeling, and they exploit these women's labour, treat them as sex objects, and even become violent and maltreat them physically and mentally.

Slave trade   The victim's point of view is dominant, for example, in a study issued by the German Federal Ministry for Women and Youth that examines 'the trafficking of foreign women and girls'. The female authors tacitly equate commercial forms of transnational marriage-broking with trade in women and that with the traffic in human beings. If you start from such a premise there is no very great distance to the conclusion that arranged marriages are closely linked to the degradation and oppression of women. It is significant, the authors claim, that 'women are procured in a degrading manner . . . They are unilaterally procured for men and not the other way round. Here it is the man who chooses and pays for the woman . . . this makes him the woman's "owner"' (Heine-Wiedenmann and Ackermann 1992: 111).

False happiness   A study by Elvira Niesner and others focuses on the situation of Thai and Philippine women who have married German men and followed them to Germany (Niesner et al. 1997). While considering the statements of their interviewees, the researchers were struck by the immigrant women's pragmatic attitudes towards marriage problems. As long as there was a basic consensus, they were prepared to put up with many impositions. Evidently irritated by this, the researchers summed up the women's attitude as one of resignation and fatalism. The immigrants, they say, 'pursue a fatalistic relationship strategy that makes it easier to accept their marriage and produces the appearance of happiness on a functional plane' (ibid.: 44). Which is as much as to say that this happiness is illusory, that it is nothing but self-deception, a pure façade behind which they conceal their true feelings. If these immigrant women could only admit the truth, they would recognize their dissatisfaction, and that would spell the end of their happiness.

But even in the interview extracts provided by the researchers we come across passages that reveal the source of the women's satisfaction. When they compare the men in Germany to those available in their own country, the Germans appear in a more favourable light. They are explicitly praised for their fidelity, their reliability and their readiness to help in the house (Niesner et al.: 43f.). The researchers refuse to take these statements seriously. They choose instead to cast doubt on the immigrants' judgement. They say they are inhibited and that they are prejudiced about the men of their own country (ibid.: 43ff.).

Forced marriages Necla Kelek's book *Die fremde Braut* [The Foreign Bride], a book that attracted a lot of attention in Germany and sold in large numbers, is a particularly egregious example of the cult of victimhood (see Beck-Gernsheim 2007b: 76ff.). Forced marriage is the dominant theme here and, as portrayed by the author, is the destiny of Turkish women in general. According to Kelek, Turkish parents pursue their own interests to the exclusion of all else when they marry their daughter to the son of an immigrant family living in Germany. They are indifferent to their daughter's well-being and are not upset if the young bride's new family mistreat and exploit her and use her like a slave. The consequences are tragic:

> The typical imported wife . . . speaks no German, is ignorant of her rights and does not know who to turn to in her hour of need. In the first few months, since she has no right of residence, she is completely dependent on a family she does not know. She will have to do whatever her husband and mother-in-law demand of her. If she fails to do as they ask, her husband can send her back to Turkey – which would mean her social or actual death. (Kelek 2005: 171)

Kelek's writing is full of large claims, and she conveys the impression that young wives are constantly oppressed and their rights are unremittingly trampled upon. But the empirical basis for her assertions is very meagre and it remains vague and unclear. The picture she gives is radically simplified and one-sided, and the facts are distorted at crucial points. By blurring the distinction between arranged marriages and forced marriages, she fails to see the diverse forms of which arranged marriages are capable, and she regards as normal what is in fact an extreme case, an extreme negative case, namely the daughter's utter subjection to the father's will. Her account of Turkish fathers runs along similar lines. In her view, they are without exception ruthless, obstinate, brutal tyrants, unfeeling monsters whose values are rooted in the distant past and who impose their will on the entire family.

In short, Kelek's book is a polemic rather than a scholarly study. It calls for sympathy with the lot of the oppressed – and combines this plea with aggressively formulated global indictments of 'the' Turks and Islam 'in general'.

Following the emergence of the women's movement, public awareness of the oppression and the discriminatory treatment of women has grown and has become a focus of political action – and for sound reasons. In consequence, marriages in which migration has been a factor have likewise attracted attention because the asymmetry of rights and resources in the relations between the sexes is particularly marked in this context. The implications of this, whether these marriages significantly consolidate the advantages already enjoyed by men, whether such marriages are instrumental in the increase in the oppression and abusive treatment of women, and, further, what scope there is for reinforcing the rights of immigrant women – all these are important questions that await answers (see chapter 7).

General Suspicion

But the writers referred to above fail to address such questions. They already know the answers. And these answers always make the same claim: women who emigrate in order to marry can expect nothing but subjugation and unhappiness. Their answer is an indictment: men as represented here exploit marriage migration in order to extend the oppression of women.

What we have, then, is a general suspicion, potentially including all men, young and old, the better-off and the less prosperous, professors and the illiterate, stamp collectors and dog-owners alike. The concern for the rights of women leads such writers to construct an image of man as the enemy. It is conceivable that the Central European men who import a wife from Eastern Europe or Asia really do fit the picture given of them in the media: a savage bunch opposed to women's emancipation, no longer as young as they were, feeling threatened by the expectations of the new generation of women,

relatively unsuccessful in their working lives, and lackir
skills. But where is the evidence?

Such evidence is not to be found in these authors. The
unhappiness and blighted hopes is a given from the very outset in the
scholarly methods they adopt. They have narrowed the focus of their
research; the data they produce has been pre-selected. Anyone who,
like them, frequents women's refuges, conducts opinion surveys in
centres for women who have suffered from abuse, and visits mosques
is unlikely to come across women who live in a harmonious relationship, who have a job and professional qualifications, and are well
integrated. They are far more likely to encounter women in unhappy
marriages, who have no jobs or training, and who are marginalized
in the unfamiliar society in which they find themselves. In other
words, if you go in search of places where victims congregate, you
will be sure to find victims.

Many media reports on the subject of marriage migration are
similarly one-sided. This one-sidedness often results from a dramatic
sense peculiar to the media themselves. The normal case, the average
version of events, is thought to be tedious. The media prefer to concentrate on the abnormal, sensational case. That is the stuff that
newspaper reports are made of. Nor should we overlook the rule that
sales are boosted by sex and crime. Love and criminality are good
for business. Reports are certain to find readers if they feature sensational headlines and appropriate photos dramatizing the sufferings
of a woman from Novosibirsk who has migrated in order to get
married, and describing in lurid detail how her husband has beaten
her and forced her to commit every conceivable kind of sexual act.
In contrast, take the case of a Russian woman who has come to
Germany and who has been living in a small town in Lower Bavaria
for ten years, who has produced two children, and gets on reasonably
well with her husband even if he is not very talkative and can be
pig-headed on occasion, who goes to gym classes and sings in the
local choir. Who wants to know about a woman like that, whose life
is completely uneventful?

The media's tendency to dramatize does not come without costs.
The emotive *mise en scène* bars the way to any rational reflection.
Texts constructed along the lines of 'Berliner beats Thai wife' can
reckon on a predictable public response: compassion and spontaneous indignation. Because individual cases directly confront the public
with tragedy and human suffering, they gain a particular immediacy.
But that is where the problem lies. It is not possible to respond with
general platitudes to the pain of an abused wife. It sounds unseemly

and even callous and dismissive if you claim that such an event is an extreme case, not the normal one.

Two Worlds

An essential feature – and a disqualifying defect – of the above texts is what we have termed 'methodological nationalism'. This means that they focus almost exclusively on the here and now; they seem incapable of transcending the horizon of the prosperous regions of the West. It follows that, when addressing the question of marriage migration, they are aware only of events that take place in the host country. The country of origin is *terra incognita*. But the lives of the women they describe are always played out in two worlds, a here and a there, the old country and the new one. Such lives can be comprehended only in terms of the interweaving of these two worlds and the tensions between the two. Once they are joined up we can see how misleading the current images are.

Women who emigrate in search of marriage are by no means just feeble, helpless creatures, sold off by men and forced to live abroad. Many have taken this path because they wished to or because they saw no other way to escape a wretched life. Emigrating in search of marriage often results from a definite decision, a conscious act of deliberation, weighing up the alternatives: staying at home and attempting to build a life there or trying one's luck as a domestic worker in the metropolises of the West – or even becoming a prostitute and earning a living in that way. If we take a realistic view of these prospects – the meagre opportunities of earning money at home or, alternatively, an arduous life as an illegal immigrant – emigrating in search of marriage may easily come to seem the most attractive option. Compared to the alternatives on offer, such a course of action may well hold out the best prospects of a better life.

If we reflect on life in the two places, it becomes apparent that not all such hopes need be mere illusions. For, ultimately, many of these women have fixed on the journey to the West in order to support their ageing parents, a task and a duty of central importance in their culture of origin. And, as the relevant studies show, many women who emigrate in order to marry regularly send money back to their families. The fact that they are able to do this despite adverse circumstances and many pressures is an achievement of which they are proud and which acts as a booster to their self-confidence. Furthermore, for the most part this achievement increases the respect in which they are held in the society in which they have grown up and to which they continue to feel attached – in other words, in their family and their place of origin. They find they enjoy a growing reputation (Constable 2005; Bélanger and Linh 2011).

From this point of view, the balance sheet can be positive for the women concerned and, as Nicole Constable puts it, 'Women can use marriage mobility to their own advantage' and to improve their life prospects (Constable 2005: 16). If so, we must cease thinking of marriage-related migration as nothing more than a trap. Depending on circumstances, it may well represent a positive option, an option, moreover, that may even be said to privilege women because it provides them with opportunities that are seldom available to men (ibid.).

Should a woman tie herself to a man to improve her own prospects? The idea is of course provocative – at any rate, as long as we measure women's situation by Western standards. The women's movement of the 1970s rightly emphasized individual freedom and aspired to liberate women from their dependence on the family. In so doing, it took for granted the social, political and economic conditions that obtained in the West – a set of assumptions that becomes increasingly questionable the further globalization advances. Anyone who considers the question of women's interests must be aware that, in the past, women's only route to security and social advancement was through marriage, and this still continues to be the case in many places. For women from poorer regions and social background, marriage-related migration is often the most effective and socially acceptable way of improving their social status and economic security. Rajni Palriwala and Patricia Uberoi, the editors of a wide-ranging international collection of essays on the theme of marriage, migration and gender, write as follows: 'Clearly, and without discounting the ubiquity of the abuses just mentioned, social scientific attention to the intersection of issues of marriage and migration needs to go beyond "victimisation" to a more balanced and context-sensitive consideration of changing dynamics in the nexus of marriage and migration' (Palriwala and Uberoi 2008: 24).

6 More Tragic Stories: Migrants as Perpetrators

In the countries targeted by marriage-seeking migrants, such marriages are surrounded by an aura of ambivalence and are commonly associated with unhappy outcomes. The more frequently encountered version constructs the stories of victimhood already described – women as the victims of male exploitation and violence. From time to time, one comes across a second narrative: women in the role of perpetrator – cold, calculating and ruthless. Such women are believed to exploit the physical and mental frailty of mostly older men. They pretend to have feelings they do not possess. They use their physical charms to procure material advantages. All they want from a man is his money, his bank account and his house. Here are two examples.

In her novel *A Short History of Tractors in Ukrainian*, Marina Lewycka tells us about the billing and cooing of an unequal couple of this kind. He is confused, no longer in possession of his senses, driven on by hormones which are close to their last gasp. She is captivating and seductive. The marriage, which is concluded in the teeth of the resistance of the husband's family, is soon transformed by the wife into a money-making machine to provide her with a car, comfort and shopping, until the financial resources dry up. When that happens the marriage is finished too.

Some of the Indian–US marriages that we have described above have also come to a premature end. These were unions between Indian men who have settled in the United States and women who were prepared to move from India. According to *Time* magazine, not a few of the young women concerned experienced bitter disappointment (the men, who were interested only in their dowry, did not hesitate to leave the women immediately after the wedding; *Time*, 22 October 2007). This quickly provoked a riposte from a reader:

> There are cases of Indian husbands becoming victims at the hands of their self-centered manipulative brides. Some women enter into overseas marriages when they have a boyfriend living in the country of their destination. They use the unsuspecting husbands as a way to join these boyfriends. Or they use the husband for professional advancement or to transplant their siblings and parents from India. (*Time*, 3 December 2007)

Where love was supposed to hold sway, we find instead the desire for money. This is the source of that ambivalent aura, the distrust that many people feel when they hear talk of marriage-related migration. Money versus love reminds us of another antithesis: the distinction between a love marriage and a marriage of convenience. This distinction always contains the assumption that the Western version, the union of two lovers, represents a higher moral stage, while the non-Western version is looked down on as a matter of material considerations, a retrograde or barbaric practice, an interpretation that applies *a fortiori* to marriage-related migration, which, so it is alleged, frequently verges on sham marriage.

Love marriage versus marriage of convenience – this antithetical pairing has been elevated to the status of a cultural norm. However, it contains characteristic misconceptions and distortions. In the first place, it is blind to the facts of history: if all arranged marriages were sham marriages, then all the royal families of Europe down to the beginning of this century would have been founded on sham marriages. Such marriages were formed in order to increase and consolidate the power and possessions of the families concerned (*'Bella gerant alii, tu, felix Austria, nube.'* 'Wars may be waged by others – you, happy Austria, marry!'). If all arranged marriages had been sham marriages, we would all be the products of sham marriages. Whether we are talking about the nobility, the middle classes or the peasantry, romantic love as the driving force behind marriage came into being only with the transition to modernity (Stone 1979; Borscheid 1986).

Romantic Love

The distinction between arranged marriages and love marriages is associated for the most part with a geographical ascription, according to which Western society is thought of as the true home of love marriages, while arranged marriage is the pattern in non-Western societies. Peter Berger has pointed out that this distinction implies a considerable dose of self-idealization on the part of the West. For, even before the romantic courtship has started up, Berger maintains that certain decisions have been pre-empted. Thus the identity of the person with whom we fall in love is not a matter of chance. On the contrary, what looks to us like a very personal attraction is rather the consequence of a certain consonance of values, preferences and interests – ranging from the canon of 'good taste' to notions of how best to furnish one's home – that have been essentially predetermined by our social origins. Thus the choice of whom to love is for the most part guided into a suitable channel. Romantic love remains within the radius of a status that is felt to be appropriate. Or, as Berger explains it: 'In other words, when certain conditions are met or have been constructed, one allows oneself "to fall in love"' (Berger 1963: 35).

The Cultural Logic of Desire

A line of argument that comes to a similar conclusion is implied in more recent international case studies, such as Nicole Constable's *Romance on a Global Stage* (2003). Whereas Berger maintained that the image of romantic love was simplistic, Constable claims that our conception of an instrumental choice of partner does not go far enough. Thus, in the case of marriage-related migration, the aim is by definition to acquire an entry permit to the First World. But this does not preclude the possibility that romantic motives may play a part in the process. On the contrary, it increases the likelihood that they will. We see the workings here of what Constable terms 'the cultural logic of desire'. Anyone who regards the West as a paradise, the Promised Land, will tend to see everything in it in a certain light, and everything that bears the label 'Western' will be transfigured by it. Studies of transnational or cross-cultural families have long since shown how myths, dreams, fantasies and seductive ideals about cultural 'others' play a subconscious part in influencing people's choice of partner (Spickard 1989; Wießmeier 1993). This is even truer today, since the hopes of would-be migrants have expanded enormously under the impact of the forces of globalization. In such conditions, fantasies about the desirability of Western men and women will have mushroomed. If so, we shall be forced to revise our ideas about marriage-related migration. Traditionally these ideas have revolved around the notion of choosing a partner with a specific purpose in mind, whereas now we could now speak of a 'dual desire' – desire for the partner *and* for the country.

An illuminating illustration of this can be seen in the documentary film *Garantiert heiratswillig* [Guaranteed Marriageable] (1993), which treats the question of marriage-related migration between Germany and Russia. One scene is set in St Petersburg, in an agency that supplies Russian women for German men. When the female film-maker asks young women what led them to choose this method of finding a partner, some reply by launching into a hymn of praise of German men and their virtues (integrity, fidelity, etc.). Their hopes are palpable to the viewer. If it is true that beauty is in the eye of the beholder, we may say that all the marvellous qualities of the German male can be said to lie in the eyes and hearts of these Russian women.

From this point of view, the contrast between love marriages and arranged marriages may be said to be not entirely mistaken, but it is not entirely right either. To regard love and instrumental motives as mutually exclusive is misleading, since they should be seen rather as the opposite ends of a spectrum in which numerous hybrid forms have their place.

As Berger has shown, it is a myth that so-called love marriages are based purely on love. The situation is far more complex. The idea of the 'cultural logic of desire' suggests that even a marriage of expediency is less one-dimensional than appears at first sight. Even a marriage of expediency is not just a matter of expediency.

This implies that the contemptuous, distrustful idea of marriage-related migration contains a fair measure of Western self-idealization. Whether they come from St Petersburg, India or Sri Lanka, women who wish to use marriage to obtain a residence permit are capable of romantic hopes and feelings. It may even be true on occasion that the desire to emigrate may lead to the blossoming of romantic feelings. If emigration is the dream of a better life, why shouldn't that dream include the idea of a better man? (Whatever 'better' may imply in this context – it may mean a man of one's dreams with a Hollywood smile; it may also have the quite modest meaning of a man who does not drink as much as ordinary Russian men.) And this raises the obvious question: if we harbour suspicions about all marriage-related migration, if we regard all such unions as sham marriages from the outset, does this not suggest that we are caught up in our own cultural beliefs and are incapable of seeing anything beyond the boundaries of the ways of life already familiar to us?

7 What Future?

The number of marriage-seeking migrants has increased in recent decades. However, if we take a closer look at this period, the picture starts to look a little different. The statistics show that this increase has slowed in parts of Central and Northern Europe and that there may even be something of a decline.

The change in the political climate is an important factor in this development. More and more efforts are being made to secure 'Fortress Europe' from encroachments from outside. Multiculturalism, formerly extolled as an achievement of modernity, has now become suspect as a naïve, unworldly utopian dream. The latest slogan is 'integration', and it has become mandatory for new immigrants. Books are piling up in the bookshops on the subject of 'women as victims' with particular reference to other religions and cultures. They deal with women as the victims of honour killings, forced marriages, circumcision and oppression; women as objects of archaic customs, ritual practices and patriarchal violence.

With this change in the political climate, the rules and regulations governing the lives of immigrants are being interpreted more stringently and more restrictively. This also applies to family members who come to join the original immigrants, especially marriage partners. In Switzerland, for example, since January 2010 only persons with the right of abode have been permitted to marry. Registrars are required to ascertain whether couples wishing to marry can provide documentary evidence of their entitlement to stay in the country ('Migration und Bevölkerung', January 2011). In Denmark a whole package of regulations to restrict the entry of marriage partners and other family members was introduced as early as 2000. According to the new rules, both partners must be at least twenty-four years old; the partner living in Denmark must have sufficient housing space; he must be in a position to support the incoming partner financially; and he must have survived without drawing any welfare benefits in the year preceding the application. The partner already living in Denmark must further deposit a certain sum as a bank guarantee to ensure that financial support for the incoming family member will be forthcoming in the future; and, finally, both marriage partners must possess a documented connection with Denmark. The success of these new regulations soon became evident. In 2001, 6,499 men and women settled in Denmark under the previous rules governing the immigration of family members, whereas by 2008 there were only 2,619 (Ritter 2010). The position in Germany is similar. Since September 2007 the immigrant partner must have reached a minimum age (eighteen) to be allowed to enter the country and must have a command of basic German. Immigrant organizations, refugee groups and church organizations have protested against this last requirement but have made no headway. The language tests are still in force, and the clampdown on the immigration of family members continues to be operated on the quiet. This has led to a drastic reduction in immigrant numbers. In the first half of 2008 the number of visas issued for married partners declined by almost 25 per cent compared with the same period in 2007 ('Migration und Bevölkerung', December 2008).

This cat-and-mouse game between would-be immigrants and the authorities in favour of a more restrictive policy suggests that, if the latter continue to gain ground, the number of marriage-seeking immigrants will shrink even further. But what does that mean? There can hardly be a return to ethnic homogeneity (whether German, French, Danish or whatever). While the gulf between rich and poor countries persists, together with the pressure to migrate that arises out of it, we can hardly expect people living in impoverished regions of the world to abandon their hopes. They will seek out other solutions – perhaps by finding other ways of bringing family members across frontiers (Bledsoe 2004; Ritter 2010) or by resorting to different methods altogether – finding illegal jobs in private households, for example.

6

Love Displaced: Migrant Mothers

When people speak of the family they tend to associate it with feelings, love, belonging and yearning, trouble and hatred. Some romanticize the family, conceiving it as a 'haven in a heartless world' (Lasch 1977). Sometimes the family features as a battleground dominated by secrets and lies. Quite a long time has now elapsed since feminist studies made us aware that the family is also a workplace. The work that is performed there covers a broad range of activities that have been summed up as the three Cs – caring, cooking and cleaning. And it goes without saying that even in the West these tasks were assigned to women until well into the twentieth century – justified by an appeal to God or nature or men (and, needless to say, the 'or' in this sentence is not an exclusive 'or').

Now, with the first years of the twenty-first century, many things have changed – and others have not. For example, men's participation in housework has not reached the levels that had been promised (setting aside Sweden, which is an exceptional case). Men have perfected two things: the verbal expression of their open-mindedness and their stubborn refusal to turn their words into deeds. The result is that, with women's greater career obligations, housework has been increasingly outsourced in order to reconcile the otherwise irreconcilable: the emancipation of women and washing the clothes, feeding the baby and changing its nappies, etc.

If we look at the family from a national perspective – in other words, if we consider the changes in family law in the different nations of the West – we perceive a trend, or at least the promise of a trend, towards greater equality between the sexes. However, if we look at the Western family from a cosmopolitan standpoint, we realize that this is at best a half-truth. In reality, the increased equality is based on 'outsourcing' essential parts of parenting and housekeeping to 'global' others – i.e., to 'surrogate mothers' and immigrant domestic workers.

This major division of labour – one operating on an international scale and involving 'global others' – is implemented in a highly concrete, direct and personal way in the inner lives of homogeneous, normal, national middle-class families and households in the United States, Europe, Israel, South Korea, Canada, and so forth. This 'fusion of horizons' is not imported into families by outside agencies, but is rather the internal precondition on which they are based, one arising from the interplay between the emancipation of Western women, male inflexibility, the lack of nurseries and the relations between the rich and poor regions of the world. The process of merging takes place behind the façade of the lives of absolutely normal families with the same nationality and mother tongue (regardless of whether they are homosexual or heterosexual, religious or secular). This means it is perfectly possible to cultivate xenophobic attitudes and simultaneously, if one's own comfort is at stake, to take into one's own employment the global others who are excluded at the national level.

This is how the conflicts of the world are introduced into internal family conflicts at the national level. The 'unequal world' has suddenly made its appearance in very personal terms behind the closed, well-guarded doors of family life and the private sphere. No wall can keep these conflicts at bay (and neither can the assertion, beloved of prime ministers and federal chancellors, that multiculturalism is now, finally, a thing of the past).

This existential dependence on global others possesses a particular feature: the global others – in other words, immigrant domestic workers – remain simultaneously 'excluded' and 'included'. They are excluded in the legal sense because they do not have the same rights as nationals, and they may even be illegal immigrants. They are included geographically, as is their labour, because they are working 'here' and their work is indispensable. A continuing state of exclusion works to the advantage of the 'emancipated' middle-class families, since it reduces the cost of the labour of such immigrants.

We shall analyse the structure of the cross-border mechanism concealed by the expression 'immigrant domestic worker' in five steps. First, we shall focus on the historical constellation that has brought about this 'internal globalization' of domestic labour: *the new form of economic immigration – the women's turn*. Second, we shall inquire into the situation of immigrant women in the host country, living their lives in the grey zones of legality. Third, like marriage-related migration (see chapter 5), immigrant domestic labour calls for a dual perspective, since it is essential to explore the situation of immigrant domestic workers in relation both to their country of origin *and* to the host country. Fourth, immigrant domestic workers themselves practise a form of 'distant love' – not merely with their husbands but above all with their children, who have been left behind in their home country. Fifth and last, immigrant domestic work poses a series of moral and political dilemmas: Are feminists, who have always called for equality between all women, becoming employers who exploit the global inequality of women for their own private emancipation?

1 A New Wave of Economic Migration

Following the destruction wreaked by the Second World War, many Western countries experienced an economic boom in the 1950s and 1960s. As the economy expanded it felt an urgent need of new workers – who, if they were not forthcoming in one's own country, could be imported from abroad. In consequence, many people left their homes in the economically weaker countries, above all in Southern Europe, in search of work and greater opportunities in the developed industrial nations. The majority took up unskilled or semi-skilled jobs in industry, and most of them were men.

For some time now a new form of economic immigration has been in evidence, starting roughly in the 1980s (Ehrenreich and Hochschild 2003). Women from Mexico find themselves working as nannies in California; Filipinas care for old people in Israel; Polish women clean, wash and iron in German households – work of this kind is performed predominantly in private families. Not a few of the immigrant workers have educational qualifications, but because of the economic situation in their homeland they have no prospects of finding a steady income there.

Inequalities of Wealth and Political Changes

This new form of economic migration has various causes. The first is obvious. It is the same as the cause underlying the first wave of economic migration, namely the gap in wealth between richer and poorer nations. But, unlike the situation in the 1950s and 1960s, the highly industrialized nations of today have little need of semi-skilled or unskilled workers. On the contrary, many industries have been hit by the economic crisis and the need to restructure. Ordinary jobs have been rationalized out of existence, and this has particularly affected the kinds of jobs previously done by immigrants.

The changes in the political map of Europe constitute a further factor. The collapse of socialism has led to the disappearance of many state-subsidized jobs in the former socialist countries. Whether in Russia, Poland or Ukraine, more and more people in Eastern Europe have fallen victim to unemployment. More and more people simply do not know how they are to provide for themselves and their families.

The escape route that was available in earlier decades – the path to the industries of the West – has been blocked. People now look to the private households of the West for its replacement.

Institutional Division of Labour in the Home

That brings us to the second cluster of causes of the new wave of economic migrants: the division of labour between men and women. In the 1950s and 1960s the so-called traditional division of labour was the norm: the man was the breadwinner while the woman looked after the family and the home. The new women's movement opposed this pattern with a different model, one which fundamentally questioned the prevailing division of labour. According to the new model, both sexes were to be involved in both spheres of activity. Spelling this out, it meant that men should help with the housework; they would have to help with the cleaning, washing, cooking and childcare.

Many things have changed since then, but it cannot be denied that, rare examples apart, the changes have been very limited.

As has been shown by a number of studies, many men of the younger generation have in fact developed a closer relationship with their children. They play with them more; they take them to kindergarten in the morning and put them to bed at night. But the same studies also show that it is predominantly women who still do most of the looking after and bringing up of children. And this is even truer of the general household chores, where men's involvement remains at a very modest level, even when the women have a career of their own. What we have in the upshot is an 'incomplete social revolution' in the relations between the sexes (Hochschild and Machung 1990: 34) – or, alternatively, an 'imbalance in the responsibilities of the sexes', as it was put in the federal government's Seventh Report on the Family (BMFSFJ 2006: 175).

Emergencies and Survival Strategies

Since career women cannot do everything themselves, they look for help elsewhere, and that means from other women. The new division of labour that has become established in the private sphere over recent decades looks like this: middle-class women, well educated and highly motivated, delegate part of the household chores to assistants. So as to cope with everyday tasks, they often engage entire networks of helpers (nannies, au-pair girls, babysitters, with sisters and moth-ers-in-law held in reserve). And these helpers come less and less fre-quently from the immediate vicinity, in the towns at least. Instead, they often come from far away. They consist largely of women from Central and Eastern Europe and the developing countries, who are in search of work in the developed countries: women from Poland or Romania, from Mexico or Sri Lanka, who work in private house-holds in Hong Kong, Rome and New York – what we are seeing is a migration from poor countries to rich ones.

This development is the consequence of a 'structural flaw in patri-archy' (Rerrich 1993: 333) in the political and institutional guidelines governing our society. On the one hand, the labour market contains structural characteristics that are inimical to the family, while both social and educational policies rely heavily on women's willingness to perform unpaid labour in the private sphere. This creates major strains in the everyday lives of millions of women with jobs. It follows that, if they can afford it, they will inevitably seek individual relief. On the other hand, thanks to immigration policies, economic migrants find that work in private households is the only work open to them. These two factors coming together have created a situation in which work is divided up transnationally between different groups of women, while for the most part men remain unaffected.

An Ageing Society

A further factor is that, in recent decades, the life expectancy of both men and women has steadily increased. Since, as people grow older, illnesses and chronic complaints also increase, the number of people who come to depend on others to look after their daily needs grows accordingly. This remains true regardless of whether people need help on an occasional basis and by the hour or whether they need assist-ance every day and round the clock. Places in old-age homes and care homes are dear and provision is often inadequate. Given this situa-tion, foreign helpers provide a welcome solution. Instead of a mass-processing system, there is the lure of personal attention round the clock at an affordable price. Few will be surprised to discover that the caring world has become a labour market for immigrant women – and that this is on the increase.

Admittedly, no one knows the exact numbers simply because many of the immigrant workers in private homes are there illegally or semi-legally, so that the relevant authorities are not in the picture. We are forced to rely on estimates, and these make it clear that we are not talking about small numbers of women migrants. In Germany, for example, 100,000 home helpers from Central and Eastern Europe are employed privately as carers for the elderly; only 2,000 of them are known to the authorities and pay National Insurance, etc. (Lutz 2007). In Italy, it is estimated that there are around 774,000 home helpers, 90 per cent of whom are foreign nationals – and most of these are employed privately as carers for the elderly (Lamura et al. 2009; Lyon 2006). At the same time, characteristic differences between the different regions of Europe can be clearly seen. In the Scandinavian countries there are few immigrant women doing domestic work or caring for the elderly; the number of such women in the Western and Central European nations is significantly greater, while in Southern Europe it is greater still. The explanation is that the welfare state is more highly developed in the Scandinavian countries, which specialize in providing a range of services promoting the family. Spain and Italy, by contrast, lack the relevant infrastructure because politics there is dominated by the idea that the family is the agency responsible for caring for the elderly and looking after children (Lamura et al. 2009; Lyon 2006; Peterson 2007).

A Win–Win Situation

This entire story can also be given a positive spin; it can be seen as benefiting everyone. Thanks to the growing numbers of female immigrant domestic workers, women in developed countries can delegate part of the household and child-rearing tasks. At the same time, women from poorer countries can use the money they earn as the foundation for a better future for themselves and their families. A fair exchange and a happy compromise, then – that is how it is judged by many of the private employers. They make speeches in which they talk of 'help and support'. Some even regard handing over the housework to immigrant women as a kind of private aid to the developing world (Anderson 2007: 253ff.). For example: 'I really feel strongly that it's a positive thing you can do for somebody . . . I think it's liberating for a girl from the Philippines to . . . leave the rice paddy fields and the village and to be able to send back huge amounts of money and to be able to get a job in (ibid.: 254).

According to such opinions, both sides profit, and we m. that this is a win–win situation. Such a view is agreeable because it masks insights that might cause discomfort to the inhabitants, both male and female, of the developed countries. Whether such an interpretation is also the truth is of course a different matter entirely.

2 Living in the Shadows

Since Western nations are adopting increasingly restrictive immigration laws in an attempt to protect their frontiers, many immigrant women find themselves in the grey area between legality and illegality. Their status is correspondingly precarious. Many of them live with the constant threat of exposure and expulsion. Since the official jobs market is closed to them, they are forced to make do with comparatively underpaid employment. They compensate for this by working harder and longer. Over and above that, they are easy prey for those out to exploit them and are scarcely in a position to defend themselves. They often have little knowledge of the relevant laws and frequently their grasp of the language is wanting. Moreover, they tend as far as possible to avoid contact with the authorities so as not to expose themselves to the risk of deportation. Some employers regard illegality as an advantage to them and make no bones about exploiting it ruthlessly.

> Especially with the illegal[s], they're so desperate to get work, they're not looking to get fired, they're looking to keep their job, so if you respect them and just let them get on with it, the loyalty that comes back to you and the hard work that comes back to you more than pays off . . . they're so frightened of getting kicked out that they're not going to pull any stunts. (Anderson 2007: 260)

In this context, Klaus J. Bade, an expert on immigration, has summed up their plight in three words: 'Hard-working, cheap, illegal' (Bade and Böhm 2000).

Immigrant women find employment precisely because they work so hard and cost so little. Those who profit from this situation include not just the women of the developed world, with their career ambitions, but also their husbands and partners, who profit at least as much. It lets them pursue their own career ambitions, unencumbered by the need to take part in the washing, cleaning and looking-after process, to say nothing of genuine involvement. There is a kind of conspiracy of silence here, a mutual agreement between the sexes not to comment on this situation: if women in the developed world succeed in coping more or less with the everyday household chores, it is alright for them to pursue their own professional ambitions and even to have careers in their own right. Conversely, if their menfolk do not stand in the way of their professional ambitions, the women can organize the private household chores by delegating them to outsiders, instead of burdening the couple's relationship with awkward disagreements.

Let us imagine for a moment: if the immigrant women from Poland or Romania, from Mexico or Honduras, were to do what the law-makers of the host countries expect them to do, namely, return to their country of origin tomorrow, then German or American men would be forced to abandon paying lip service to the values of equality between the sexes. Instead, they would find themselves confronted to a far greater extent by the daily consequences of those values. This would lead to such concrete questions as: When will you actually do something? When will you clean the bath? When will you help to look after Grandpa? When will you take our daughter to the physiotherapist?

By taking care of all the background work in the family, immigrant women stabilize the precarious state of peace in relations between the sexes.

The state and the politicians also benefit from this state of affairs, as do local councils and other officials in charge of immigrant women. They too find that such women relieve them of the need to perform vexatious tasks. Let us imagine the situation once again: if these immigrant women did not exist, the intolerable conditions in old-age homes would be even more disgraceful and even more visible. There would be no escaping public anger. This would produce a highly explosive situation, since affordable solutions are nowhere in sight. Those responsible know this full well, and it explains the schizoid practice which has by now become established. Officially, entering the country to take up jobs in private households or in the caring professions is 'illegal'; it is condemned and indeed criminalized. Unofficially, it is tacitly condoned on a massive scale, tolerated consciously and systematically, and has long since been accepted as normal. Klaus J. Bade has described this situation as 'the great hypocrisy' (Bade, cited in Metz 2007).

In other words, here too there is a conspiracy to look the other way, a tacit agreement, this time between politicians and the families concerned. It has been made possible because immigrant women are providing the emergency cover where provision is lacking. They are invisible, these silent helpers in the system. And they are the indispensable, essential supports enabling people to cope with everyday chores in modern Western societies.

3 Broken Care Chains

Many of the women who go abroad to work in the West have families of their own at home. They have left their husband and children behind because earning a living there was more or less out of the question. 'Transnational motherhood' is the term that has become accepted to describe this group of immigrant women, and an entire branch of research has grown up round this subject (Ehrenreich and Hochschild 2003; Gamburd 2000; Hochschild 2000; Hondagneu-Sotelo 2001; Hondagneu-Sotelo and Avila 1997; Madianou 2012; Madianou and Miller 2011; Parreñas 2001, 2005a). Their findings indicate that in many cases it is the children that provide the impetus to emigrate. The women want to earn money to give their children a better future. To achieve this they are prepared to put up with long periods of separation and also with life in a foreign country with all its difficulties. In former times, it was staying together through all the vicissitudes of fortune that was thought to be the proof of love, whereas nowadays, in the globalized world, the opposite imperative holds good: a man who loves his family leaves them behind in order to establish the foundations of a better future elsewhere. A novel by Michelle Spring sums this up succinctly: 'for migrant workers the world over, love means having to go away' (Spring 1998: 63).

Inhabitants of the prosperous nations of the West do not experience the compulsion to leave. To their minds that is a story from a distant world, an extreme case and a rare exception. Things are different in the rest of the world. There, such statements as Spring's are not unfamiliar; more and more families live their lives separated against their will from their loved ones by countries or even whole continents. Here some figures tell the story.

According to the data supplied by the Sri Lankan Office of National Statistics, one working-age woman in eleven was working abroad, and this was the case as early as the mid-1990s (we have reason to believe that there has been a marked increase since then). Some three-quarters of the emigrating men and women were married, and, of the married women, the vast majority (90 per cent) had children they had left behind in Sri Lanka (Gamburd 2000: 39). In the Philippines it is reliably estimated that 9 million men and women (10 per cent of the population) have gone abroad in order to earn money, the majority of them women with children. The upshot is that between 6 and 9 million children have fathers, mothers or both parents working abroad (Conde 2008; Parreñas 2005b: 317). Or let us take Eastern Europe. There entire villages have lost all the mothers, and a term has even been coined for the children that have been left behind: they are called EU orphans (Burghardt et al. 2010: 48ff.). In Romania alone, according to UNICEF, around 350,000 children have one parent living abroad and 126,000 children have both parents living far from home (ibid.). In the Republic of Moldova every third child grows up without one or both parents because they are abroad working to earn money (Brill 2010).

New Communication Media

Distant love thus becomes an everyday reality for ever more families. This contradicts the classical image of the family with its connotations of closeness and community. How do family members cope with enforced separation? What sort of life do they lead? In particular, how can we envisage the relationship between mother and child?

Despite geographical distances from their children, transnational mothers make every effort to maintain their emotional ties to them and to be close to their everyday lives and the process of growing up. They use every means possible – video messages, regular telephone calls, email greetings and presents both large and small – to continue to dispense love and affection, to keep memories alive and, if need be, to admonish and punish. They devise personal rituals, their own versions of 'transnational intimacy' (Parreñas 2005b: 317; Madianou 2012; Madianou and Miller 2011) – in short, they do whatever they can to carry out the tasks of maternal care. The new media play an important role in all this – mobile phones, text messages, email and Skype (Parreñas 2005b; Vertovec 2004). They make it possible to maintain regular everyday contact; the children can tell them what happened in school and about their friends and whatever else is worrying or exciting them, and their mothers can follow the events of their lives at least in part. In the Philippines it is said that, by now, one child in three has its own 'mobile-phone Mum' (Burghardt et al. 2010). Needless to say, if major or even minor crises arise (difficulties in school, drug problems, illness, accidents, etc.), the limits of these mediatized forms of maternal love at a distance are soon reached. The new media are 'sunny day' technologies. In troubled times, closeness and actual presence become essential, especially for children. Thus, according to a twenty-year-old Filipina whose mother has been a domestic worker in New York for ten years: 'There are times when you want to talk to her, but she is not there. That is really hard, very difficult. . . . There are times when I want to call her, speak to her, cry to her, and I cannot. It is difficult. The only thing that I can do is write to her. And I cannot cry to her through the emails and sometimes I just want to cry on her shoulder' (Parreñas 2003: 42).

The Global Hierarchy of Caring

What we said above about love at a distance between adult partners holds good also for distant love between mother and child. It's love without the daily routine (see pp. 49ff. above). The practical demands of looking after children – washing, cooking, cleaning, bathing, dressing, etc. – cannot be satisfied globally and transnationally. They call for immediate personal contact. According to recent studies, new forms of the division of labour have been developed to cater for this. As a rule, emigrant mothers will try to make use of other women in their home town – grandmothers, sisters-in-law, neighbours. By sending them money and presents, they attempt to ensure that the care of their children is maintained. This gives rise to 'global care chains' spanning countries and continents (Hochschild 2000). The chains may look like this: in a developing-country family the eldest daughter looks after her younger brothers and sisters; this liberates their mother to look after the children of another woman, thus enabling her to earn a little money; this other woman has emigrated to one of the affluent nations of the West and obtained a job as a nanny. Such cross-border care chains may arise, for example, as a consequence of the population movements between Eastern and Western Europe. Women move from Poland to Germany to look after children in middle-class families, while simultaneously Ukrainian women move to Poland to look after the children of the Polish women who have emigrated to work in the West.

The American sociologist Arlie Russell Hochschild has summed up the course of such movements in a single sentence: 'As mothering is passed down the race/class/nation hierarchy, each woman becomes a provider and hires a wife' (Hochschild 2000: 137). Put more generally, a new global hierarchy is emerging in the age of globalization. Private care is being spread from top to bottom at the level of nations, skin-colours and ethnicity. In the process the opportunities for appropriate provision and care worthy of human beings disappear as one proceeds from one stage to the next until, having reached the lowest rung, nothing remains at all. When Polish women migrate to Germany in order to do the chores in German households, and when Ukrainian women migrate to Poland to perform the chores in Polish households, who does the everyday household chores in Ukraine? Who looks after the children of Ukrainian women and who takes care of their parents?

For all those at the lower end of the pecking order the costs are considerable. For example, for the children left behind at home, the grandmothers, aunts and elder sisters are not always up to the challenge; they may lack the time or the energy or be too old or ill to cope with the additional demands. So the children may be left more or less to their own devices or else are pushed from pillar to post between different households. The fathers are of little use in this situation. Many of them will have abandoned the family years before and left the responsibility for their children to the mothers; others are unable to come to terms with the new situation, with the fact that the wife is working abroad and that it is she who is the family bread-winner. This destabilizes them to the point where they become unwilling or unable to look after their children. The children, in consequence, may suffer from emotional neglect.

4   Motherly Love and Other Emotions

Historians disagree about the mother–child relationship and its historical development (Rosenbaum 1982; Shorter 1976; van Dülmen 1990). Various answers are forthcoming to the question of whether a close emotional bond between mother and child has been a feature of all epochs and societies or whether it made its appearance first in the transition to modernity – whether, in short, mother love is an invention of the modern world. This much is agreed: motherhood grew steadily in importance in the European discourse of the nineteenth and twentieth centuries, not merely as a biological fact but as an emotional relationship. Philosophy and theology, politics and art evoked, eulogized and transfigured motherhood and motherly love. It was the object of countless poems, novels and plays, a recurrent motif in both art and kitsch. It was felt to be an elemental, natural, close and eternal emotional bond. Mother love was pure, selfless, sacrificing, consoling and healing, inexhaustible and irreplaceable. In this form, mother love was cult and culture, myth and fairy tale, a home in a rapidly changing, increasingly homeless world. It was an ideal and also a self-evident duty, ascribed and prescribed to women in equal measure. 'The mother belongs to the child' – this was declared to be the supreme task of woman and as such it was anchored in a programme in which gender roles were polarized (Beck-Gernsheim 2008).

In the late 1960s, at a time when more and more women completed their education, took up careers and became increasingly reluctant to restrict their activities to the home and the family, a change began to take place in relations between men and women and mothers and children. A new model gradually became established in the following decades after lengthy, often bruising debates about the division of labour, gender roles and a mother's duties. Today the omnipresent mother is no longer the ideal; instead, a woman is expected to go out to work. But, because she spends part of the day on other activities, a mother is now expected to make up for this by lavishing even more affection on her children. As the current slogan has it, the new programme for mother and child focuses on 'quality time'. This means that, although she is no longer confined to the family and the home, a higher value is put on the emotional tie between mother and child. Women may rise further up the career ladder, they may succeed in politics and even win the Nobel Prize. But the term 'a mother's love' continues to possess a special aura.

And, as many studies show, the same thing holds good for the home countries of women who emigrate in order to earn their living as domestic workers. By setting out for foreign lands and leaving their children behind, they enter certain taboo areas. Their behaviour is a provocation, an emotionally charged challenge to the fundamental rules – a combination that everyone involved finds perplexing. Mother love, which used to be defined as a self-evident tie, as a woman's love for her own biological offspring, as an integral part of her being, now acquires a global dimension, thanks to the new situation of a transnational division of labour between women. On the one hand, mother love is a duty she has to perform; on the other, it is the object of wishes, hopes and fears. All of a sudden, a woman has become an insecure, controversial resource, one that is fought over and bought. Love from nearby and at a distance, yearning and jealousy, reproaches and counter-reproaches – when you read through the relevant studies you become aware of a tangle of feelings and expectations. These merely provoke further, similar questions: Which mother loves which child? And which woman enjoys the child's love? Who should love, may love? Which mother loves too much and which too little? Which one loves the wrong child? And, not least, which mother has forgotten about a mother's love? Which mother neglects her child?

Jealousy

The majority of children feel great longing for mothers who live far away (Nazario 2007; Parreñas 2005a). Many dream about an ideal mother; they imagine a mother as a larger-than-life figure, at all times full of patience, affection and understanding, inexhaustible in her care for them and her love (Parreñas 2005a: 120ff.). Many are jealous of the 'other' children, those in the distant land, those for whom their mother is employed as a nanny and who are able to enjoy her company every day (ibid.: 129). That is what Floridith Sanchez felt, the eighteen-year-old daughter of a Filipina who works in Taiwan as an immigrant nanny: 'Very jealous. I am very, very jealous. There was even a time when she told the children she was caring for that they are very lucky that she was taking care of them, while her children back in the Philippines don't even have a mom to take care of them' (ibid.: 129; Parreñas 2003: 42).

The mothers in their turn – that is, the migrant workers – feel disturbed in two respects. They worry about whether the person to whom they have entrusted their own children will prove to be dependable. They regularly shower them with rewards and presents to keep them sweet (thank-you letters, money, clothes, etc.) (Hondagneu-Sotelo and Avila 1997: 560f.). At the same time, the migrant women also have the opposite worry, namely that their delegating the tasks of motherhood might succeed only too well – so well that the children gradually forget their real mother and become attached to their carer, with whom they build up an increasingly powerful inner bond (ibid.: 561).

A similar ambivalence is often felt also by the other mothers – i.e., mothers who employ an immigrant worker. On the one hand, American women prefer to employ immigrants from Latin America as nannies, on the basis of their origins and the national character associated with it – qualities such as joie de vivre, spontaneity and warmth, which can be regarded as advantageous in looking after children (Hochschild 2003: 23).

On the other hand, many parents watch the nanny like a hawk to see whether the bond between her and the child has become too close, too affectionate. Dominique, an immigrant who earns her keep as a nanny in New York, says that '[The parents] want us to be father and mother to these children. They're the ones who brought the kids into the world, but then they don't have time to raise them. So the kids get attached to you because you're the one who's always there. Then the parents get angry' (Cheever 2003: 35).

To reduce the potential for conflict in the relationship with their employers (parents or mothers), the immigrants must perform a daily balancing act. Because many mothers who delegate the task of bringing up the children also have guilt feelings and anxieties, calming their fears is one of the chief duties of the migrant workers. They therefore have to convince the mothers that they will protect the child as if it were their own, that they will look after it to the best of their ability, and that the process of delegation is in the child's best interests. But when the child, grateful for all the attention, begins to show affection, the migrant women must keep these feelings carefully in check. They need to keep the child at a distance because, if they do not, they may be made to feel the parents' anger and jealousy. In short, the migrant workers need to walk the tightrope of showing their love for the child that has been confided to their care while at the same time withholding it to some degree because the child's love is meant for the parents alone.

A Global Heart Transplant

One emotion surfaces again and again in those involved in these transactions. It is the fear that love might take the wrong turning and become attached to the wrong person. As interviews confirm, such fears are by no means groundless. This applies in the first instance to the immigrant workers' children. If the mother is absent for years on end and is unable to visit even for a short time, they become estranged from her; family togetherness is supplanted by alienation (Hochschild 2003: 15ff.). It's the children's good fortune if they have access to another person (an aunt, a grandmother or a sister) who not only provides them with food and drink but also cuddles them and shows affection. Some children then build a bond with this person while the memory of their actual mother gradually fades (Gamburd 2000: 196). In short, they begin to love the substitute mother instead of the real one.

The situation is no simpler for the mother working abroad. Studies show that women suffer agonies from being separated from their children. They miss their children dreadfully; they feel depressed because they are not there to see the children growing up; they worry constantly that the children are not being properly looked after by the grandmothers, aunts or neighbours to whom they have entrusted them. At the same time, they feel lonely in a foreign country; they are isolated, emotionally exhausted and have scarcely any private life outside their work (Hochschild 2003; Hondagneu-Sotelo and Avila

1997). In this situation, the children that are not their own but with whom they spend the main part of the day may well become one of the few pleasures of their lives (Hochschild 2003). They enjoy the liveliness and the laughter of the child entrusted to them, the feel of their skin and the physical closeness; it reminds them of their own children. With some women this reaches the point where they transfer the love they feel for their own children to the children of their employer (Gamburd 2000: 199ff.; Hochschild 2003; Hondagneu-Sotelo and Avila 1997: 564f.). Their interview statements read like confessions from the heart.

Vicky, for example, a Filipina, has left five children behind in order to earn money in the United States: 'the only thing you can do is give all your love to the child [in your care]. In my absence from my children the most I could do with my situation was to give all my love to that child' (Hochschild 2003: 22). Then there is Rowena, also from the Philippines and now working in the United States; she says about Noa, the small daughter of her American employer, whom she looks after from morning to evening: 'I give Noa what I can't give to my children.' And she finds herself duly rewarded by Noa: 'she makes me feel like a mother' (ibid.: 16). Or, again, there is Maria who left the Philippines to go to California: 'I love Ana more than my own two children. Yes, more! . . . I work ten hours a day with one day off. I don't know my neighbors on the block. And so this child gives me what I need' (ibid.: 24). Hochschild describes this as a 'global heart transplant' (ibid.: 22). Mother love which has been so highly prized and is said to be irreplaceable is withdrawn from children of poor regions, re-routed and used for the benefit of the children of the affluent.

What we read in these interviews casts doubt on the assumption of Western employers that the warmth, sincerity and love that migrant women display towards the children entrusted to them is a more or less natural bonus derived from their earthy, rural origins and the culture of their homeland. Such statements demonstrate that the qualities ascribed to such women arise, in part at least, from their situation of love at a distance – from their separation from their own children and their loneliness in their new environment. In Hochschild's view, the picture drawn by American employers is alto-gether too rosy and bland. If we listen to the voices of the immigrant women themselves, the picture takes on a much darker hue: what we see then is that 'theirs is not an import of happy peasant moth-ering but a love that develops partly on American shores . . . through the intense loneliness and longing for their own children (Hochschild 2003: 24).

Recriminations

Maternal feelings and mother love still enjoy considerable prestige in our own day. Since mother love is simultaneously many things – an ideal, an indissoluble bond, an allotted duty – and above all because mother love is closely bound up with gender roles and the division of labour based on them, the behaviour of migrant women – going away, leaving the children behind – is tantamount to a revolution. It threatens the foundations on which the entire organization of everyday life is built. It flies in the face of our received ideas of the nature of male and female. We must expect such a far-reaching reversal of existing conditions to trigger irritation and resistance. And, in fact, not everyone from the same social background as the migrants approves of their leaving. The women are sometimes the object of fierce disapproval and are condemned as 'heartless' for neglecting their most important duty, namely taking care of their own children (Gamburd 2000: 199; Hondagneu-Sotelo and Aviva 1997: 552; Parreñas 2003). Moreover, many migrants struggle with self-reproaches and guilt feelings. Here, for example, is an immigrant Filipina in Rome:

> When the girl that I take care of calls her mother 'Mama', my heart jumps all the time because my children also call me 'Mama'. I feel the gap caused by our physical separation especially in the morning, when I pack [her] lunch, because that's what I used to do for my children. . . . I begin thinking that at this hour, I should be taking care of my very own children and not someone else's. (Interview in Parreñas 2003: 41)

The immigrants do not find it easy to brush off such reproaches and self-reproaches. In the interviews we have quoted they attempt to justify themselves, evidently in response to criticisms they often have to contend with. To start with, they point out that their going away is by no means the same thing as voluntarily abandoning their children, a deficient sense of responsibility or even callousness (Hondagneu-Sotelo and Avila 1997: 557). Three distinct lines of defence can be identified: a traditional one, an innovative one and one in which they go on the attack.

In the traditional defence, migrant women represent their going away as a sacrifice, one that they make not out of self-interest or to gratify their own desires but for the sake of the family and above all the children. As the woman quoted above says in a later passage in the interview: 'the work that I do here [in Rome] is done for my family' (Parreñas 2003: 41). Such a line of argument is traditional because, in emphasizing her selflessness, she touches on a familiar theme much emphasized in the past and turns it into a crucial element in her decision.

In the case of the innovative line of defence, the migrant women point out that their going away is not the result of a free choice but rather of the force of circumstances, the changed world order. To cite the words of a Mexican woman, now working in California: 'It's something you have to do' (Hondagneu-Sotelo and Avila 1997: 563). If the men no longer have jobs, the women have to help out. If women go abroad nowadays, that is because it is the only way to enable the family to keep their heads above water. For example, a migrant woman from Guatemala who has been working in Los Angeles for years says:

> One supposes that the mother must care for the children. A mother cannot so easily throw her children aside. So, in all families the decision is that the man comes [to the US] first. But now that the man cannot find work here so easily, the woman comes first. Recently the women have been coming and the men staying [behind]. (Ibid.: 558)

We see then that migrants do not spurn the ideal of mother love and its associated obligations. On the contrary, they acknowledge it fully, while reinterpreting the obligations that follow from it by pointing to the changed conditions surrounding it: in the here and now, going away offers the best chance of doing justice to one's role as mother (Hondagneu-Sotelo and Avila 1997: 563). By leaving home, a woman broadens the radius of maternal duty, pushes the boundaries even further and helps to create a new model of the 'good mother' (ibid.: 567), one that comes to terms with the alien world in the internal space of motherhood.

In cases where migrant women defend themselves by going on the attack, they reject the accusations levelled at them and simply pass them on to others. This means that other mothers, namely the employers, become the target of criticism (Cheever 2003: 35; Hondagneu-Sotelo 2001: 25, 40f.; Hondagneu-Sotelo and Avila 1997: 565f.). They, the migrants, claim that they acquiesce in the separation from their children only because of external pressures. Their employers, however, are in a different position. They have a career because they have chosen to have one, for the sake of the career itself and in order to achieve self-fulfilment. Their motives in leaving the house every morning and abandoning their child to another woman are alleged to be purely egotistical. Alternatively, they do not even work but wish simply to luxuriate in the enjoyment of their own free time. It is the employers, then, who display callousness and lack of feeling. Listen again to the immigrant from Mexico: 'I love my kids, they don't . . . what they prefer is to go to the salon, get their nails done, you know, go shopping, things like that. Even if they're home all day, they don't want to spend time with the kids because they're paying somebody to do that for them' (Hondagneu-Sotelo and Avila 1997: 565f.).

Thus the women migrants cling to the traditional ideal of motherhood as a full-time occupation as far as financial circumstances allow. With this last proviso they proclaim the legitimacy of their own behaviour on the grounds that they are acting only out of necessity. They can claim, therefore, that they are heeding the unwritten laws of motherhood and mother love – while at the same time abandoning the cardinal rule of motherhood: immediate proximity to their own children.

Care Drain

It follows from the above that the topic of immigrant domestic workers involves not just the situation of families in rich countries but also the migrants' homelands, countries geographically remote from the developed world but inextricably bound up with it, as well as the consequences for their families. If we broaden our gaze to include these homelands, we suddenly see a very different picture. We realize that the history of immigrant domestic workers is a history of loss rather than of profit. We are familiar with the term 'brain drain' to describe the emigration of highly qualified personnel and the problems resulting from their departure for the societies affected by it. But few people realize that there is also a 'care drain' (Hochschild 2003) – i.e., the departure of people responsible for taking care of everyday work in families – and that this leads to scandalous gaps in provision in the deprived regions of the world.

5 Asymmetrical Gains

Whoever employs a migrant as a domestic worker, whether to take care of ageing parents, to look after children or to do the housework, tends to view the employer–employee relationship in a positive light, namely as a boon for everyone concerned (as an easing of the burden of work for the employer and as aid to developing countries). This harmonious view of the matter is faulty:

- For one thing it overlooks the fact that costs and benefits are unevenly distributed. The very thing that makes life easier for families in rich countries creates correspondingly intractable problems for families in the rest of the world.
- Second, the employment of immigrants as domestic labour creates new forms of social inequality; the wealth gap between poor and rich nations is extended to the kitchen and nursery.
- Third, using immigrants for domestic labour confronts feminists (whether male or female) with a problem. They call for the equal treatment of all women. However, they now find themselves in the position of employers who exploit the global inequality of women to promote their own private emancipation.

At the same time, we must reckon with the increased probability that further forms of such international interaction will make their appearance. If frontiers become more porous, if rich and poor nations come closer together (and even a determined protectionist policy will scarcely affect the outcome here), the affluent nations of the West will continue to exert a magnetic force. As long as poor countries lack the public infrastructure that would enable their own women to have equal rights to a career, these women will continue to look for private solutions and survival strategies.

In the 1970s, when the new women's movement was on the rise, one of its chief slogans was 'the personal is the political' (Hanisch 1969). In other words, the patterns of private life are not merely a private matter; they are a political fact. They are a keystone in the structure of society, not least in the structural inequality between the sexes. Today, in an age of worldwide migratory movements, we can add: 'the personal is global' (Hochschild 2003: 30). Freely translated, this means that the transformation of everyday work in the family and the emergence of a transnational private shadow economy in the grey areas of legality is not just a matter of personal lifestyle or the contents of private purses. It is directly linked to questions of global justice and the global distribution of resources. 'And Grandpa will be looked after by a woman from Eastern Europe.' This development would be unthinkable in the absence of the political, economic and social hierarchy between the nations.

7

Male Hegemony in Decline? Why Women Gain Power in World Families

Many people claim that migration and women's emancipation have little in common. Migration, it is thought, is the product of poverty and deprivation, while emancipation is a sort of luxury. Many people believe that the disadvantages of women would increase, and increase dramatically, as a result of migration (Han 2003: 281). Many assert that forced marriages would lead to women being sent abroad by their families and treated like slaves (see pp. 92f. above; Kelek 2005).

Is it true, then, that the old bonds and shackles continue to thrive even in the context of migration and within world families? Are women failing to make progress in their emancipation and are they still unable to improve their position in society? Has the hierarchy between the sexes remained unchanged wherever women decide to move?

Such claims miss the point. Following migration, men and women invert the traditional rules governing gender roles and invent new ones. 'Like the men, the women reported wanting to migrate "to know other places" and to earn a target amount of money' (Hondagneu-Sotelo 1994: 87). Migration can effect a shift in the power relations between the sexes and set new negotiating processes in motion. The traditional power relations become eroded. What comes next may well be an open question in the first instance (Treibel 2004). This means that we have to look at the balance of power between the sexes in different kinds of world family. To anticipate our conclusions: we expect that women in world families will make gains in the pecking order.

1   Geographies of Migration

We can approach the question of the changes in relations between the sexes by asking 'From where to where?', or, more accurately, by looking at the direction of the route taken by migrants. Since women's rights are significantly further advanced in Western than in non-Western societies, women who travel (or marry) from East to West (or from South to North) generally achieve an expansion of their rights, whereas those who migrate from West to East (or from North to South) must reckon with a considerable diminution. This holds good at the level of social institutions (such as education and the law) as well as in private life and relations with a partner.

Western Women Lose Autonomy

Women who marry a man from a non-Western family frequently find themselves confronted with a world in which no great importance is attached to autonomy and independence, at least as far as women are concerned. This has the effect of a profound psychological rupture for women who have enjoyed a successful career and have shaped their lives in accordance with their own wishes and ideas. They find their rights significantly curtailed in the public sphere; they may even be unable to enter public spaces on their own, unaccompanied by a man. Many make the discovery that that they have not married a single man but a family – or, more precisely, an extended family, with highly developed hierarchical structures, fixed rules and ubiquitous controls. They find themselves tied into a hierarchy of the sexes in which, because of their status as women, they are at the bottom. The existence of this hierarchy comes as a shock to a wife who follows her husband to his home country. But it can also reveal itself if the couple remains in the West. And it can all start on the wedding day, since from that point on the male family members may well feel authorized to issue instructions to the newly wed wife.

A study of Anglo-Indian couples contains an Englishwoman's memories of such instructions:

> What I didn't expect, however, was that the act of marriage would instantly transform the way in which certain relations treated me. On our wedding day we threw an impromptu party for sixty or so people and the next morning the house was littered with flowers, wine glasses and dirty dishes. My brother-in-law, visiting from India, who up until that day had treated me very courteously, looked askance at the debris and shouted, 'What a mess this is – get on and clear it up!' I was

completely taken aback that he now felt that he had the right to order me about in what I regarded as my own house. (Joshi and Krishna 1998: 182)

In many non-Western countries, such as India, an age hierarchy exists alongside the hierarchy of the sexes. This hierarchy of age lays down rules for the relations between the younger and the older generation. The older a person is, the higher his or her status and the more the younger generation has to show its respect. Respect and obedience are mandatory. The consequence is that the English or American woman who marries an Indian man finds herself, often unexpectedly, tied into a second hierarchy, a hierarchy of women among themselves. And once again she is bottom of the pile. At the top end of the pile is the mother-in-law, who expects respect and submissiveness from the young, and hence immature and ignorant, daughter-in-law. Her son, the newly wed husband, is also expected to show his mother the same respect. Whether in India or Britain, the rule is always the same: the family has priority. The mother-in-law reigns supreme.

An Indian married to an Englishwoman recollects the first days of his own marriage:

the day we got married Catherine and I left with my brother, mother and cousin in the car. It didn't seem incongruous to me, but to Catherine it was a violation of all that she had been brought up to expect. The next morning, just after our marriage, I took my cousin to the airport and saw him off. It was really hurtful to Catherine, but I didn't realize that. Then we went on our honeymoon for a few days and came back to London because my mother had a throat problem. It wasn't incongruous to me to break up the honeymoon and then go back again, but to Catherine it was. (Joshi and Krishna 1998: 174)

The mother-in-law's power is at its greatest when the young couple move to India and live in the house of the extended family. It is the mother-in-law who possesses the superior wisdom, the knowledge that brooks no contradiction, regardless of whether the issue is one of cooking or of bringing up the children. This is what underpins her right to exercise total control. She has the right to read letters and monitor telephone conversations; she can oversee how the money is spent, she can redecorate the young couple's bedroom without consulting them and can specify which clothing and which jewellery are to be worn on which occasion (ibid.: 181).

We can guess at the shock felt by young Western women on finding themselves in such a situation – these women will include young lawyers, doctors and biologists. Women who have grown up in the belief that they can make their own choices about their life suddenly discover that what counts is hierarchy instead of equality, subordination instead of autonomy. This calls for enormous effort and reserves of self-discipline and constitutes a threat to their self-confidence and their self-respect. The study referred to above contains reports in which young women explain again and again what an effort it has cost them to play the role of the deferential and subservient woman, and to do so with a smile and without letting anyone see them fuming inwardly. It is not just that they recoil from acting as a servant to their new family and their mother-in-law; experiences of this kind damage their sense of integrity and their very identity (Joshi and Krishna 1998: 184).

In mixed-nationality marriages in which the woman moves from West to East she is subjected to considerable pressure. A study of Danish–Japanese marriages reports that the pairing of a Danish wife with a Japanese husband is highly susceptible to conflict, while the reverse pairing, of a Japanese wife with a Danish husband, is as a rule far more harmonious. This is borne out by the divorce figures, since divorces are far more common in the former case than in the latter (Refsing 1998: 204).

Non-Western Women Gain Autonomy

Whereas migration or marriage that involves moving from West to East often results in a loss of autonomy, the opposite is true for people migrating to the West. They are winners in a number of respects, personally as well as in economic terms. In Western societies women enjoy the same rights as men – from the inheritance laws via educational opportunities to divorce. In the West there are facilities for sex education and access to reliable forms of contraception. Sexual violence towards women is punishable, and even within marriage sexual intercourse without the wife's consent is a violation of the law and renders the husband liable to prosecution.

Such rights and opportunities extend to women but often only with reservations. In reality a right cannot always be enjoyed. This does not detract from the fact that women in Western societies enjoy far greater autonomy both in the public sphere and in private life. The benefits can be seen especially in certain immigrant groups: unmarried women, lesbians, single mothers and divorcees – in short, women who do not fit into the normal pattern of wife and mother and who would enjoy even less respect and even fewer rights in their homeland than married women. The road to the West can provide new life chances to women who are marginalized in their own country.

But emigration can offer the yearned-for way out even for married women – the way out of an unhappy marriage. Divorce is a near impossibility in many non-Western countries because the legal hurdles are too high, the economic drawbacks are extremely serious, the social ostracism is inevitable and, over and above all else, women must reckon with severe sanctions, such as the enforced separation from her children. It is irrelevant that the husband may be an alcoholic who constantly deceives his wife or beats her regularly; women have to put up with it. All that changes when they start to live in the West, since they will have been able to escape from an unbearable marriage.

An illuminating illustration of this can be found in a Swedish study (Darvishpour 2002) which claims that the divorce rate among Iranian immigrants was significantly higher than in the Swedish host society. According to Darvishpour, two factors explain the difference. First of all, many of the Iranian women had long been unhappy in their marriages but did not venture to contemplate divorce. All this changed once they found themselves in a new country. They now found that they had the same rights as men, not least in the matter of divorce. Furthermore, they were now able to obtain work and to stand on their own two feet financially, so that they no longer depended on their husbands for their survival. Second, many men experience the situation of exile as socially demeaning, as a loss of both status and income. This leads to a shift in the balance of power within the marriage. This shift creates additional scope for conflict and leads to a further rise in the number of divorces.

The fact that women experience living in the new country as a liberation becomes even clearer from yet another finding in this study. The Iranian immigrants were asked whether they would return home in the event of a change of regime in Iran. The result was unambiguous: whereas almost all the men said they would return, almost all the women said they would not. They feared that, were they to return, they would lose all the benefits that emigration had brought them and that had so strengthened their position (Darvishpour 2002).

Other studies of migrants returning home come regularly to the same conclusion. Whenever this subject is raised, the men are for it and the women are against (Darvishpour 2002: 278; Pyke 2004: 262). And so it is in real life too. No sooner has the possibility of a return appeared on the horizon than the women start to procrastinate and invent reasons for further postponement; they even think up all sorts of ruses to torpedo the man's plans to take the family home. Even when they fail to gain acceptance in their new country or have to make do with poorly paid work with no job security, the women are loath to give up the freedoms they have so recently gained.

This is very telling. It shows that women do not just simply accept the change in the relations between the sexes resulting from migration. They attempt to exert an active influence so as to achieve greater equality. This becomes even clearer when it comes to the question of choosing a partner. It then emerges that men too regard the question of equality or inequality in the relations between the sexes as an important criterion when choosing a partner, though in their case it is from the opposite point of view. To anticipate our findings: where relations between the sexes are not set in stone by tradition but have started imperceptibly to shift, choosing a partner becomes the terrain on which the laws governing the family are renegotiated and reshaped for the future. The choice of partners becomes the place in which to introduce new patterns of behaviour in relations between the sexes or else to protect existing ones from change.

2   Strategies for Choosing a Partner

Ever since the waves of immigrants began to reach Europe, i.e., countries that had thought of themselves hitherto as homogeneous nation-states but have now developed into ethnically mixed societies, the question of integrating the incoming groups has moved to the top of the political agenda. That was accompanied by the question of the newcomers' attitudes to marriage. Do the migrants marry one another, or is there a growing tendency for marriages between members of the majority population and the ethnic minorities?

Whether we look at Turks in Germany, members of the Indian subcontinent in Britain or Indonesians in the Netherlands, the answer is more or less the same. Even when they have already been settled for years in their new country, the majority of immigrants do not join the majority in the host society; they find a partner from their country of origin. Traditional sociological explanations offer a variety of interpretations for this which, even though they draw attention to a number of factors, all have one thing in common: they remain imprisoned in the framework of particular nation-states, in a nation-based methodology. This trend began with Robert Merton, who was one of the first to discover the topic of 'intermarriage'. He analysed the socio-cultural assumptions (and barriers) underlying the choice of partner that arise from the demographic characteristics of the group (i.e., the size of the group; the proportion of men to women; their age profile; and, finally, the closeness of contact to other groups;

Merton [1941] 1976: 220). According to Merton, it is factors such as these that determine the probability of finding a partner in one's own group or outside it. More recent writers have refined his analysis and pointed especially to so-called structural factors (e.g., Klein 2000; Spickard 1989: 6ff. and 361ff.; Vetter 2001), as well as cultural norms and barriers.

Such factors are supposed to explain why marriage behaviour frequently complies with the pattern of homogamy – that is to say, why most people marry within their own social group. The motto for such behaviour is 'birds of a feather flock together', a motto valid also for migrants, so it is assumed. This line of argument is typical. For a long time, it was customary to regard the findings of studies based on men as universal laws governing human actions and to transfer these results automatically to women. In the same way, findings obtained from the study of people in the nation-state were simply extrapolated to migrants – that is, to people who cannot be located within the frontiers of a single nation-state. Looked at from this standpoint, the tendency to choose a partner from one's country of origin is hardly surprising. If Vietnamese immigrants living and working in the United States predominantly choose women from Vietnam as marriage partners, the situation is much as it is in Bavaria, where people choose to marry other Bavarians, or among Catholics, who tend to marry other Catholics, or members of the middle class, who marry members of the middle class, or farmers, who marry other farmers. They all tend to marry people from their own social group. If we adopt the national point of view, we should rather ask the opposite question: What is so remarkable about a Vietnamese immigrant in the United States marrying a woman from Vietnam? Isn't that just the normal situation?

Such an assumption seems perfectly plausible at first sight – and yet it is based on a highly dubious premise. It is tacitly assumed that there is a natural fit between immigrants and the population of the relevant country of origin. This implies that Turkish immigrants in Germany form a coherent group with the Turks in Turkey, just as Moroccan immigrants in France are all of a piece with the Moroccans in Morocco.

That these assumptions are open to question is made very clear by the findings of many of the more recent studies in migration. Migrants of Turkish origin in Germany (or Pakistani origin in Britain) are not simply Turks or Pakistanis. With their experiences, expectations, needs and values, they form an independent group, namely that of Turkish Germans or Pakistani British. The way they live their lives is not a straightforward continuation of traditions they have brought with them from their mother country and unpacked ready for use in their new home. Their lives are marked by the experience of migration, of their arrival in a foreign country, and by its social, political, legal and economic circumstances. This creates a dual frame of reference, a state of tension between 'here' and 'there' from which new hybrid cultural forms emerge (Baumann 2002; Kibria 1993; Tietze 2001).

That is precisely what is omitted by conventional attempts at explanation. They ignore, push to one side or dismiss as unimportant whatever defines the particular situation of immigrant men and women. They remain blind to the fact that immigrants perpetually find themselves in a state of tension between two societies, countries and cultures. This is the exact point on which we now wish to focus. We wish to show that an essential component of the life of immigrants is the need constantly to observe, compare and relate two different worlds, the new country and the country of origin, and to realize that this is their great opportunity. By comparing the two worlds, their advantages and defects, by noting what each has to offer or where each has a deficiency, immigrants can construct their own options and discover their own opportunities for action. Depending on the astuteness with which they proceed and the flexibility with which they respond, the fact that they are members of two different worlds can be the source of significant benefits. This is true in economic terms, but also in the private sphere – for example, when it comes to their choice of partner.

Imagined Husbands, Imagined Wives

As the findings of numerous studies suggest, when immigrants make a decision, they frequently have a particular contrasting image of the following kind in their minds. On the one hand, they see their country of origin as the repository of tradition; on the other, they see the host country or the ethnic community in the host country as the locus of a new permissiveness and new morals. Such expectations provide the background for their choice of partner. They supply a kind of marriage compass, signalling why a person may find it to his or her advantage to look for a partner in one world or the other.

Such contrasting images acquire clear contours if we consider the motives and wishes of young men in search of a bride. The traditional family contained a hierarchy of the sexes; the man had precedence and authority. The new ranking of the sexes in the host country, on the other hand, implies a greater sexual equality. In other words, men are stripped of their privileged position – or, at least, many of them believe this to be the case. How should they compensate for this loss? One obvious option is to look for one's future wife in a place where equality is not yet so firmly established – in one's country of origin. And, in fact, such a line of thought frequently does emerge from the relevant studies – in the case of immigrants from Pakistan, from Turkey, from Vietnam and from Morocco (Autant 1995: 173f.; Lievens 1999: 728; Reniers 2001: 29; Shaw 2001: 330; Thai 2003). In their eyes, the young women who live in the host country are too spoiled and too permissive in their attitudes. It would be better, therefore, to find a bride in one's home country. 'She knows the customs. . . . She won't stand up to you' (Shaw 2001: 330).

We may infer from the foregoing that young women from immigrant families find themselves in the opposite situation when they come to look for a marriage partner (if indeed they have the right to decide this for themselves). They have passed through the school of the West both literally and figuratively, and they frequently do not regard serving a husband and children as their sole purpose in life. Hence they are unlikely to be attracted to the idea of marrying a man from their country of origin, who is probably wedded to the old traditions. If that is the case, why do so many young women in immigrant families nevertheless find themselves taking a man from their home country as a marriage partner? It is widely supposed, especially among the majority population, that they are married off in this way. Pressure is put on them and they are forced into such marriages.

This may in fact be what happens in many cases, but it is hardly the norm. This has been shown by the relevant studies of young immigrant women from families from Turkey or North Africa (Autant 1995: 174ff.; Kofman 2004: 251f.; Lievens 1999: 717, 728; Munoz 1999: 117f.). These studies show that the women concerned are not simply compliant victims, even when their marriages have been arranged within the family itself. On the contrary, they have themselves chosen to marry a man from their home country. They have carefully weighed the advantages and disadvantages of such a union beforehand – and have given their consent. Why? Because they hoped that this would give them room to manoeuvre in their dealings with traditional expectations and controls. Because they hoped to shift the balance of power in the marriage to their own advantage. To put it bluntly: precisely because they are unwilling to fit into the hierarchical, patriarchal relationship between the sexes, they are ready to enter into a marriage with a man who comes from their home country.

This may seem paradoxical at first sight, but is not without its own logic. For, if the man comes to join her from abroad, the woman will already have a head start on him. As a rule, she will be able to speak the language of the host country; she will know her way around its institutions, its way of life and its regulations. This means that the balance of power in the family can be shifted in her favour. Furthermore, her parents-in-law will be far away, at a safe distance – an advantage that is not to be despised. Hence there is no need to move in with them, to acquiesce in their control of the situation or to be forced to obey them all the time. Looked at in this light, the balance of possibilities veers towards the young wives. By way of summary, we can say that a woman may indeed marry an 'imported husband' in order to protect the freedom she has garnered for herself.

At the beginning of the twenty-first century, as many commentators have noted, relations between the sexes have undergone a major shift, at any rate in the Western world. Its ramifications extend into many aspects of life, not least those of immigrants. In the younger generation of immigrants, among both men and women, we can see strategies for choosing marriage partners that all follow a similar goal: given the changing circumstances, they all strive to achieve a new equilibrium in the relations between the sexes. Men and women alike put their hopes into finding a marriage partner who comes from their country of origin. Whether such hopes are justified in the everyday life of a marriage, whether or not the man who follows his future wife in fact moderates his assertion of power, whether or not the woman who follows her future husband in fact becomes more tractable and obedient – that is another question (Lievens 1999: 728f.; Thai 2003: 248ff.). What is crucial here is that such unions possess strategic advantages in the minds of both sexes.

Thus for both men and women it is the possibility of comparison that is the determining factor. Whereas all comparisons would seem to be ruled out from a 'national' perspective – the separate worlds of 'us' and 'them' seem incomparable – such comparisons appear unavoidable inside world families, and the results of these considerations help to create a new balance of power one way or the other. In this sense world families are *families that make comparisons*. In such families – and this holds good both for the active participants and for the social scientist observing them – the values, standards and power exercised by both men and women can no longer be inferred from the national context. They have to be investigated by a process of comparison – i.e., by systematically relating to each other the separate but conjoined worlds of the marriage partners. This means that the 'age of comparison' that Nietzsche predicted 150 years ago has now become everyday reality.

3   Different Horizons

In *Gender & Society*, the Korean journal of women's studies, an essay was published in 2008 devoted to Vietnamese and Philippine women who immigrate to Korea in order to marry. It describes the ordeals experienced by these women. Although they try hard to learn the Korean language and to adopt the customs of their new environment, their efforts receive little acknowledgement. They have to do a lot of hard work, they must obey their mother-in-law implicitly, and their husband provides scarcely any understanding and support. Although many women find themselves exposed to harsh conditions and puni-tive discipline in their new country, they rarely resort to divorce. Why not? The explanation put forward by the author of the study is that they stay put because they have to; they have no alternative (Shim 2008: 66).

Another sociological study examines the situation in the countries of origin of women who have emigrated to Korea in order to marry. This produces a very different picture. Following their emigration the women gain in power both in their family of origin and throughout the entire region.

> Narratives and survey results suggest that remittances significantly increase emigrant daughters' status and power in their native house-holds . . . In contrast, young men, particularly those deemed to have little value on the money market, such as the poorer and unemployed ones, find themselves disadvantaged and experience marriage migra-tion negatively. Overall, the 'gender balance sheet' suggests significant social transformation and a reconfiguration of gender power relations, attributable, in part, to international marriage migration. (Bélanger and Linh 2011: 60f.)

The mother of a marriage migrant tells how her daughter gained the right to a say in all decisions affecting the family:

> Before, when my daughter did not earn any money, I never asked her anything. I used to make every decision on my own. Now, since she is the one who supports the whole family, I have to discuss with her about family affairs, such as buying valuable furniture, building a house, organizing a wedding for my son or opening a shop . . . (Ibid.: 65)

Daughters who have been married off abroad not only take part in decisions affecting the economic well-being of the family (such as the purchase or sale of land, the purchase of expensive household goods, etc.); they also have an important say on matters concerning the future of other family members, their education, health or marriage. Because, with their move from a poverty-stricken region to a prosperous country, their marriage has given these immigrant women an improved transnational status, their status in their original family rises simultaneously. Their position in the hierarchy moves from powerless to powerful. Here are some typical statements from interviews: 'Everybody in the family has to obey her'; 'Having money means prestige and authority'; 'If the family wants to buy or do something, they have to phone her to ask for money' (Bélanger and Linh 2011: 67).

This in turn has implications for the lives of younger sisters. The fact that the elder sister has had such success and has reaped such recognition inspires the younger ones to want the same thing. They dream of finding their own foreigners and achieving the status of successful wife. Marrying abroad becomes the shining ideal to which the younger sisters also aspire.

The indigenous men are the losers here. They find they are devalued in the local marriage market. Since many Vietnamese women now seek foreign husbands, Vietnamese men are little in demand as marriage partners (Bélanger and Linh 2011: 71). In order to have any sort of a chance, they have to look to even poorer regions for a bride. Because the women weigh up their opportunities for improving their lot by considering whether to marry a local man or a foreigner, the men are left with far fewer options. A competitive process of repression sets in among men in their hunt for women. It might well end in toppling one of the characteristic features of traditional societies, namely the privileged position of the son. What is the point of the male line if the real contribution to a family's survival comes from the daughter's money? Does it mean the days are numbered of the practice, widespread in India and China, of aborting pregnancies if the embryo is of the wrong sex – i.e., it is a girl?

Thus we have two studies of Vietnamese marriage migrants which tell two different stories. The first is a story of unhappiness and suffering, the second is a success story. Which one is right?

It is impossible to answer this question without knowing the details of the study. Both could be right in their own way – i.e., for the sample that they are discussing. The two studies are concerned with the well-being of Vietnamese marriage migrants, but they have very different focal points. The first describes only the situation in the host country, in this instance Korea, while the second describes only how it is in the country of origin. It may very well be the case that both narratives are true – i.e., that the women experience humiliation in their new country and an increase in power and status at home.

At any rate, it is not disputed that an improved status in one's country of origin does not inevitably imply a similar improvement in the host country. On the contrary, we obtain a glimpse here of a discrepancy in transnational status between the social situations 'here' and 'there' – a highly typical consequence of migration, as the relevant studies have shown in the case of other groups (Goldring 1997).

4 Loss and Gain

Exploitation, misery, loneliness, these ingredients come up in studies on transnational motherhood and transnational families time and again. Yet, on closer inspection, a few studies also point out moments of a different shade. While by no means ignoring the loss and pain that comes with geographical separation, these studies question the 'dismal view of transnational households' (Parreñas 2005a: 30ff.) and caution against both the 'dramatizing features' (Rerrich 2012: 89) and the 'horror story genre' (Gamburd 2000: 209ff.) made of abused women, incapable fathers and neglected children. The stories they present speak of 'ambivalence' (Madianou 2012; Madianou and Miller 2011: 42ff.) – not total loss but, along with the loss, also some gains.

So what might these gains be? How do we explain that, as claimed by a Filipina migrant, having come to London was 'the greatest blessing' of her life (Madianou and Miller 2011: 34)? For a preliminary answer, in the material given in empirical studies we find two major groups of positive effects.

First, a way out from an unhappy relationship (Gamburd 2000: 144ff.; Hochschild 2003: 20f.; Madianou 2012; Madianou and Miller 2011: 40ff.). Quite often, women migrants, when describing their life back home, speak of relationships gone sour (a drunken husband, domestic violence, etc.). Yet in the Philippines, one of the major countries of female migration, there is no legal divorce. In other countries divorce, though legal, comes with a heavy social stigma for women, and having a child outside marriage brings a similar loss of reputation. So, in their native countries, these women have been trapped. In a context dominated by a traditional family model and a gender-based division of labour, their prospects of finding a husband, or finding a better husband, are severely reduced. At the same time, they are also deprived of the economic benefits that come with marriage and a male provider. For these women to start a new life, a new relationship, maybe even a new family, there is only one option: the way out. Looking for a better future means leaving behind their native country and trying their luck elsewhere.

Second, migrant women, whether running away from a dysfunctional relationship or not, may enjoy further benefits. Often for the first time, they gain some independence. In the new country they may have to follow the whims and wishes of their employers, yet they are no longer subject to the direct control of husband, father or wider kin. For some women at least, their identity begins to become transformed, in subtle yet deep ways (Madianou 2012; Madianou and Miller 2011: 69ff.).

They begin to enjoy their new independence and personal freedom (Sassen 2003: 259). Over the years, they find ways to adapt to their new surroundings, making new friends, learning to appreciate the geographical distance from everyday life in the close-knit family, sometimes maybe even appreciating the anonymity of urban life. For working long hours and working hard, the women migrants receive little money. Yet it is money nonetheless; what is more, it is their own money and, even better, money at their own disposal. They decide how much to send home and how much to keep, how much to spend now and how much to save for the future. In the new country, they are labelled 'illegal' and stuck at the low end of the social hierarchy. Yet, in their home country, migrant women gain social status and authority. Because most prove loyal to their families, sending money home regularly and often also sending generous gifts, the reputation of transnational migrants rises, changing from 'morally dubious' to 'successful and hardworking'. In their family, neighbourhood, native village, they are now met with respect (Madianou and Miller 2011: 34f.).

Two conclusions suggest themselves from what we have said. First of all, the initially simple question of the balance of power between the sexes soon turns out to have greater complexity. We need therefore to set out the different dimensions of the situation: the power relations in the country of origin and in the host country and the power relations between the couple, the family and society in general. A characteristic feature of the migrant experience is that these different contexts are anything but identical. The typical experience of migrants is that their social status in the host country is significantly inferior to the status they acquire in their home country – thanks to their emigration. For this reason, we cannot answer questions about the shifting balance of power if we look only at one or the other social hierarchy in isolation – the effective social hierarchy in the new country or the old. We have to look at them in context, and we must constantly examine the social situation in both societies.

That leads, second, to the problems of methodological nationalism. Anyone who looks at world families, whose lives are marked by border crossings and multiple citizenship, exclusively through the prism of the nation-state will fail to grasp the reality – i.e., the motives, values, constraints and opportunities of the men and women in those families.

In other words, in global families we cannot speak of 'the' social position of women or men. There is always a dual position in the social hierarchy, for women as for men, one in the host country and one in the country of origin. However, these two strands in the experience and actions of migrants are completely intermeshed, forming a third strand in its own right. It is this meshing together of the two strands – gain in social status in one country, loss of status in the other, with both processes taking place simultaneously – that creates the discrepancy. Migrants may encounter discrimination and even contempt in their new country, while gaining in respect and influence in their homeland. Only by bringing these mutually exclusive national contexts into focus will we be in a position to decode migrants' behaviour and, in particular, their behaviour in relations with the opposite sex.

8

Transnational Family Networks: Winners of Globalization?

In everyday life as in the social sciences and politics, two assumptions about couples and families predominate in the West. First, the family and globalization are mutually exclusive; second, networks of relations are anachronisms, too cumbersome and immobile in the face of a global capitalism that calls for the 'flexible human being' (Sennett 1998) – who, ultimately, is the human being who stands on his or her own two feet (see chapter 4).

What we see in reality is the exact opposite of this. The flexibility of family networks makes it possible for world families to take advantage of the opportunities provided by economic globalization in order to exploit the capital created by trust between family members to bridge national disagreements and thus to build up transnational enterprises on a greater or lesser scale. Refugees from poverty-stricken regions make use of the opportunity to create cross-border family networks so as to open up niches in the world market. The transnational nature of economic networks enables world families to evade or exploit state regulations by distributing their economic and cultural capital in different locations abroad for the benefit of family members.

1 Are Transnational Family Enterprises Anachronistic?

When we speak of world-family enterprises we are talking about the collaboration of different 'regimes' – families, nation-states and the global economy – that intersect, that mutually influence one another and that either restrict or enhance the flexibility of family networks.

It is widely believed that families in non-European regions of the world are no better than mute participants in the projects of the hegemonic West and should be regarded as the victims of globalization. It is our contention, however, that we should explore the extent to which family enterprises – whether in the shape of the new Chinese wealth or as a response to the growing impoverishment in large parts of Africa, Asia and Latin America – are playing an active role that runs counter to the global hierarchy. In their explorations of the cultural and political landscapes of the global economy, they have proved adept in turning the stereotypical images of them current in the West ('oriental man' as depicted by Edward Said) against Western hegemony and at the same time casting doubt on the validity of such images of their own nations and of the 'other'.

A preliminary conclusion is that the modernization path of the 'family' seen in the West – and more specifically in the European welfare states – and declared to be the functional family of modernity, is just one of several options. It is well known that 'modern families' have a variety of historical antecedents, and it is believed that these earlier forms can be found today in regions outside Europe. In consequence, they are all arranged in an evolutionary hierarchy and analysed on a scale leading from the 'traditional' to the 'modern', in which the traditional forms are regarded as less valuable and the modern forms as correspondingly more valuable. This leads to the forecast that the force exerted by family relations and the economy in the transnational space will ensure that, sooner or later, these families will approximate more closely to the ideal type of the normal family to be found at present in the West.

The facts, however, point to a very different conclusion. The so-called modern family of the West can make no exclusive claim to modernity. It is being undermined from within by a variety of trans-national effects (cross-cultural marriages, immigrant domestic labour, baby tourism, etc.). Even the contrast between national, territorially limited forms and mobile, transnational ones is becoming blurred.

The monocultural, one-nation family presupposes the uncoupling of the family household from the 'economic sphere' that Max Weber described as the key characteristic of the modern capitalist and industrial society. But Weber's assumption is becoming increasingly questionable today. In the age of globalization, the union of the family and the world economy, previously thought of as mutually exclusive, is gaining new significance.

World families and one-nation families are very different, indeed antithetical, as far as the role of family networks and their significance for the material circumstances, emotional ties and help in times of crisis are concerned. Nevertheless, the importance of these networks is waning in normal 'indigenous' families. Many observers think they are anachronisms. In contrast, such family networks are gaining significantly in importance in family enterprises in the global economy. They become the cultural adhesives that make it possible to expand and consolidate trust and solidarity beyond national frontiers.

2 The Relationship between the Individual, the Family and the State

Normal one-nation families are founded on what is felt to be a self-evident bond between the individual and the state. To exaggerate slightly, in mobile networking families the question of which nation-state one belongs to becomes almost arbitrary. Loyalty to the family dilutes the individual's loyalty to the state and to himself. These forms of the family set limits to individualization. Simultaneously, they develop strategies to exploit world markets for the purposes of the transnational family economy. Taking the impoverished and the excluded members of world society as examples, we can say that, having from birth been banished to regions of the world where there are no prospects, they construct 'transnational escalators' that increase their chances of eluding that fate.

In countries of the European centre the individualization of the family continues to make strides. We see this in the diversity of life patterns, the rise in the number of families not based on marriage, the growth in the divorce rate, the decrease in the number of children, the normalization of homosexual partnerships, the increase in one-person households, and so forth. It cannot have escaped the attention of the Western observer that in many ways the Western ideal of the family is better satisfied by the non-European families, with their involvement in the global economy, than by the European route of greater individualization. People in non-European regions marry one another, they divorce more rarely, produce more children and uphold family values.

As we have noted, loyalty to the family and loyalty to the state mainly go hand in hand in one-nation families – they are mediated by patriotism and national identity. The passport symbolizes this as much as the much cited readiness 'to die for one's country'. World families are formed when the connection between family solidarity and loyalty to the state becomes attenuated. The strategy of immigrants and managers on the move is aimed at evading the regulations imposed by nation-states. They achieve this by choosing different locations for their investments, their jobs and their families.

Such new positioning in transnational space must not lead us to conclude that world families are disloyal to their countries of origin or their host nations. Their primary loyalty undeniably goes to keeping the family together. When family loyalty comes into conflict with obligations to nation or state, it is the family (so we must assume) that provides the yardstick for what constitutes right and good actions or wrong and wicked ones. By analogy with nationalism, we can call this a kind of economistic 'family-ism', since the combination of family, globalization and economics gains the upper hand over all other individual, social, moral and political considerations. What we might call a sub-political orientation towards the family is based on the principle of 'keeping it all in the family' – a principle that brings together the energies of the immediate family and more distant relations in order to serve their common interests.

3   What Binds World Families Together?

The morality of world families finds its classical expression in staying power and hard work, obedience towards one's parents, and the subordination of women and children. Family discipline of this kind is what has made possible the phenomenal transformation of Hong Kong, for example, into a giant of production (Ong 2005). But it has also enabled many families in poor countries to overcome situations in which they were hopelessly underprivileged.

The ties binding individuals to the family business are informal, non-legal and mutual. In the formal labour market, the observance of contracts between employers and employees is regulated by law, which is why it is possible to take offenders to court for any breaches. For workers in the transnational family businesses, in contrast, there is no appropriate legal protection, and hence in the last resort there is no recourse to the law, because in transnational space there are neither laws nor courts that could exercise effective control over informal family arrangements. The consequence is that, as far as wages, working time, etc., are concerned, there is no institution to protect family workers from crass exploitation. In this sphere it is individuals, human beings – or, more precisely, fathers – who have the crucial say-so, not laws and justice. The father–son relationship is decisive, not just in the family but also in the world of work.

Bosses in such families are always bosses twice over: as bosses and fathers. This means that the sons cannot simply say, 'I don't agree with this, I'm leaving'. You cannot leave your father in the lurch. Nor can you switch to another firm or set up in business on your own. Since a man's status – his income, his position and his future – is determined by his place in the family hierarchy, anyone who attempts to cut himself off jeopardizes his overall status in both work and the family.

The combination of networks welding together the immediate family, more distant relations and the business calls for effective discipline within the family, on the one hand, and open-mindedness as regards business contacts and the acquisition of a different nationality, on the other. The aim is always to achieve access to finance or to exploit niches in the world markets. The chief priority, however, is to mobilize the resources of social, cultural and economic capital for the benefit of all members of the family collective in order to increase both collective and individual opportunities within the transnational space ('transnational escalators').

The creation and maintenance of discipline to promote the family has resulted in two successes. On the one hand, worldwide ethnic colonies and diasporic communities have come into being and enjoy increasing prosperity (even if they are still relatively poor when compared with the standard of living of the host countries). On the other hand, immigrants support their countries of origin with the remittances that they send back home via informal networks. We are looking at sums that reach around $250 billion annually – i.e., more than the total amount of money given in state aid to all underdeveloped countries. There can be no doubt that, globally, these remittances must make some contribution to reducing the gap between the rich and the poor.

4   Relation to Democracy

We may inquire in the case of both rich and poor world-family businesses how far this transnational, market-orientated family consciousness pursues its interests independently of the democratic nature of the state and the well-being of nation-based societies. Or how far world families' experience of the world brings about the emergence of a kind of cosmopolitan realism from below, with implications for their thinking, their moral consciousness and their political actions (see chapter 11).

According to Aihwa Ong, the growth of Chinese networks and Chinese wealth in Asia has given birth to

> a narrative of Chinese triumphalism that transports the myth of fraternal solidarity across the oceans. Yet the discourses about the neo-Confucian foundations of Asian capitalism have provoked the protests of Muslim politicians in South-East Asia who have launched a counter-discourse about a new Islam that is perfectly compatible with capitalism. On a wider regional plane, Asian countries share a common moral standpoint in opposition to neo-liberal orthodoxy's claims to an epistemic monopoly: say No to the West. At the same time, they cast a veil over the fact that they are themselves part of global capitalism. We must conclude that in Asia globalization has brought forth both national and transnational forms of nationalism that not only oppose the hegemony of the West but are also designed to promote the rise of the East in pan-religious, cultural discourses. (Ong 2005: 30f.)

The retreat to family-based economics, however, remains ambiguous. Even people who attempt to enclose themselves completely in ethnic relationship networks remain dependent for their success on transnational information and practices, and above all on the legal guarantees provided by the nation-state. Family members break with the state's monopoly on loyalty; however, they are able to do so only by switching between different countries – i.e., by taking advantage of citizenship rights in more than one country. In other words, multiple, flexible nationality is especially reliant on the fact that citizenship rights are anchored in the law. Wherever bureaucratic, authoritarian or xenophobic institutions attempt to stem the rising tide of transnational enterprises, these are predestined to fail. Strictly speaking, therefore, world-family businesses cannot isolate themselves in family-based economic units to the exclusion of wider considerations. It is in their own interest – i.e., the interest of globalized members of the family or of family investments – to support civil rights, open-mindedness and hence the division of powers and democracy.

9

My Mother Was a Spanish Ovum: Baby Tourism and Global Patchwork Families

1 Wanting a Child and Medical Technology

In 1978 Louise Brown, the world's first test-tube baby, was born. That was a historical turning point. For the first time in the history of mankind, a child was conceived outside its mother's womb. It was a sensation that unleashed a storm in politics and the media, the world of science and the public sphere. Passionate debates raged in many countries about whether this method of conception should be allowed or prohibited, whether it was progress or sacrilege.

Today, a few decades later, in vitro fertilization (IVF) has long since become everyday normality. We now have other developments and new techniques of reproductive medicine making the headlines: 'Seventy-year-old Indian woman gives birth to twins'; 'Embryo created with two mothers and a father'; 'Gay couple commissions child from Russian surrogate mother'.

Such announcements, arriving over our morning coffee, point to a profound change in the history of mankind. The combination of medicine, biology and genetics opens up vistas of utterly new interventions in human life, a transformation of human reproduction and parenthood that would have appeared inconceivable as recently as thirty years ago.

For thousands of years, birth and motherhood were regarded as anthropological givens, immune from human meddling. Yet these biological foundations have now gravitated into a zone where they are subject to the influence of technology, the world market, global inequality and the international division of labour. Suddenly the familiar coordinates of father–mother–child have started to crumble. All sorts of controversial issues have arisen. Is motherhood divisible? Can it be sold, bought, commodified? What about 'surrogate motherhood'? Can it be outsourced like jobs – i.e., to places where legal buffers and wages for 'rent-a-womb mothers' are kept as low as possible, while the profits for transnational 'birth companies' (clinics) are correspondingly high? Where does the private sphere of the family stop? Where are the boundaries drawn? Who forms part of the family, and who doesn't (the sperm donor, the egg donor, the surrogate mother)? Where do we draw the line and why? What feelings, what attachments are expected from whom? Which feelings are painfully missed by whom and which are repressed? Which feelings become risks because they do not comply with the world market – with birth as a commodity? In the light of the global market and the prevailing inequalities, what forms should love assume between multiple parents and children? When parenthood is split into separate parts and the basic pattern is designed by economic rules and global inequality, how will this affect the relationship between parents and children, how will it affect their ways of love and bonding?

To be sure, these medical options have hitherto been used only to a limited extent, since the legal and financial framework varies from country to country. While some countries permit almost everything that is technically possible, others – like Germany, for example – have established clear legal limits. Medical treatments are expensive – the costs vary likewise from country to country – and state institutions are seldom willing to shoulder them.

It is precisely from such differences in national contexts that baby tourism has sprung up. Anyone who encounters difficulties in his or her own country may find more favourable conditions elsewhere. Globalization presents opportunities for people unwilling to abandon their longing for children. National frontiers and laws can no longer stop them.They are undeterred by national frontiers and laws; they simply travel to wherever their dreams can come true.

Thus far, the consequences of all this can only be guessed at. But we may at least say this: baby tourism leads to new kinds of family bonds that literally 'embody' transnational relationships, not on the macro-level of politics and the economy, not at the level of our private space, but in us, in the innermost core of the family. The statement 'the global other is to be found in our midst' gains existential, genetic significance here (see chapter 3).

Medical Tourism and Baby Tourism

Medical tourism is flourishing. In this age of globalization, people from wealthy countries travel to the poorer regions of the world to get their hips, teeth and eyes fixed. At the same time, the (few) rich people from poor countries travel to the medical centres of the Western metropolises to have their ailments attended to.

In recent years baby tourism has become established as a special branch of medical tourism, a branch with high growth rates. Having children, so people said, is the most natural thing in the world. In pursuit of this natural desire, people set out for foreign parts, and even foreign continents, so as to produce 'a child of their own' with the aid of medical interventions and a new version of the international division of labour (egg donor, surrogate mother, or carer). This special breed of tourist includes women and men, couples and single persons, the young and the old, heterosexuals and gays and lesbians, practising Muslims and atheist Protestants, the Egyptians and the French, the Americans and the Dutch. Their destinations are to be found in South America and India, in Ukraine and the Czech Republic.

Superficially these people may seem to resemble one another – they are all travelling abroad in search of a child – but the motives driving them may be very different. Some want to perpetuate the traditional model of the family, with father, mother and child, and vehemently reject any alternatives. Others have abandoned the traditional model; they live together without getting married or else as a homosexual couple or alone, but none of them is willing to renounce having children. Some women are desperate to have a child because in their society they are thought inferior and are discriminated against if they do not experience motherhood. Other women have spent years concentrating on their careers and now want personal ties and a family of their own, complete with children.

In short, baby tourism is the product of many motives and assumes very different forms; it leads from the most varied starting points to a plurality of goals. Sometimes the aim is to overcome physical defects and health problems; sometimes the quest for medically assisted reproduction is related not to physical problems but rather to the social situation of the client; and in some cases the clients' wishes collide with the professional ethics of medicine. Furthermore, when reproductive technology leaves the realm of scientific research and academic competition and becomes applied science and a treatment offered by doctors, it undergoes a fundamental change. Social circumstances combine in ways that are liable to enter into conflict with the professional ethics of medical science – and not just in the laboratory. In their practical application, too, the services provided by medical technology collide with pre-existing social and cultural guidelines, commandments and prohibitions, hopes and fears, that are coloured by nationality, religion, class and sexual preference. In her study *Local Babies, Global Science* (2003), the anthropologist Marcia C. Inhorn has provided a detailed analysis of this entire complex. She examines the use of in vitro fertilization in Egypt and provides a detailed analysis of the interweaving of medical technology and social context.

In Egypt the services provided by advanced medical technology are far too costly for most people. Poorer people, often barely able to survive, with no money to spare, have no access to them. Even middle-income groups often find them too expensive and would like to increase their earnings so as to avail themselves of them. This leads them to seek work in one of the countries of the Arabian peninsula, where wages are significantly higher. As soon as they have saved up enough they return to Egypt – because treatment costs there are lower, because they have greater faith in Egyptian doctors, and because they are at home and feel safer there. The situation is very different for couples in the Egyptian upper class, who have far greater wealth. Whenever they have need of medical assistance to make their dream of having a child come true, they travel to Europe or the United States – because they have greater trust in the competence of Western doctors, because they believe this will give them greater chances of success, and because they are undeterred by the high prices obtaining in the West.

This example highlights the fact that it is not only the inhabitants of the Western world who avail themselves of the products of reproductive medicine. On the contrary, IVF centres are particularly numerous in the Middle East. Large numbers of clinics have sprung up not just in Egypt, but also in Lebanon, while, in proportion to its population size, neighbouring Israel is one of the world's leaders in IVF centres and IVF treatments (Inhorn 2003; Waldman 2006). Nevertheless, we shall focus predominantly on the situation in Europe and North America, where far more material is available. We shall proceed in five steps.

We shall start with the question: How was such a development possible in so short a time? What were the social and cultural preconditions that made in vitro fertilization and similar advances in reproductive medicine acceptable? We must look first of all at the public controversies surrounding modern reproductive medicine and then at the crumbling of the traditional model of the family and the emergence of new patterns. The next step is to take a closer look at the state of baby tourism and, especially, the trade in transnational reproductive medicine. Third, we shall also examine the participants in that trade and their motives, including the financial costs involved and the legal restrictions imposed. Fourth, we shall scrutinize the rhetoric employed by the relevant medical centres abroad to attract a global clientele and build a global reputation. Fifth and last, we shall focus on some of the consequences. We shall ask how the new options offered by reproductive medicine have started to influence, indeed to change, our basic concepts of family and mankind.

2   Moral Issues: Contested Territory

If the biological foundations of mankind are increasingly subject to change, a new world of possibility will open up. Where previously there was destiny, the iron cage of biological necessity, we are now able to a greater extent to shape, select and decide on the features we want for our descendants and for ourselves.

The existence of such options quickly became controversial territory, prompting widely differing factions to assert their interests, worldviews and values. For that reason many states passed laws so as to retain some control over developments arising from reproductive medicine, prenatal diagnosis and gene technology. In a similar vein, the representatives of the great religious faiths have responded with policy statements on reproductive technology, issuing instructions about how to use or not use its applications. Last but not least, representatives of science, interested parties and health organizations have all given expression to their wishes and misgivings.

One basic problem of such discourses was quickly brought to light. Since medical technology has opened up hitherto inconceivable possibilities, the time-honoured values and norms which various groups of people invoke now are worlds apart from the issues and dilemmas inherent in the rapid advances of that technology. A gulf always remains, one that can be bridged only by more or less convincing, more or less fanciful interpretations. The consequence is that most of the debates in this field follow similar lines. Time and again, they are based on a rhetoric of highly sophisticated twists and turns, definitions and suppositions. For the pressing questions at hand, their answers are built on shaky ground: the questions that are raised are of the following kind.

Is in vitro fertilization a procedure for creating life, a way to counter the suffering of childless couples who have remained childless through no fault of their own, and therefore worthy of social support and active promotion? Or is it a procedure that offends against our notions of human dignity, sanctions risky manipulations and has far-reaching, unpredictable consequences? Is embryo screening a form of eugenics or is it a legitimate and efficacious way of preventing serious hereditary disease? Or is it permissible in certain circumstances but not in others – and who defines those circumstances?

Unambiguous answers to such questions are not to be found among the established authorities – regardless of whether we look at the Koran, the Ten Commandments or the Constitution of the Federal Republic of Germany. Their precepts are always formulated in highly general terms that allow for divergent interpretations and conclusions. All commandments and prohibitions find themselves labouring under the burden of such principled controversies, which, mutually exclusive in part and laying claim, therefore, to universal validity, impinge on the foundations of any ethics of what it is to be human. Looking at the public statements of various authorities, we find a rivalry between conflicting universalisms and controversial interpretations to the point where it seems absurd to insist on taboos. On the one hand the (former) German Federal Chancellor Gerhard Schröder came out publicly in defence of embryo research, stressing its potential for innovation (Schröder 2001). On the other hand Jürgen Habermas, the most famous philosopher in the country, with a worldwide reputation, issued warnings about an instrumental view of the embryo and any kind of research not recognizing the dignity of human life (Habermas 2001). When German specialists in reproductive medicine called for the relaxation of current legislation, the president of the German Medical Council instantly criticized such demands (Bethge 2001). Whereas Gordon Brown, while he was still British prime minister, stated that certain aspects of stem-cell research and practice were beneficial and indispensable, in Germany these very lines of research were taboo, forbidden by the Embryo Protection Act (Brown 2008). Leading representatives of Islamic Shiites have declared that egg donation is permissible, while leaders of Islamic Sunni have ruled that it is not permissible (Inhorn 2006). Given all these conflicting views, it is not surprising that the public should be perplexed. The to and fro of argument and counter-argument renders all points of view suspect; each helps to undermine the other. Many people gain the impression that the subject matter is confusing and that no one has a monopoly of the truth. That raises the question: If all the opposing views seem to be well founded, how can we formulate generally acceptable policies? The effect of these disagreements is to undermine the law's effective claim to legitimacy, so that people feel they have little incentive to identify with it. Prohibitions and decrees are increasingly drained of their authority.

This process of destabilization has been intensified by the enormous rapidity of the advances made in medical technology. Even specialists are frequently unable to keep up with events and feel they are being left behind. The perplexity among those without medical qualifications must be correspondingly greater. How are ordinary people supposed to appreciate the various developments in medical technology, such as IVF and ICSI, egg donation and surrogate motherhood, prenatal screening and pre-implantation genetic testing? On the one hand, individuals are supposed to be regarded as adult citizens able to make their own decisions; on the other hand, they feel caught up in a jungle of concepts and options that turn even experts into laymen.

A further factor is the rapid expansion of the range of medical treatments. The basic pattern is familiar from many branches of medicine. It has turned out that certain procedures, developed initially for narrowly defined purposes, may be effective in other, often very different situations. Normally, such changes occur step by step, but, in reproductive medicine, prenatal screening and genetic testing have been compressed into a few years. A striking example is that of in vitro fertilization. This began as a procedure for women who were unable to conceive because of a blockage in their Fallopian tubes. It was rapidly extended to embrace a broad spectrum of medical indications – for example, where the man is the cause of infertility (i.e., where the quantity or quality of sperm is insufficient); in the case of couples where the causes of infertility are unknown; in conjunction with embryo screening, in couples who are at increased genetic risk, so as to select embryos which do not possess the relevant genetic predisposition; again in conjunction with embryo screening, in couples with a sick child, in order to produce a genetically suitable sibling and also to harvest the necessary cell material required for therapy.

The faster the pace of expansion, the less time remains to investigate where limits should be set. Should in vitro fertilization be permitted at all? Is it reconcilable with our ideas of human dignity? Is its application justifiable in the case of couples who have remained childless, but an intervention to be condemned in the case of those who wish to avert a genetic risk? Which form of application is allowed and which prohibited? If one type of application is very close to another, how can we distinguish between them? And how can such distinctions be upheld when each advance follows hot on the heels of the previous one? We are tempted to conclude that medical progress itself is responsible for undermining its own ethical foundations (Beck, Bonß and Lau 2005).

3 A New Diversity of Life Patterns

'Love, marriage, baby carriage' – in the 1950s and 1960s that was the classic formula involved in establishing a family (see chapter 4). At that time, in the so-called Golden Age of marriage and the family, there was a generally recognized life pattern, practised by the majority of people. It was that of the 'normal family', consisting of an adult couple with their children. It went without saying that the adults would be of different sexes – i.e., man and woman – that they were married and that they would remain married until death did them part. The wife was responsible for looking after the household and for bringing up the children, the man for dealing with the outside world, his profession and public life.

Tempi passati, as far as partnership is concerned. A few decades ago, gay and lesbian couples were still criminalized and pursued by the law. Today they can have their partnerships officially registered in many countries, and can even marry in some. For heterosexual couples the trend goes in the opposite direction. Many of them do not see why their relationship should require the blessing of the state and will have no truck with the register office. Even if they do marry, their lifelong union is often ended prematurely. Or consider divorce: this used to attract a stigma and exclusion from respectable society, whereas now it has become socially accepted. A child born outside marriage was formerly a 'bastard', and this was a catastrophe, especially in the life of a woman. Today the children of unmarried parents are not only accepted as a matter of course in the majority of countries in the West but are also increasingly treated as equals before the law. In short, within a few years a pluralization of lifestyles has taken place. Types of unions and relationships that were regarded as deviant or defective only a few decades ago are practised nowadays by more and more people. Most importantly of all, they have found acceptance. Much of what used to be morally condemned now passes unremarked, as just one behaviour pattern among others.

But if more and more ways of life become socially accepted, why should people who live beyond the bounds of the traditional family renounce the right to have children? If others have the right to parenthood, why should not they as well? Singles, gay and lesbian couples; women who have never had sexual intercourse; women over sixty who discover on reaching pensionable age that they would like a child; women whose partner is dying or already dead and who want his child; women who have been sterilized after they had had children and had thought their family was complete but now, after divorce and a new beginning, would like a child from their new partner; couples who want to determine the sex of their offspring – all of these people can now have the children they yearn for with the assistance of reproductive medicine.

'Appetite is aroused by possibility' – this was the view expressed decades ago by Hans Jonas, the philosopher of technology (Jonas 1985). This is confirmed by the current growth in the wish for children. The greater diversity of life patterns is expanding the clientele of reproductive medicine.

The greater the demand, the more products become available. Clinics now offer all kinds of services, from IVF as a standard product right down to the choice of the baby's sex, from catalogues with pictures of sperm donors and egg donors, right down to the procuring of surrogate mothers, complete with snapshots and biographical profile.

4   Children as 'Commodities'

As we have noted, taking up such offers often comes up against legal and financial barriers. But things that are obstacles to some people are opportunities for others. Many of the clinics set up in order to help would-be parents acquire children consciously aim their marketing at foreign customers. Communication via the internet is swift and unproblematic; a few mouse-clicks and you are in touch with fertility clinics in Russia or Turkey, India or Denmark. The services on offer are typical of those available in outsourcing capitalism generally. They can be tabulated as follows:[6]

---

[6] In 2008 we searched the internet for the websites of typical international clinics and took a closer look at around sixty such websites. To avoid bias we consciously sought out clinics in a wide variety of locations – from India to Russia, from Israel to South Africa and the United States. We then looked for claims commonly encountered in the promotional material put out by these clinics. We were concerned in particular with such matters as the medical treatments on offer, the nature of additional services, the particular features or benefits claimed for each clinic, and the extent to which an international clientele was addressed, as well as the pricing structure and the legal framework. This enabled us to form a picture of the typical services and promises on offer. The material underpinning the following account is derived from our scrutiny of the information provided by the clinics that advertise on internet websites, as well as Pande (2010) and the documentary film *Google Baby* (2009).

- The ideal locations are those where staff costs are low and restrictions minimal.
- Legal requirements in the country where the clinics are based are referred to by such positive epithets as 'modern', 'enlightened' and 'liberal'. A Greek clinic, for example, is described in this way: 'the legal framework in Greece is among the most progressive in the world and makes Greece the ideal destination for foreign couples seeking treatment not available in their own countries.' Freely translated this means: You will have no inconvenient problems with regulations and our services will answer all your needs.
- Where necessary, it is often stated that, if services are required that are not permitted in the client's own country, it may be possible to cooperate with another clinic abroad.
- Many clinics provide the option of communicating with them in as many as six different languages. Emphasis is placed on the international composition of the team, consisting as it does of multilingual doctors and support staff. In other words, clients need have no fear of language barriers; communication in their native tongue will be available.

The services provided extend beyond medical facilities proper; clinics frequently offer a variety of additional benefits:

- Putting clients at their ease: 'individual treatment and personal attention', discretion and understanding.
- The tourist attractions of the region: 'abundant sunshine, wonderful surroundings and extensive beaches'. In some instances, much is made of 'shopping and culinary opportunities' as well as excursions and sightseeing.
- Many clinics have a psychologist on the team or even an entire psychological department to provide support and relaxation and help to reduce stress.
- Many clinics offer legal assistance to ensure that their clients are spared the vexations of legal complications.
- Many clinics have different versions of their services, depending on the financial situation of their clientele. These range from the luxury service (chauffeur-driven car from the airport), through the standard version, right down to the pared-down basic provision for those of lesser means.

Not least among the repertoire of services on offer are those designed to guarantee the health and optimal well-being of the hoped-for child. To put it bluntly, the child people long for has to be a quality child.

- Strict standards are maintained in the selection of egg donors, surrogate mothers and sperm donors. The criteria include the donors' health, medical history, family status, and, depending on the procedure envisaged, psychological stability, intelligence and education, appearance and ethnic origins.
- During pregnancy the surrogate mother's health, eating habits and lifestyle are regularly monitored (several times a day or round the clock, depending on the client's financial resources) to ensure that she will provide the best possible environment for the prenatal development of the child.

With the aid of such services, infertility treatment has ballooned into an international business with high growth rates. It has become a market with a global future or, as one clinic has formulated it, rising demand from abroad has 'simply forced us to expand internationally'. Depending on the treatments and financial resources available, Germans travel to Turkey, Egyptians to Lebanon, the Dutch to Belgium, and Americans to Romania. German women have the ova of Spanish women implanted in them (Truscheit 2007); American women have ova sent from Italy or Greece (Withrow 2007); Lebanese women make use of eggs donated by American women (Inhorn 2006).

More and more people desperate for children – men as well as women, single people and couples – travel to India in the hope of making their dream of a child of their own come true.

India – World Capital of Outsourced Pregnancies

India is a deeply divided nation. At its apex there is a tiny group of rich and powerful people. Below them is a still small but gradually expanding middle stratum. Below this is the mass of the poor, with no access to education, secure work or adequate healthcare – many, many millions with no prospects of ever escaping destitution.

In consequence, ever increasing numbers of women, above all, the uneducated and women from the countryside – in other words, those who are most disadvantaged – are willing to place their bodies at the service of the fertility clinics (Hierländer 2008; Hochschild 2009; Zakaria 2010). According to specialist studies, there are at least 350 clinics in India that provide surrogate motherhood. Surrogacy, it is said, has become a significant growth industry; India has become a 'womb at the most affordable prices', the 'world capital of pregnancy delegation'. Whereas surrogacy is prohibited in many countries, in India it is officially authorized and even viewed positively as a contributor to the economy (medical tourism is actively promoted by government media campaigns). Whereas in the United States the total cost of surrogacy is $70,000 to $100,000, a child can be obtained by the same service in India for $12,000 to $20,000.

Of that sum the surrogate mother herself receives between $5,000 and $7,000 – more than many women earn in years. In exchange, they are forced to submit to a strict regimen. The contracts frequently stipulate that they should cease living at home during the pregnancy, follow a strict diet, abstain from sexual contact with their husband, and leave their own children in the care of others. In order to monitor their progress, the clinics often provide their own communal quarters or dormitories to house the women during pregnancy. Rules to protect the rights of surrogate mothers scarcely exist.

For some women, then, the paying customers, comfortable surroundings are the norm. For others, the women who make their own bodies available for pregnancy services, there are regulations, surveillance and control.

Legal, Illegal, Translegal

Are the practices of the fertility industry legal or illegal? Our answer is that what is going on here cannot be captured by traditional concepts. We need a new conceptual framework to grasp the novel aspects of such activities. Such practices are essentially 'translegal'; they are neither allowed nor prohibited (Beck 2006: 103–5). They exploit the gaps in the law arising from differences in national legislation. They spread as national frontiers decline in importance and distances are reduced in significance by modern methods of transport and rapid forms of communication. Those who have learned to play on the keyboard of legal distinctions will soon discover how to seize the opportunities provided by globalization. Such people belong among the new 'frontier acrobats'. Or, as an Austrian fertility clinic elegantly expresses it: 'we overcome . . . restrictions through our transnational activities'.

This is the essence of outsourcing capitalism, which replaces what was previously thought of as the harmless extension of trade and distributes its activities across the world in accordance with the rules of the international division of labour and global inequality, organizing them so as to subvert existing legal obstacles, minimize costs and maximize profits (see also chapter 4).

It is likely that many of those who escape abroad in this way do not have any sense that they are doing anything wrong, but feel rather that their actions are legitimated by the constraints of the situation. If even experts disagree about what is permitted and what is forbidden, why should they allow dubious prohibitions to deprive them of their life's happiness? If countries such as Germany refuse them their basic rights, they are surely entitled to seek them abroad. If they are treated unfairly in Germany, it must be morally permissible to seek justice elsewhere.

5   Designing Confidence

As described above, many fertility clinics in India and Eastern Europe make a living from baby tourism and foreign clients. They thrive on their ability to provide what is forbidden elsewhere. This means, of course, that in order to lure customers from abroad they have to face up to a climate of scepticism and disapproval. They need to win over men and women who have been told by doctors in their own country that this or that procedure represents an abuse of medical progress and serves only to gratify the parents' selfish wishes.

Fertility clinics based in Ukraine or India have to dissipate such doubts and misgivings in their clients' minds. As long as they succeed, the number of clients will doubtless continue to grow; if they fail, demand will soon dry up. In other words, they have a job of persuasion to do.

The web pages of the relevant clinics read like a response to this situation; they are exercises in confidence-building. They take issue with the criticisms levelled at them in order to present a counter-narrative: a positive rhetoric.

Who Owns Morality?

The fertility clinics rebut the common criticism about the moral ambiguity of their treatments by countering with an accusation of their own. Its basic thrust is the assertion that the laws in other countries are far too narrow; they are an anachronism with no appreciation of the suffering of people who are childless through no fault of their own. In contrast, we are progressive and liberal. We take up the cudgels against false and arbitrary rules. We fight to defend the most natural of all rights. We commit ourselves to helping our clients realize their dreams of children's laughter and parental happiness.

The founder and proprietor of a surrogacy agency in Russia has formulated this in exemplary fashion. The business is called 'Right to Life' (see Jeska 2008), and its name is also its programme. The clinic's owner has provided a simple, clear answer to the question of the moral principles governing his clinic. He believes that whatever helps to gratify his clients' desire for a child is moral; everything that attempts to prevent it is immoral. It follows that there is a higher morality than the restrictive laws that hold sway in other countries. The services provided by his agency are not simply permissible, they have moral force.

We Want to Help

The criticism that the services provided in these clinics are in conflict with basic principles of morality and human dignity is sometimes met by an appeal to the Most High. The relevant texts seek the aura of sacral authority in the Bible. The story of Sarah and Hagar in the Book of Genesis is turned into an early form of surrogate mother-hood, and the corresponding services of reproductive medicine are interpreted as modern versions of ancient practices. This implies, it is suggested, that surrogacy is morally unexceptionable and even that it has divine approval.

Far commoner is a different, secularized form of the claim to the moral high ground. This is an appeal to altruism, charity and human-ity. All those involved may be said to be altruistic. 'We want to help you'; we are 'doing good to others'; we want 'to make people happy' – this is the promise made by clinic proprietors, surrogate mothers, egg donors and sperm donors alike. They all belong to a club of self-less helpers, ceaselessly active in the service of charity and aiding their fellow human beings.

A Win–Win Situation

Social inequality is an essential foundation of baby tourism. Anyone who travels to a poor country to obtain a child on the cheap is clearly profiting from the global disparities between rich and poor. Is it rep-rehensible to take advantage of such opportunities? Does it make you an accomplice in exploitation and oppression? The owners of baby tourism centres offer an alternative interpretation to counter poten-tial criticisms of this sort. They speak of a win–win situation – i.e., one from which both sides profit.

The customers of infertility centres tend to find similarly optimistic interpretations convenient. They too emphasize the positive aspect, the mutual benefits. For example, a homosexual man from Israel who, together with his partner, has arranged for an Indian woman to act as surrogate mother for his child insists that the money the woman has earned in this way will ensure a better future for her and her own children. He regards the arrangement as fair because he 'feels it is two people who are helping each other out'. They intentionally chose India because it was 'an opportunity to help someone in India' (Gentleman 2008). Here the potential criticism of taking part in global exploitation is transformed into its opposite. Baby tourism – like the situation with regard to marriage migrants (see chapter 6) – becomes aid to the Third World.

6   The Global Patchwork Family

In the 1980s, when commercial surrogacy was still in its infancy, there were complications that made international headline news. Some surrogate mothers wished to keep the babies to whom they had given birth and refused to hand them over in accordance with their contractual obligations. An especially well-known case was that of 'Baby M'. The dispute about ownership caught the attention of the public worldwide. It was a case that aroused extreme feelings and provoked bitter disagreements, culminating in kidnapping. A judgement was finally passed following protracted legal proceedings, involving expert opinions and counter-opinions and consideration of the material and emotional circumstances of both parties, as well as their health, to say nothing of the myriad documents and files that accumulated. Finally, the child was awarded to the clients, while the surrogate mother was granted the right to visit the child once a week (e.g., Lacayo 1987).

This case shows that advances in medical technology create both new conditions with manifold cosmopolitan origins and implications that provide scope for the most varied interpretations (see chapters 4 and 11). What is the meaning of terms such as 'father', 'mother' and 'family' in the case of a child who is conceived to order in the lab, using 'biomaterial' derived from alien people who live 'somewhere else', in a distant land? Who has what rights and obligations here? To whom does the child belong? Which mother is supposed to produce motherly love? Where does love become its opposite, turning into a conflict of interests? In what follows we wish to show by a series of examples how a free space opens up in the global patchwork family in which incompatible expectations, fantasies and claims can lodge.

Maternal Feelings as a Risk Factor

Negative headlines, such as those about Baby M, are off-putting, and a disaster for those eager to make a business out of surrogate motherhood. Such headlines obviously represent a threat to a market keen to expand. They revive misgivings that the positive rhetoric was just labouring to overcome. It is for this reason that the representatives of the various clinics and agencies have attempted to alter the course of the procedure and build in security thresholds in order to be able to calculate the economic risks that the surrogate mother might form an emotional tie to the child. The measures widely adopted to prevent this include the following:

– Division of labour: the breaking down of surrogate motherhood into different tasks that are assigned to different women – in other words, multiple motherhood. This means that one woman provides the ovum (egg mother) and another goes through the pregnancy and birth (surrogate mother). Experience teaches that maternal feelings risk running out of control if the egg mother and surrogate mother are one and the same. In such cases the preventive measure is to make sure that the pregnant woman does not give birth to her own biological child but always to someone else's.
– Family status as a criterion for selection: only women who are already married and have a child of their own should be accepted as potential surrogate mothers. This reduces the likelihood – so it is supposed – that the birth mother will develop maternal feelings – in other words, an inner bond with the foreign child of the foreign parents.
– Partitions: many clinics have built-in partitions – i.e., a curtain is hung over the body of the women in labour, concealing the lower part of her body and preventing her from seeing the child to whom she is giving birth. The parents who have commissioned 'their' child take possession of it on the other side of the curtain.

But even such precautionary measures cannot entirely eliminate the risk that maternal feelings and ties might develop. Reports and interviews make it clear that some women find it hard to suppress every internal feeling and to regard the pregnancy as no more than a business transaction (Hochschild 2009; *Google Baby* 2009).

Of course, it is questionable whether disciplining one's feelings in this way is truly desirable. Suppose we think of the pregnant surrogate mother as an employee like any other, more or less conscientious, more or less concerned with her own interests. If surrogate motherhood were to be reduced in this way to a purely commercial transaction, this might eliminate an internal motivation that is really indispensable for the well-being of the child. External controls alone, we may suppose, are scarcely enough to guarantee that the pregnant woman will do nothing that has the potential to harm her child. And if certain patterns are established prenatally and the child already senses feelings in the womb – as indeed recent research believes – it may well prove detrimental if the surrogate mother has nothing in her mind but the agreed cash payment.

This invites us to ask with some urgency how 'maternal love', 'child love' and also 'paternal love' will fare in the age of proliferating technical development.

Children's Fantasies Against Parents' Fantasies

Egg-donating began only in the 1990s, while artificially inseminating a woman with the sperm of a stranger had been possible long before that, although it was socially taboo for a long time and became widely accepted only with the development of IVF treatment. In the United States up to now, around a million children have been conceived anonymously with the aid of sperm banks. In Germany the number is estimated at around 100,000. Thus the number of children conceived in this way is considerable. However, since most of them are still fairly young, there have been scarcely any authoritative studies on their development and their lives as adults.

International adoptions began significantly earlier, and this explains why there have been more studies and field reports. But because both adoption tourism and organized pregnancy tourism have their roots in the desire for children, and because donor children are frequently compared with adopted children, we have decided to begin by referring to the research on international adoption.

We know that many cross-border adopted children develop fantasies to fill in the gaps in their origins. These fantasies regularly revolve around a similar core, whose basic motif is: 'What if I had not been adopted, if I still lived with my physical parents?' (Honig 2005). Here, for example, is a young Vietnamese woman who has been adopted by a Swedish couple:

> What if my birth mother had been able to keep me? What if I had stayed in Vietnam and had not been brought to this place where I am

so different? What if I were growing up in China right now? What if
a family in India had been able to adopt me? (Ibid.: 215)

These are stories that revolve around the possibility of a life not lived
– dreams of a life with one's biological parents, in a family of one's
own, which the subjects think of as poor but loving. Above all, and
this is crucial, such a family is thought to provide an unshakable
support; it is an unquestioned given, a biological fact and not the
product of selection and decision.

The adoptive parents likewise may also develop fantasies of the
same sort: 'What if . . .?' But they have quite different images in mind.
Their fantasies generally take the line: 'What if we hadn't come
along? Your life would have been terrible; you would be living a life
of poverty, would go hungry and would have received no education.
But for us you would probably have come to a sticky end.' These are
all fantasies of rescue, with the parents taking the role of the saviours
of children in need.

Parents' Wishes Versus Children's Rights

Similar contradictions, though in a more acute form, can be found
in families that have come into being with the aid of sperm donations.
One theme above all runs through the reports put out on the internet:
Who is the unknown man who happens to be my biological father?
If, as is frequently the case, the father has remained anonymous, the
children have hardly any information on which to build – no more
than is contained in the questionnaire filled in at the request of the
agency, e.g., by Sperm Donor No. 1772/09, with standardized boxes
and data on health, education, hobbies, height, colour of eyes, etc. If
no further information is forthcoming, the young man or woman
concerned has no choice but to speculate. Do I have the same strik-
ingly blue eyes as my aunt? Did I inherit my big feet from my grand-
father? Did my grandmother also have freckles? Am I so unmusical
because that's what my Dad was like?

These questions are tied up with feelings of loss, sadness and
pain. Again and again we hear wistful talk of longing to know about
the other half of one's origins of which one had been robbed when the
biological father vanished into the obscurity of anonymity and the
files, thus rendering the entire paternal line invisible – grandparents,
uncles, siblings, cousins. To appreciate the savage rage such people
feel, you have to hear the original voices. Here are three examples.

I was angry at the idea that where donor conception is concerned,
everyone focuses on the 'parents' – the adults who can make choices

about their own lives. The recipient gets sympathy for wanting to have a child. The donor gets a guarantee of anonymity and absolution from any responsibility for the offspring of his 'donation'. As long as these adults are happy, then donor conception is a success, right? Not so. The children born of these transactions are people, too. Those of us in the first documented generation of donor babies – conceived in the late 1980s and early '90s, when sperm banks became more common and donor insemination began to flourish – are coming of age, and we have something to say. I'm here to tell you that emotionally, many of us are not keeping up. We didn't ask to be born into this situation, with its limitations and confusion. It's hypocritical of parents and medical professionals to assume that biological roots won't matter . . . We offspring are recognizing the right that was stripped from us at birth – the right to know who both our parents are. (Clark 2006)

I am very sad today, with a grief that is not talked about. It is not allowed. Because I had two loving parents. . . . Well . . . what . . . are you complainin' about?? You got everything you wanted. You had so many presents at Christmas and your birthday that it was supposed to buy your happiness. You were supposed to forget about your mother. You had everything. Why would you want more? WE GAVE YOU EVERYTHING. I had everything . . . everything but my mother. (Internet blog, quoted by Singh 2009)

Paul McCartney once said, 'all you need is love', however despite what many in the donor conception community wish to believe, it's not true. There seems to be an overwhelming majority of recipient mothers that truly believe that just so long as they love their child, that he or she won't feel any loss of their biological father. I would like to stand up and say that this is nonsense. (Greenawalt 2008)

Again and again outbursts of rage and despair; the tone is sometimes soft, sometimes loud and shrill, but the message is the same. It is full of accusations, vehemently expressed, against the adoptive parents. Their constant theme is: you have acted only to satisfy your own desire for children, without regard for our interests. You speak constantly of your love for us, but what we want is our basic existential rights; we want to know about our origins and our inheritance. Love is the myth by which you justify yourself, by means of which you have set yourselves up as the creators of new life and by means of which you have made us. However, we say to you: love is not enough.

The internet now contains a growing number of websites with such names as 'Donor Conception Network' or 'International Donor Offspring Alliance', in which donor children exchange experiences and make efforts to track down their own biological fathers. A 'Donor Sibling Registry' has been established in the United States, a website where the children of sperm donors can register in order to find other children by the same donor. This website has attracted many visitors. Even if the identity of their biological father remains a mystery, they can often discover at least a (half-)brother or (half-)sister, who is at any rate a connection of some sort to a physical family and a biological origin.

It may be objected that such internet forums do not provide a representative selection of voices. No doubt, the young men and women who speak up about their situation are not the ones who are contented with their lot, but the others, the ones who are furious, unhappy, emotionally insecure and perhaps also unstable. That is bound to be true. But is it a sufficient reason simply to ignore such voices and to see no significance in their complaints and accusations? Is it not rather a good reason to look more closely at the underlying reasons for their despair?

International Pregnancy Industry: Where Do I Come From?

'Sperm father', 'egg mother', 'surrogate mother' – these are verbal constructs that fail to yield up their secrets. Instead, they help to normalize the process. Let us take 'sperm father' as an example. Is 'father' simply a meaningless appendage to 'sperm'? Can 'paternity' be reduced to the sperm, its biological substrate? And, if so, to whom does that apply or not apply? To the (non-)father anonymously present in the 'sperm child'? To the fatherless 'sperm child'? To the 'sperm-impregnated mother'? These verbal façades surely conceal questions of identity, dilemmas of identity that have failed to burst to the surface only because the necessary concepts were missing. Or perhaps there will be a cold intimacy, lacking in identity, that speaks of 'sperm fathers' when it means 'fatherless sperm'?

Must we conclude that the international pregnancy industry produces nothing but medical, economic and legal questions and dilemmas? Or are we witnessing the emergence of an unintended consequence, namely a volcano that one day will erupt in the midst of our civilization, spewing out moral conundrums and questions of identity? In either case, we would be well advised to remind ourselves that words that come all too easily to our lips remain silent about the realities, the questions of meaning that they contain and conceal within themselves. Perhaps what we are seeing is the birth of a Brave New World, and no one can say today whether in hindsight we shall discover that it has really been the birth of an age of inhumanity.

If we consider the experience of adoption and sperm donation, and the feelings and the searches undertaken by the children, we shall have good reason to believe that the question of origins affects more than a few of the children of the international wave of baby tourism. What should they ask when they feel frightened by the alien component of their origins? What should they look for, or who or how, if all they know is that 'my mother was a Spanish ovum'? Or my father a Danish sperm donor? Or that an Indian surrogate mother gave birth to me? Or that I am a combination of all these ingredients, the product of a kind of Spanish–Danish–Indian joint venture? What kind of narrative can be combined with a Spanish ovum? What geographies of kinship, what transnational landscapes of origin and family connections, family yearnings and family fantasies will come into being in the wake of this so-called baby tourism – a euphemism par excellence, since the combination of two terms with positive associations ('baby' and 'tourism') has been coined to obscure the immolation of a piece of human history and the creation of a grotesque piece of Frankenstein-like reality? And what feelings will arise when the children growing up learn one day that whole worlds have been fused to make up their identity and that the hierarchy of global inequality has been built into their lives? Will they feel rage because their parents have bought them, in a faraway place, at a relatively favourable discount because the indigenous inhabitants – in the country where they were born – ask little in return for their contribution? Will they feel an inner kinship, something of the order of a physical solidarity, with the people living there? Or shame because part of them belongs to the 'others' – i.e., the beggars and slums of the world?

To be sure, we can also imagine a different scenario. Gazing into the future, we must also ask whether the desire to find out about our family and cultural origins is part of a fundamental supra-historical human need. Or whether perhaps a time will come when the question of our origins no longer holds any meaning for us. Let us make a conjecture. If we were to assume that conception with the aid of sperm donors or donated eggs were increasingly to become the norm, would children who had been conceived in that way keep on wanting to find out exactly which people were connected with these biological materials? Or might such curiosity come to seem remote and exotic to people living in future centuries?

We are concerned here with the assumptions underlying the basic needs of human existence. Is our knowledge of our origins an anthropological constant or is it an expectation that can change over time? Is that expectation the expression of a desire to know exactly where one belongs and to enjoy the resulting sense of security? Is it possible to conceive of a common-sense diversity in which being at home in a number of countries and languages could be taken for granted? Can we conceive of a society in which people stop inquiring into the identity of their biological father, their biological mother, and the place and country in which they were born, so that the quest for identity and the sense of belonging can be pursued along quite different paths?

10

The Intimate is Global: The Model of Distant Love

The Normal Chaos of Love (Beck and Beck-Gernsheim 1995) deals with relationships between the sexes inside and outside marriage – with each other, without each other and in conflict with each other – with unmarried couples living together, childless marriages, single parents, divorce, second marriages and my, your and our children, partners of the moment, part-time cohabitation and same-sex partnerships. In the light of such circumstances, answering even simple questions becomes a highly complex matter. For example, what is a *couple*, if a couple is no longer defined as the union of a man and a woman, whether by marriage certificate or simply by sharing a common household.

The French sociologist Jean-Claude Kaufmann has devised an ingenious answer to this question. A couple is a couple when two people buy a washing machine. That is when the really important questions and disagreements begin. What counts as dirty when the question arises as to who washes the dirty clothes? Who makes the decision? Who does the washing for whom? Is ironing a duty, etc.? (Kaufmann 1994).

This question – a washing machine for two people – is obviously not the best way to define the nature of love at a geographical distance. But it does lead one to ask what changes characterize the transition from the 'normal' chaos of love to the 'global' chaos.

Our reply is that love and family lose their tie to *a single* place and instead seek their fortune in the diversity of the world. This gives rise to a distant love that is both geographical and cultural. Either here or there, either us or them – both these alternatives disappear from the horizon of love. Few absolutely insuperable dividing lines remain:

not the colour of one's skin, one's nationality or religion, or even the distances separating countries and continents. On the contrary, it is the geographically distant other that contains the alluring new possibilities of love. Love has sprouted new wings.

What is the crucial characteristic of the different forms of life and love that we have brought together under the concept of the global chaos of love? What features are common to distant love, mixed-nationality couples, marriage migrants, immigrant domestic workers, surrogate mothers, etc.? What enables us to bring them together under the general heading of 'world families'? Do they share similar goals, similar conflicts, similar challenges, similar forms of development, similar constraints, resistances, contradictions and dilemmas? And how are these to be distinguished from those of normal 'nearby' families living close together, given that the diversity of the latter already far exceeds anything to be found in traditional ideas of love relationships?

Do world families bring us closer to a social era in which national distinctions and antagonisms lose their force? Do we find ourselves on the road to a future that seems to some to justify their hopes of putting an end to the spiral of force and counter-force, while appearing to others as an elemental threat, as the destruction of the natural order and meaning of the world?

Such are the great questions that are swirling around before our eyes. We showed in the last chapter that we find ourselves in the midst of a fundamental, historic change in the forms of love and life confronting us. This change is generating a new dynamism and a diversity that can be encapsulated in the idea of 'world families' as a model. This model contains five (interconnected) dimensions that we shall discuss under the following headings:

- The distant other is in the midst of our family
- Cross-border communication
- Global inequality acquires names and faces
- Beyond National Law
- Your families, our families: clashing ideals[7]

[7] The following dimensions of the world families model were arrived at by induction. They are part of our diagnostic theory of world families (see p. 8 above). These dimensions – and this is our thesis – are the necessary preconditions of the existence of world families. Whether other dimensions are also indispensable, what they are and how the totality of dimensions fits together theoretically – these are all matters that await further clarification. For example, the key question of what keeps world families together has been rather put to one side in the present study. It might well be argued that a 'multiple memory' (see pp. 186ff. below) is also one of the features of world families.

1   The Distant Other is in the Midst of Our Family

To explore the new landscapes of love, intimacy, family and the household in the age of globalization we have in the preceding chapters contrasted two different models: nearby love and national families, on the one hand, distant love and world families, on the other. We have shown that the transition from national families living close together to world families living far apart from one another belongs to a development characteristic of the age of globalization in general. The excluded other lives in our midst. Family relationships come into being across national, ethnic and religious boundaries.

This development enables us to identify one characteristic feature of world families. Whether the individuals concerned like it or not, they find themselves confronted with the world in the interior of their family. This changes the coordinates within which socialization occurs and identities are formed. Hitherto, these processes have been registered in the social sciences as part of the interaction between self and others, in which these 'others' have been regarded chiefly as 'identical others'. In contrast to that, we are now concerned with a situation in which the interaction between the self, the 'other others' and the world becomes the focus of attention.

The confrontation with the foreign world that now takes place in the interior of love and the family is displayed in a variety of ways in the various forms assumed by world families. Let us take immigrant domestic workers as an example. They cook and clean for families of the (affluent) host society and look after their children and the elderly. The excluded others – the illegal immigrants, the migrant men and women, the foreigners – are present in the kitchens and nurseries of indigenous middle-class families in the United States, Europe, Israel, South Korea, Canada and elsewhere. Many of these normal middle-class families could barely survive without their new domestic servants with foreign accents and different appearance. This is closely linked to the changes, more properly the partial changes, in the relations between the sexes in Western countries. These changes include above all the increased participation of women in the labour market, on the one hand, and, on the other, the still very limited involvement of men in the housework and the chores of looking after children and the elderly. To counteract the effects of this inequality in the relations between the sexes, the inequality of the world is invoked (see chapter 6) and exploited. This global inequality is imported into the normal lives of national families in the shape of immigrant domestic workers.

It must be admitted that the situation of these immigrant domestic workers is remarkably contradictory. They have now become a fixture in the ordinary lives of many Western families. At the same time, they are excluded – because for the most part they are not here legally and do not enjoy the protection of the law, and also because their world and their own children remain invisible to the families that employ them. Furthermore, interaction with the employer's family is fundamentally asymmetrical. The immigrant women are not independent and, where they have no legal standing, they are open to exploitation. Whereas they have to place themselves in the situation of the child or older person for whom they are caring in order to do their job, their employers have no need to practise empathy but can preserve an emotional distance. For this reason the families of both rich and poor are existentially bound to each other – and yet separated by chasms.

2   Cross-Border Communication

There is one thing that communication across borders isn't, namely a topic specific to world families. It is one of the fundamental preconditions of life in society and particularly so in the globalized world. Intercultural communication manifests itself in every sphere of human activity today; it permeates everyday exchanges in education and work, the economy and politics, tourism, TV, the internet, and so forth. Nevertheless, particular conditions obtain in world families. In world families, cross-border communication (with its accompanying dangers of misunderstanding and incomprehension) is not simply one element among many, but rather the indispensable precondition for coping with everyday challenges in love, intimacy and the family.

Thus world families are a testing ground for what are lauded in celebratory speeches as the skills of the global age. Such skills are referred to in seminars as 'soft skills' and practised as such. Partly of necessity and partly of their own free will, world families acquire through their lives skills that are elsewhere taught in classes, paid for and confirmed by certificates. World families are pioneers of interculturalism.

It goes without saying that there are also many sources of misunderstanding in nearby and national families, especially in tensions between men and women or between old and young, and these tensions may become more acute in times of radical change. However, such conflicts are played out in a common language, a shared political

and legal system, and a shared nationality. In world families, compli-
cating factors are provided in these conflicts by antagonisms on a
world scale – different languages, different pasts and different political systems. However, this means that people live suspended above
abysses of incomprehension, abysses that are partly ignored, partly
taboo and partly bridged by people struggling to improve mutual
understanding. This is a situation that can lead to an adventurous
journey full of discoveries.

Basic, everyday situations – eating habits, giving presents, the significance of holidays, ideas about time and punctuality, a grasp of
who belongs to the family and who doesn't, who is worthy of respect
and what 'respect' means, right down to such questions as the
meaning of climate change and an understanding of which foodstuffs
contain harmful substances and are to be avoided – all such basic
questions of ordinary life inevitably mean different things to different
people and can rarely be resolved by recourse to a fund of shared
meanings and values.

National families can frequently rely on shared assumptions that
enable them to make preliminary decisions and establish rules. In
contrast, the answers that facilitate world families' everyday continuity have to be clarified in the course of 'cross-border communications', through the permanent dialogue between the various family
members. This dialogue must needs lead to overall agreement, but
the agreement does not entail express understanding or a tacit consensus. It may imply a kind of moratorium so as to get round disputed
points by a pragmatic agreement to disagree and for each family
member to retain the ability to act.

Cross-border communication – and this is an important postscript
– includes both dialogue and silence. Communication across borders
can point to 'reflexivity' – i.e., the silent confrontation with the
stranger in one's own life – but also 'reflection' – i.e., meditation,
interrogation, and discussion of one's findings.[8]

In any event, the opposing worlds that collide in world families
have to be negotiated. For normal couples (i.e., single-nation couples)
there are published guidebooks that will tell you how to turn silent
partners whose marriages have fallen into a rut and been stifled into
husband and wife with a lively, talkative marriage. Similar guides for
mixed-nationality couples and world families are few and far between;
in fact, it may not be possible to produce them. For what would such
a collection of Golden Rules look like if the partners come from

---

[8] On this distinction between 'reflexivity' and 'reflection', see Beck, Giddens and Lash
(1994).

different cultures? What kind of Golden – i.e., shared – Rules could there be that might decide who has the right to name a child and which festivals are to be celebrated, etc.? It means that the procedures and conditions involved in making decisions would themselves have to be negotiated. World families find themselves forced to invent their own procedures and practices through a process of *reflexive negotiation*.

This presupposes at the very least the first steps towards changing their point of view and making the effort to see their own world through the eyes of the other person. The ability to empathize with the other person, who is both loved and also a stranger, is desirable not just for the sake of one's partner but also for the sake of the love they both feel – in other words, it is also a matter of self-interest.

3   Global Inequality Acquires Names and Faces

World families are not merely the stage on which the dramas of love are played out. They are also the point at which we see how national frontiers intervene in the lives of the various members and produce demarcation lines that run straight through the family. Some members are privileged, others are discriminated against. To give an example, here is the story of I., a Flensburg doctor who was born in Iran. When he first met Claudia ten years ago while they were both studying medicine, they were in Italy, where both were foreigners and were seen to be foreigners; both spoke only elementary Italian. They have been married for two years and now live in Germany, where their respective situations have completely changed in opposite ways. Now only he is the foreigner; he speaks German with a definite accent and attracts attention by virtue of his features and the colour of his hair. He has constantly to report to the police to have his work permit extended and is repeatedly picked on in stop-and-search situations. When he flies to conferences in London he has to stand in a long queue for non-EU citizens. Or take the case of M., an eight-year-old boy who lives with his parents and older siblings in California. Whereas the other members of his family live illegally in the United States, he, the youngest, was born there and therefore has US citizenship. Because he is the only one who can exit and enter without difficulty, he has become the ambassador between the two worlds. He spends the summer holidays in the small Mexican township in which his grandparents, his parents' siblings and the majority of his numerous cousins live – a journey that he finds a nuisance but for which he is envied by the family members who remain in the United States. When he returns to California, he is bombarded with questions and has to keep telling and retelling what things are like at home and how the different members of the extended family are getting on.

When we consider the inequalities between richer and poorer nations, the history and present state of colonialism and imperialism, the rules governing membership and exclusion in different countries and legal systems – we must surely inquire how all these things are reflected or refracted in world families.

In everyday life, in politics and sociology, the relation between the family and social inequality is usually described in completely differ-ent terms. In textbooks on social structure it always has been and still is customary to think of members of the family as belonging to a single unit and then to assign them a common position in the social hierarchy (so that the Berger family are treated as a middle-class family and the Keyser family as part of the marginalized lower class). Seen from this standpoint, within the framework of the nation-state, one family has greater status while the other family is ranked lower. But all the members of the family are given the same ranking. Reduced to a formula, we could say that there is inequality externally, in society, and equality internally, in the family.

It was for this reason that the family was mistakenly regarded as a 'leveller', an institution in which individual family members were treated (broadly speaking) as a unit. This assumption was exposed as a myth as early as the feminist studies of the late twentieth century. The fact is that it completely obscured the unequal distribution of rights and duties, to say nothing of the power hierarchy within fami-lies and the enormous inequalities between men and women, between parents and children and, where relevant, between siblings (between the first-born – the heir – and the brothers and sisters who arrived subsequently). These radical inequalities have undoubtedly been weakened in Western countries as a consequence of changes to family law. But new inequalities have arrived to take their place because, with the emergence of world families, global inequalities have made their entry into the interior of the family. The inequalities of the world now have names and faces; they determine the dynamics of intimate relationships.[9] But how are people inside a family to withstand, nego-tiate and survive pressures that separate whole worlds from one another?

[9] This has failed to make any impression on sociology, which equates family with the national family and thinks of the household in local, culturally homogeneous terms. In tacit agreement with the host society, a sociology still imprisoned in methodological nationalism occludes the transnational shadow economy, which directly chains the households and human destinies of the poorer and richer parts of the world to one another.

The world's inequalities are not refracted uniformly in 'the' world family. Instead, different family members 'are the embodiments' of different countries and so assume correspondingly different positions in the social hierarchy. A striking example is seen in the relation between nationality and the franchise. People who have lived and worked in Germany for decades but who do not have German citizenship cannot vote even in local elections.

Another example tells us that anyone who has not mastered the language of the country he has entered, or speaks it inadequately, becomes a second-class human being. The inability to speak the language constitutes a kind of social disability. Anyone who lives in a country where a different language is spoken is forced to depend on the assistance or support of other people for many of the activities of everyday life. 'These people' may include an individual's own children, who have to act as translators.

What the host society may think of as 'integration' means something different to the minority. It means how much of my own language and origin do I have to forget in order to gain acceptance? How can this be resisted?

The perception of social inequality is always determined by national frontiers. This focuses on the inequalities within a society (e.g., the level of pensions in eastern Germany as opposed to western Germany). These inequalities are emphasized, magnified and made the basis of political demands. In contrast, social inequalities between different societies (such as the level of pension provision in Germany as opposed to Russia) are ignored and treated as a kind of natural fate. This distancing process becomes dubious if global inequality is manifested within the family – for example, in the shape of a daughter-in-law from Thailand or an adopted child from the Brazilian favelas. This is because it violates the basic principle of the family: solidarity. Looking the other way is morally not acceptable. Here it is people's duty to help one another out.

We see similar questions constantly re-emerging in world families. They assume almost classical form and are basically insoluble. Are we obliged to provide help globally and, if so, then for whom, how often and for how long? The German husband of a Thai wife may understand that he must help to finance an eye operation for his wife's brother who is threatened with blindness. But if one of her many cousins twice removed faces a similar fate, he may feel his wife's urgings as inappropriate and may even reject her pleas with the comment: you haven't married the social worker responsible for the whole of Thailand!

Stereotypes of oneself and others can be found in every society. They become effective on initial contact, when you meet someone for the first time. A spontaneous sorting procedure begins as soon as someone stands out from the crowd. The locals hear a foreign-sounding name and become aware of unusual facial features, gestures or style of clothing, and this is quickly translated into the message that this person doesn't come from here, he is not one of us, he comes from somewhere else.

Such messages may be deceptive in the age of globalization and mixed families. Anyone who was born and has grown up in Germany, who has a German mother and a German passport, but who also has a Turkish surname because his father comes from a solid middle-class family in Istanbul, studied in Germany, fell in love with a German woman and married her – any person with such a family background knows exactly what to expect when he meets someone for the first time. No sooner has he given his name than he finds himself the object of a quick, scrutinizing glance, a moment of irrita-tion or surprise, inevitably followed by the identical question, either explicitly or left tacitly hanging in the air: 'Where do you actually come from?' He may interpret this as a sign of open-mindedness, an approach to him, the foreigner. But in fact he isn't a foreigner; he is a native, a German, someone born in Stuttgart or Cologne. But, when faced with the question 'Where do you actually come from?', he is confronted again and again with an identity that does not fit his image of himself. His interlocutor's look turns him into an outsider, literally excluded and pigeonholed along with other foreigners. His surname functions as a signal of his deviation, his not-belonging (Battaglia 2000).

The power of such stereotyping is immense, both for those directly affected and for their families. In families with members both of the host society and of ethnic minorities, it creates boundaries and can have a destructive effect. Where the family members with the foreign-sounding name or the foreign-looking appearance are regularly exposed to questions about their origins, those with ordinary names and appearances experience nothing of the sort. They do not know what it means when people you have just met – on the bus, in the lecture room, at a party – react automatically with questions about your family history, a history that often enough is scarred by poverty and war, expulsion and flight, separation and loss. In this way the question of origins can become a source of irritation not simply to those directly affected but also to other members of the family. This happens when family members whose name and appearance trigger no reaction have only the dimmest idea of what their closest relatives experience every day, whether in the shape of the question about their origins or in the various kinds of discrimination to which they are subjected. In such situations, various forms of estrangement can quickly develop inside relationships – for example, if a wife thinks that her husband is hypersensitive or even hysterical in his reactions and, if her partner notices this, feels misunderstood and retreats into himself.

4 Beyond National Law

The state should keep out of people's bedrooms, according to an ancient piece of political wisdom. The fact is, however, that the state is to be found in people's bedrooms, as well as in their living rooms, nurseries and kitchens. Whether we are talking about laws forbidding incest, laws granting maternity or paternity leave, or laws recognizing homosexual partnerships, love and life relationships are not fully free and unconstrained and left completely in the hands of the individuals concerned. Instead every state has a system of rules known as family law that sets the framework for what is permissible within the family and what is not. This set of rules is said to help protect the weaker members of society.

However, we see increasingly that family law fails to keep pace with developments in love relationships and the forms of love. This is particularly true when globalization is involved. The legal systems of nation-states are poorly adapted to the needs of world families. In many respects world families find themselves positioned at odds with the conceptual framework of the nation-state. They fall between the cracks in the demands made by the nation-state and are caught between the conflicting guidelines of different legal systems. Such grey areas and gaps can be actively exploited so as to further one's own interests, but, by the same token, they can also lead to the loss of state guarantees and safety nets, and so to an existence in which individuals are exposed to the arbitrary actions of other people or the interference of the state.

Fake Marriages?

Cross-border love does not fit into the legal systems of the nation-state. The shadow of suspicion it cannot shake off – sham marriage, forced marriage – has a structural basis. Love that seeks to cross frontiers offends against the national monogamy commandment: thou shalt have no native country but me!

In the West the state, the law and the judiciary tend increasingly to withdraw from the lives of individuals. Whether you marry or just live together without a marriage certificate is left to individuals to decide. Homosexual partnerships are acquiring quasi-marital status. It is up to couples to decide among themselves who is responsible for the housework and for raising the children. But when the basic right to love crosses the frontier, the nation-state's tolerance comes to an end. The traffic lights turn red and the burden of proof shifts the other way. The suspicion of guilt now comes into play. Indeed, cross-border marriage becomes a potential crime. The accused, whether man or woman, has to prove his or her innocence. But how should they go about it?

A blonde man from Munich discovers a black woman with whom he wishes to share his life in the Dominican Republic – a marriage of convenience just to be obliging? Does she really love him? Or did she use her feminine wiles to turn his head? Why did he not marry Katharina, whom he had known from childhood and who was so very much in love with him? Parents, relations and friends can't help asking questions of this sort.

Nor indeed can the authorities, who set out to judge the legality of this marriage. Anyone who wishes to contract a cross-border marriage rouses the suspicions of the guardians of the law. If a couple of the same nationality wish to marry (the same language, the same skin colour, the same citizenship), scrutiny lasts no more than a couple of hours. But when an international couple wish to marry, let's say a German woman and an Arab man, they come up against a wall of objections, prejudice and harassment – and it can go on for months.

Bureaucratic doubts are graded according to colour. The poorer the country or the darker the skin colour, the more likely that people will be refused certification, the keys that open the doors to an officially licensed marital bliss. Who will trust the blonde Markus and his dark complexioned Catalina? (German) red tape has a field day. Please provide a notarized copy of your parents' marriage certificate, proof of your parents' descent, a residence permit, a certificate of the applicants' legal capacity to marry, alternatively an exemption from this requirement approved by the court, but to be replaced by a 'certificate of no impediment'. 'Is there really no official record of the future bride before she reached the age of eleven? That's a fine state of affairs! Who can guarantee that the woman the caring state is going to confide to the care of one of its citizens and thus allow to take her place in the community of the nation is in fact the person standing before him now and not someone else entirely?' In the administrative court in Cologne in 2009 there were 1,500 appeals pending against decisions to refuse visa applications to would-be marriage partners. A court hearing to decide on Markus and Catalina's 'marriage application' cannot be expected any earlier than June next year. By that time the daughter whom Catalina is expecting will be almost one year old.

Unintended Consequences

In the 1950s, Germany was ethnically speaking a largely homogeneous country. Foreigners amounted to no more than 1 per cent of the population. Today the proportion of foreigners is a good 8 per cent. That does not include the large group of people with a German passport but also with an 'immigration background' – in other words, people for whom immigration is part of their own life history or the history of their immediate family. If you add the two groups together, one in five of the total population must be counted among 'people with an immigration background', while, for children under six, the figure is one in three. The Federal Republic of Germany has become the 'Rainbow Republic of Germany'.

The decisive impetus for this demographic change was provided at the institutional or, rather, political and legal level. Above all, we must refer to two historic but antithetical decisions that paradoxically both produced the same sort of outcome. These were the decisions first to recruit and then to stop recruiting foreign workers. In the wake of these decisions Germany became a country of immigration, or, rather, a reluctant country of immigration, with millions of world families – immigrant families of Turkish-German, Italian-German, Greek-German origin. Here is a brief account of the historical development (Bade 2000: 314ff.; Herbert 2003).

In the mid-1950s, Germany had an urgent need of workers in order to maintain the progress of the Economic Miracle. Because of the shortfall of workers in Germany itself, the first recruitment scheme was signed with Italy in 1955. This was followed by further agreements with other Mediterranean countries, in particular with Turkey in 1961. Expectations in Germany mirrored those of the Italian (the Greek and the Turkish) signatories. The workers recruited in this way, so German politicians assumed, would abide by the so-called rotation principle. They would spend a few years working in Germany and then return home, to be succeeded by a new wave of recruits – should the German economy still have need of them. This idea chimed with the expectations of the newly recruited immigrants. They arrived with the hope that they would soon be able to save up enough from their earnings to enable them to make the leap into a better future, build their own house at home or acquire a shop and make themselves independent.

As everyone knows, things worked out differently. Many of the immigrant workers had underestimated the time it would take to earn enough to finance their dreams. Many began to live a commuter's life, living alone in a hostel in Germany, separated from their family for eleven months of the year. For this reason, many immigrants returned home after their (for the most part short-term) contracts had come to an end, coming back to Germany after an interval on obtaining a further – short-term – contract. All this went well as long as the economy was booming. The first great turning point came when the economy was hit by crisis and the numbers of the unemployed started to grow. For the German government, this signalled the end of the 'guest-worker' era. The immigrants who had been recruited were now supposed to return home. To make sure they did so, a ban on further recruitment was introduced in 1973. It was helped along by a 'repatriation bonus' for immigrants who left Germany of their own free will.

This meant that immigrant workers in Germany had two courses of action open to them. They could remain in Germany, but in that case they had to do so on a continuing basis, without any gaps between job contracts and without spending time with their families at home. Or else they could choose to go home to stay with their family once again. But, if they did go home, the way back to Germany was blocked by the recruitment ban.

How did the immigrants respond to these alternatives? They discovered a third way. Some did return home, to Portugal, Greece or Italy. But many wanted to keep their jobs in Germany while not wanting to be separated from their families permanently. They resolved to bring their wives (in rarer cases their husbands) and their children to Germany. The process of family reunification had begun. The immigrants abandoned the company hostels and rented flats. Children were brought to Germany from Turkey or Greece. Additional children were born in Germany, grew up there and established families of their own.

In this way, the recruitment ban fired the starting pistol for a new era. The phase of the 'guest worker' on a short-term contract now lay in the past; the era of the immigrant family settling in Germany for the long term began. This meant that the political intentions underlying the recruitment ban had turned into their opposite. The others, the immigrants, did not disappear. On the contrary, they settled down for the duration and acquired children and grandchildren in their new country. First recruitment, then recruitment ban. The combination of these two steps was the prelude to the internal pluralization of a monocultural society.

The Global Chaos of Divorce

Why international couples decide to live in one country rather than another depends not least on the onerousness of the legal and bureaucratic obstacles to such marriages. If later on they decide on a divorce, they find themselves facing more decisions, though of a different sort. Now, each member of the couple that no longer wishes to be in the relationship asks him- or herself where the most favourable conditions for a divorce are to be found. Which legal system will afford me the greatest protection from the (unreasonable) demands of my ex?

We see here a situation that could well be named the 'global chaos of divorce'. More and more often, married couples own several passports and houses in different towns in different countries. Where they are intent on divorce, the battle begins with the question of which legal system should, may, or must be appealed to. Should the divorce be conducted according to the conditions and procedures prescribed by the husband's nationality and the corresponding divorce legislation (and what if he has dual or even triple nationality?)? Or should the wife's nationality be decisive (and what if she has two or more passports?)? Or is jurisdiction to be determined by the law of the country in which the partners have lived longest (or most recently)?

Moreover, it's not just peanuts at stake. On the contrary, it is often a matter of large sums of money, of the obligation or lack of obligation to pay millions. Who has the right to maintenance, how much and for how long? Who is owed financial compensation for past contributions to the marriage, or failure to contribute? Should pre-nuptial contracts be recognized, or should they be declared null and void, either because they disadvantage the economically weaker partner or because they are liable to bleed the financially stronger partner dry (Croft and Peel 2010; Hodson and Thomas 2009)?

Since the rules for maintenance and financial compensation and the guidelines for making awards to divorced spouses vary from one country to the next, the negotiations involve sums that are large even for the affluent middle class, while they rise astronomically in the ranks of the rich and the super-rich. Depending on the law of the land, money, houses and other possessions may be awarded to one partner or the other or shared out between the two.

The consequence of the differences between legal systems is that, following the breakdown of the marriage, the global chaos of divorce begins with a highly specialized form of divorce tourism. Frequently there is a competition between the parties and their legal representatives. Each side tries to launch proceedings in a country whose laws would favour their own client (and consequently result in a less favourable settlement for the opposing party).

For example, where the aim is to achieve a division of property between the (former) married partners, it happens to be the case that British law seeks to protect the rights of the economically weaker partner. This means in practice that the interests of women are better protected, significantly better than in other countries. This has led to a long series of court cases in which the wife has won very generous awards. Soon afterwards there was a rapid growth in the number of cases where the husband urged his legal team to launch the divorce proceedings as soon as possible in another country, before the wife could begin proceedings of her own in Britain. Similarly, more and more cases involve (ex-)wives who have received only a modest settlement in other jurisdictions and who attempt therefore to have the proceedings re-run in Britain so as to obtain a more generous ruling in their favour.

5   Your Families, Our Families: Clashing Ideals

The more the floods of immigrants swell, the more variegated and mixed populations become, and the more the new media make remote and alien worlds familiar to us all, then the more will the world religions and the individual values of modernity tend to impinge directly on one another. This sets new wars of religion alight that strike at the heart of everyday experience. They centre on the question of what is an 'ideal family'.

For some, patriarchy is the natural foundation of a good family; for others it is a tool for the oppression of women. For some, equality between the sexes is the top priority; for others it is an aberration, a violation of the natural order of the world. For some, sexuality is the expression of intimacy, sensuality and self-knowledge; for others, it is inseparable from the imperatives of religion and reproduction.

Here one view of the world collides with another. The groups that embrace these views often regard each other with mutual contempt, each accusing the other of perpetuating a false, amoral or repressive notion of the family.

Members of the Western host societies often regard immigrant families as patriarchal, authoritarian and contemptuous of women, governed by rigid and obtuse fathers and aggressive elder sons, all of them hostile to the values of the Enlightenment and the modern world, all of them believers in forced marriages and honour killing. Conversely, the charge levelled against the West by many immigrant groups is that it has betrayed the laws of the family. From their perspective, it is they, the immigrants, who are the guardians of the family and society and concerned with their preservation. In contrast, the families of the host society lack authority and create a pervasive climate of indifference and lack of affection.

A major empirical study asked immigrant Turkish women what they thought of the Germans and invited them to compare Turks and Germans. The chief features of German families, according to these Turkish women, were a deficient sense of hospitality, absence of respect for the elderly, and a failure to appreciate friendship and neighbourliness. They described German women as self-centred loners (Gümen 2000: 343). A study by Deutsche Shell, *Jugend 2000*, reached similar conclusions. There was little sign of rebellion on the part of Turkish youth against what Westerners saw as the authoritarian upbringing at home. On the contrary, most of the interviewees were critical of the way in which German families raised their children. They interpreted German customs not as the expression of liberalism but as proof of the parents' indifference towards their children. In their view, their own parents' strict rules and setting of boundaries showed that they truly loved their children and took pains with them. Inevitably, this meant that their parents sometimes forbade them to do something or other and made sure they didn't do it. As a young Turkish woman put it, 'I don't think German families are much good. The children can do as they please. Then they get stuck somewhere or other and can't get out. Too much freedom' (Deutsche Shell 2000: 13).

Such judgements represent more than mere disagreement about different forms of the family as expressed in kitchens, bedrooms, living rooms and the political arena. What they point to is a competition between cultures and religions. They all lay claim to the right to sanctify the 'ideal family', the power to define right and wrong, good and evil, in everything concerning sexuality, freedom and the equality between men and women. They all know what God's will is and what is of the Devil.

Thus it is not only the family that is at stake here; it is the future of humanity. The assertion of belief in this or that idea of the family or view of love has long since assumed a quasi-religious character, even in secular societies.

This gives rise to new divisions between your families and our families. All these global images of the 'ideal family' assume concrete form in world families. They cause conflict within individuals and tear families apart.

11

Are World Families Pioneers of Cosmopolitanism?

To understand the meaning of love today, it is not enough to understand the meaning of love today. We must also understand how the self, frontiers, the world and love all interlock. This book has for its subject a new chapter of social history, one in which love, the family and the alien world often enter into paradoxical unions.

Should we think of the concept 'world families' in universalistic terms? No. In our view, there is no meta-language capable of addressing the differences in the heterogeneous and tension-filled sphere of world families. It is rather the case that the meaning of 'world families' changes depending on the cultural contexts in which it is found. 'World families' is the term for this cultural diversity. It bridges the divisions separating the developed and the developing world, the centre and the periphery, the modernities of the West and the non-West – wherever these divisions are manifest in people, in the private sphere, in love relationships and in the bosom of the family. World families are the empirical proof that such dualisms are drained of their significance in the intimate and private realm, or, rather, they reorganize themselves and form new syntheses.[10] In this sense world families must themselves become multilingual. They must learn through what Charles Taylor calls 'the dance of understanding' to love and live with cultural differences.

---

[10] World families, which have only just been made visible in conceptual terms as a historically novel social reality and unity, are exemplary as a research field that transcends methodological nationalism. The present book attempts to construct the foundations of a methodological cosmopolitanism for the sociology of love and the family (Beck 2006; Beck and Grande 2010).

In this sense, our diagnostic theory of distant love and world families (see p. 8, above) is post-universalist and post-Western. We do not operate on culturally neutral terrain (as Jürgen Habermas formulated this with reference to his theory of the public sphere). If an uncontextualized understanding of the family leads to false generalizations, it is even truer to say that the uncontextualized understanding of world families will lead us astray. We must conclude not only that there are innumerable kinds of world family but also that there are very many different ways of understanding the different types of world family (see pp. 17ff. above).

How open-minded are such world families? Are they the precursors of a post-national solidarity, solidarity at a distance, friendship at a distance? Are there historical parallels? In the nineteenth century the increasing popularity of newspapers contributed to the strengthening of national consciousness. May it be argued similarly that, at the beginning of the twenty-first century, the communication media – the internet, Facebook, Skype, etc. – are contributing to the rise of distant love and world families? Do world families help to create a style, a future? Are they an early form of world society?

As we have repeatedly emphasized, it would be an egregious mistake to make the intellectual leap from world families to open-mindedness. Quite the contrary: since world families cast doubt on the fundamental tenets of tradition and nature, counter-movements arise which attempt to salvage the old order of love, sexuality and the family. It follows that world families may act as breeding grounds not only for open-mindedness but also for globalized, fundamentalist, anti-modern, closed minds. Indeed, it may well be a feature of world families that they combine open-mindedness with the tendency to retreat into fundamentalist convictions. For the fact is that what we call 'fundamentalist' is itself the product of a dialogue with modernity which has always been present in the dialogue conducted among world families.

Perhaps the most surprising feature of world families is that they constitute a stage on which daily surprises are acted out. The unquestioned, self-evident convictions that help to give our lives stability are constantly put in doubt.

Some people wish to escape their isolation; they seek a companion and in the process they drag the world into bed with them unawares. Others want to fall in love with the whole world, but stumble over their own roots in their everyday lives with their partner and are forced finally to admit to themselves just how provincial they are and, even worse, to confess their satisfaction with that.

Heterosexual couples who are childless without wishing to be so, as well as gay and lesbian couples, find themselves yearning for ordinary, normal, 'natural' lives – in other words, they want to experience the delights and travails of having children of their own. Having obtained children by means of the world markets, they raise 'biological world citizens' whose origins embody the inequalities of the world.

Some sing the 'new Internationale of Love', others the 'new Internationale of Hatred'. Sometimes it all comes together in the cacophony of the world-family choir.

It may be true that, the more identities you conceal within yourself, the simpler it becomes to comprehend the position of the excluded others. Perhaps we can venture to predict that, the more children from world families form couples with other children from world families, the more natural it will seem to live together with the excluded 'others' (who by then will have ceased to be excluded others).

It is clear, then, that world families are by no means autonomous and stable. Their fragile existence depends on many factors – above all, on the stereotyping and hostile views propagated by the host society or the basic rights that they have been granted or denied. A historic example, of course, is the way in which German citizens were turned into Jews in Nazi Germany.

The fundamental truth is that immigrant domestic workers and substitute mothers working illegally are citizens of the world – they all possess civil rights and human rights. It is not our intention to discuss further the relation between world families and human rights. And yet it is of fundamental importance to state that, for mixed-nationality marriages, distant love, immigrant domestic workers and surrogate mothers, etc., who fall between the different stools of national legal systems, we can find values in the catalogue of human rights that form part of our elementary conception of modernity. These human rights are the Pole Star that enables us to find our bearings in an age of cultural relativism and to make solidarity possible. Just as with the Declaration of Human Rights or the facts of man-made climate change or the decoding of the human genome, so too the emergence of world families forces us to ask what it is that constitutes the inalienable core of humanity.

1 Children of Postmodernity?

Are world families a typical product of postmodernism? Doesn't the combination of Spanish ovum, Danish sperm and Indian surrogate mother point to the cultural arbitrariness and the absence of clear distinctions that constitutes the trademark of postmodernism? Don't

men and women in world families practise forms of symbolic ethnicity that deploy origins and traditions merely as the décor and the
colourful stage sets for the drama of their everyday lives? Is this not
just another instance of postmodernism's playful treatment of the
worlds of style, symbol and meaning? Won't this specious diversity
keep on collapsing into a general confusion in which everything is
mixed up with everything else?

And does this not mean that what in this book we have called
'world families' is in reality no more than a minor family branch of
the global culture industry, one that, to exaggerate only slightly, can
be reduced to a single characteristic, namely inauthenticity? If even
normal families are less and less able to lean on a body of tradition
that can be taken for granted, may we not suppose that world families
are likely to form milieus of childhood without memories because
they have lost the images and stories of their background and country
of origin?

These arguments, taken together, would lead us to the conclusion
that world families have no sense of time and continuity. Globalized
families might well make use of the imagined vestiges of their origins
and their past but would not be able to orientate themselves in history
as world families. The do-it-yourself imagination, the mental bond
that keeps world families together, is either trivial and superficial or
else rooted in particular origins, which means that world families end
up as second-hand hybrid cultures.

2 The Multiple Memory

This accusation of a haphazard postmodernity overlooks the fact that
there is such a thing as a bastion of non-arbitrariness, namely human
rights. These cannot be dismissed as the expression of a postmodern
synthetic culture; their roots go back to the earliest beginnings of
Europe, to Greek philosophy (Habermas 1998; Levy and Sznaider
2010).

Moreover, the charge of world families' lack of memory is based
on the questionable assumption that individual identity can be developed only in the context of collective memory. According to this view,
anyone who cannot situate himself in a collective tradition and collective memory will be unable to develop political consciousness and
identity.

People who live, love, think and act transnationally have to decide
between different forms of historical memory. This holds good for
the crucial questions: Where should they live and where should they

want to live? Which mother tongue should they learn? Which religion inherited from their parents should they practise?, etc. It applies also to concrete questions and occasions, such as the festivals they celebrate, the calendar they adopt, the rituals to be followed, the songs to be sung, the relatives to be invited, etc. If in the process the historical memory is disrupted, with its one-sidedness and its assumptions about what is expected, then the horizon opens up and the false simplicity of national memory loses the ground beneath its feet.

The end effect is decisive. It is not the absence of memory that characterizes world families. What marks them out is the simultaneous presence of different lines of memory that have to be related to one another. The accusation of lack of memory is based on a false alternative: either a shared collective memory or none at all. World families show signs of multidimensional or plural memory forms whose monopolistic claims tend to cancel one another out, at the same time as challenging individuals to reconsider their position. This means that each and every person is constantly forced to decide between different traditions, loyalties and narratives. Life and love in world families are suspended between the different offerings of the historical memory, and these can or must be weighed up and negotiated by individuals or else combined in new ways of thinking and remembering.

Looked at in this way, one thing can be said with certainty of couples, marriages, families and grandparents who have been compelled to experience and endure the traumas of world history in their own lives – German-Jewish, German-Polish, French-Algerian, Israeli-Palestinian, Japanese-Chinese, Chinese-American, etc., including their origins and pasts, wounds and stereotypes. If one thing is true of them, it is that they are not superficial and lacking in memory. Even if they come to grief on the reefs of the past, what unites them is a miniature world of cosmopolitan enlightenment. This is the arena where what defines world families is contested and experienced: universal human rights plus the love of difference.

The contrary view is obvious. At a time when complaints are spreading about 'lazy Southerners' and 'bankrupt Greeks' and where everything that is not 'national' becomes a negative stereotype; at a time when Islamophobia has reached the heart of society and even presents itself as a form of enlightenment – is it not entirely unrealistic to speak of open-mindedness, a utopianism from inside the ivory tower?

It may well be utopia. But not just inside an ivory tower. In Berlin of all places, a city where the failure of multiculturalism can be seen on every corner, Gustav Seibt has discovered a remarkable example of open-mindedness. In Schaubude, the children's theatre, they are doing Goethe's *Faust* in an unexpectedly 'open-minded' way. This play, which is the quintessence of German national culture, has been brought to life in a new way not by actors from distant continents, speaking foreign languages, but by Germans – Germans of every colour – and, more particularly, by German children of every colour, but all speaking excellent German. They are middle-school pupils – i.e., between nine and thirteen years old – and they have taken on the whole of *Faust*, including the almost unplayable second part. The young actors and actresses are girls in headscarves, little macho Turkish boys; they have Indian faces or else they are black Germans together with cheeky-looking Berlin kids without any 'immigration background'.

> The performance began with a diminutive theatre director who came on stage wearing a top hat and explained who this man Goethe actually was . . . This was followed by a brisk dramatic action full of bumping and banging, lightning flashes, explosions and hissing sounds lasting ninety minutes. The 'rival song with brother spheres' echoed through the heavens, Mephisto joked around with God whose voice reverberated from the ceiling, a Faust who was not quite up to his part learned a vast amount, but still ended up understanding nothing – every schoolchild knows how that feels. A constant parade of children, some chubby, others gangling, entering and exiting, representing the human race in every conceivable colour. (Seibt 2011: 3)

For the audience there are magical moments. The yearning for a Germany open to the world becomes a visible, palpable reality. The audience finds itself enchanted by half-earnest, half-amusing rituals of a Faustian children's theatre. The multiculturalism of the young actors enables them to rediscover a German national treasure in an unfamiliar, transformed guise. It may sound trivial and stretch the great idea of a 'multiple memory' to excess. But 'the first names of the young actors, musicians, designers and stagehands are a foretaste of the Germany of the future: Antonina and Israa, Meliha and Adela, Fatma and Noah, Max and Jos, Dragan and Nabil, and many, many others. Altogether they have put on a performance of the best that Germany has to offer the world: Goethe' (ibid.).

3 Postscript from the Future: the Two Commissions on Love

We shall now skip a few decades and conclude with the speech given by the chairman of the Nobel Prize Committee, parts of which were reprinted in the *International Herald Tribune*.

Oslo, December 2061. Archival data show that around the year 2010 a dispute broke out concerning the nature of the real utopia of love, which continues to agitate people even today. Beginning in 2016, two groups formed under the banners of 'Distant Love' and 'Nearby Love', each starkly opposed to the other. This made it clear that the battlefield of love has ceased to be dominated by religious disputes or disagreements between the sexes. Instead, cutting across these tensions and divisions, there was an explosion in the conflicts between geographical and cultural distance and proximity in love relationships, in families and among couples.

The surprising aspect of this was that these disagreements arising from love relationships were no longer played out in private, but could increasingly be seen instead in talk shows and internet forums, in ministries, political parties, parliaments and governments. This was even followed by the emergence of social movements in support of distant love and nearby love. Statistical data underpinned what later became known as the 'lovers' rebellion': according to a census conducted by the US Federal Office of Statistics in 2010, for the first time in American history, fewer than half of all households consisted of married couples. Whereas married couples represented 74 per cent of all households in 1950, this had now dwindled to 48 per cent. In addition, traditional families – i.e., married couples with children – now amounted to only one-fifth of all households, whereas in 1950 they had still formed 43 per cent of the total.

Similar developments could be seen in many other countries. There was a rapid fall in the birth rate, which it was widely feared would constitute a threat to the continued survival of the population, as well as to the nation's political establishment, economic strength and cultural identity. At the same time, the number of marriages was in decline while there was a steep rise in the divorce rate – a trend interpreted by the public as a symptom of a growing lack of love and joie de vivre. The countries where cultural pessimism had long thrived looked as if they might be swamped by the visions of doom purveyed by journalists and other writers. Furthermore – and this was decisive as far as the political parties and governments were concerned – the conflict between the different cultures of distant love and nearby love became the subject of statistical analysis, and the figures were as hotly debated as the numbers of the unemployed had been in earlier times. In this instance, the figures pointed to a dramatic growth of distant love.

This triad of the falling birth rate, the decline in the marriage rate and the increase in the incidence of distant love became known among social scientists as the 'global challenge of distant love'. The political parties quickly recognized the scope for action – or, in other words, the electoral potential – and the experts perceived a new opening for their own activity. The result was the 'Commission for Sustainable Love Ethics', which was established in 2041 on an EU-wide basis and with a number of institutes in different countries.

Needless to say, there was public controversy about the choice of experts to sit on the commission. Everyone could see that love researchers and psychologists should be represented. But experts in classics and languages had to work hard to prove their case. They succeeded by demonstrating that the differences between distant love and nearby love could be traced back through history and were of course reflected in the language ('the discourse') of love from time immemorial. It was the literary scholars who made particular use of this argument. Somewhat surprisingly, women literary scholars were especially quick to adopt this theme.

The sociologists queuing for a ticket to enter the prestigious institution could demonstrate their professional competence and their indispensability by focusing on the social and global conflicts characteristic of the subject. Inevitably, church representatives and religious dignitaries of the most varied kinds were chosen (albeit the selection of individuals was said to be 'a delicate matter').

There were bitter disagreements about whether to admit specialists in 'foreign' forms of love, experts on the early practices of the Kama Sutra or (a highly controversial topic) the tradition of free love in Islam. They had finally to make do with seats from which they might readily be ejected. Physicists and other scientists were disappointed to have their applications rejected. They failed to make any impression with their argument that reflecting on the 'physics of love' was indispensable. In contrast, and as a compromise, animal biologists were given access, since the sexual behaviour of both rats and lions formed part of their expertise. Indeed, in one institute the post of deputy chairman was filled by a scientist specializing in the sexual behaviour of lions (in order to strengthen the scientific credentials of the commission as a whole).

As detailed historical studies have shown, quarrels broke out in the Commission for Sustainable Love Ethics soon after its establishment. Two opposing camps gradually came into being. One camp based its position on the premise that salvation lay with distant love. The other side took the opposite view as its starting point, namely the assertion that salvation lay in nearby love. The Commission for Sustainable Love Ethics soon split into two factions in every country where it was represented, so that both a 'Distant-Love Commission' and a 'Nearby-Love Commission' came into being.

The advocates of distant love emphasized the deficiencies of nearby love. They had no difficulty in producing empirical evidence, which they summed up under the heading 'the coefficient of the stultifying effect of nearby love'. This played well in the media. According to their studies, couples who spent more than fifteen days per month together were four times more likely to split up than distant-love couples over the same period of time. One researcher summed up this finding in the succinct formula 'nearby love is a drag', a formula that doubtless owed something to his own experience. According to the central perception, in love relationships based on proximity there was a drastic diminution in the couple's willingness and ability to converse with each other. Such couples exchanged on average no more than 27.5 words a day. As the sociologists were at pains to stress, this was not due to any fault or failure on the part of the individuals concerned. It must rather be ascribed to the nature or, as the sociologists would say, the 'structure' of nearby love. The consequence of this near absence of communication was that eroticism, intimacy and sexuality would inevitably wither away. Surprisingly, even the experts on the sex life of lions were able to confirm this finding with the aid of a rather daring parallel argument and some impressive statistics.

The psychological, political and sociological therapies proposed by the commission dedicated to distant love covered a broad range of therapeutic techniques designed to immunize people against the debilitating symptoms of nearby love. Trade-union representatives spoke up in favour of what later became popularly known as 'ovulation leave', for which there was great demand. Catholic dignitaries seized the initiative by calling for ten free fertility treatments (using the frozen sperm of the male partner). Furthermore, couples separated by more than 500 kilometres were to be allowed to collect 'heart points' that would be valid on trains and planes.

An alliance of IT specialists and liberal sex researchers proposed to help rejuvenate the now ageing technology of Skyping by introducing a novel multi-sense TV screen that would make its users more seductive. The sex researchers devoted to the promotion of 'sexual realism' supported this hi-tech vision by suggesting ways in which the so-called practices of 'distant gratification', which were still in their infancy, might be brought to the point of 'orgasm at a distance'.

The commission decided unanimously that the emancipation of love from the shackles of nearby love should be encapsulated in the 'Ten Golden Rules of Distant Love'. As one commission member declared facetiously in the course of the debate: 'Nearby love spells the ruination of love.' And yet, according to the unanimous resolution of the Distant-Love Commission, what was at stake was not an absolute choice between love and the end of love, but a paradigm change from nearby love to distant love that was to be adopted by society as a whole.

The Nearby-Love Commission took the opposite line. It put the extremely high infidelity coefficient of distant love at the heart of its programme and supported it with a wealth of theoretically based and methodologically sound findings. According to these, couples who lived at a distance greater than 500 kilometres from each other or who were born in two different countries had an 'infidelity coefficient' 170.7 per cent greater than that of comparable nearby-love couples. A significant number of the commission's members referred to Sven Hillenkamp's book *The End of Love*, a work that had been translated into many languages. In a theoretically dazzling combination of behaviourist and utilitarian approaches, this book demonstrates that the flaws in distant love are insuperable. In the further course of its work, the Nearby-Love Commission backed up its arguments with increasingly detailed and rigorous studies. Its conclusions were summed up in the succinct formula: love and nearby love belong together by their very nature. All attempts to separate them are therefore doomed to failure.

It is important to note one critical reservation with regard to the nearby-love faction. It did not shy away from occasionally resorting to the general xenophobia that became so prevalent in times of globalization. Distant love was dismissed as a kind of multiculturalism; some even proclaimed the 'death of multicultural love'. Others called for a statutory national marriage monopoly and took Goethe's verse 'See, goodness lies so near' as the motto for their campaign.

The Nearby-Love Commission's recommendations were original, though frequently provocative and controversial. Internationally renowned sex experts, who in their labs had studied brain activity and dopamine emissions, as well as the blood supply and erectile function of the male sex organ, were forced to concede that their empirical findings confirmed the existence of the so-called stultifying effects of nearby love. These multidimensional studies arrived at eminently practicable proposals. They culminated in a plea for publicly financed feel-good hotels that would act as 'refuges from the everyday'. Their visions of a renaissance of nearby love included love massages on prescription, aphrodisiac foods, sex toys (with pensioner discounts), and so on. Admittedly, some of the proposals contained in their 'Ten Golden Rules of Nearby Love' provoked public outcries. One example was their call for 'masked sex' or 'lingerie instead of baggy trousers' (the opposing faction talked of pornography and misogyny). This contrasted with proposals that were universally welcomed, such as financial bonuses for nearby-love couples. The whole process culminated with businesses being dragged in and put under pressure. They were called on to promote mobility for professional couples and provide posts for couples in the same location in order to stem the tide of hostility towards nearby love characteristic of global capitalism.

Today, in December 2061, the Commission for Sustainable Love Ethics has been awarded the Nobel Peace Prize. According to the jury's citation, 'Our intention is to honour an outstanding historic achievement and an indispensable contribution to the development of humanity. The Commission for Sustainable Love Ethics, the representatives of the Commission for Distant Love and the Commission for Nearby Love have with their efforts laid the foundations for the most important love movement of the twenty-first century.'

References and Bibliography

Alberoni, Francesco (1983) *Verliebt sein und lieben: Revolution zu zweit*. Stuttgart: Deutsche Verlags-Anstalt.

Alibhai-Brown, Yasmin (2001) *Mixed Feelings: The Complex Lives of Mixed-Race Britons*. London: Women's Press.

Almeling, Rene (2010) 'Selling Genes, Selling Gender: Egg Agencies, Sperm Banks, and the Medical Market in Genetic Material', in Eileen Boris and Rhacel Salazar Parreñas (eds), *Intimate Labors: Cultures, Technologies, and the Politics of Care*. Stanford, CA: Stanford University Press: 63–77.

Anderson, Bridget (2007) 'A Very Private Business: Exploring the Demand for Migrant Domestic Workers', *European Journal of Women's Studies* 14(3): 247–64.

Appadurai, Arjun (1991) 'Global Ethnoscapes: Notes and Queries for a Transnational Anthropology', in Richard G. Fox (ed.), *Recapturing Anthropology: Working in the Present*. Santa Fe, NM: School of American Research Press: 48–65.

Autant, Claire (1995) 'La tradition au service des transitions: le mariage des jeunes Turcs dans l'immigration', *Migrants-Formation*, no. 101: 168–79.

Bade, Klaus J. (2000) *Europa in Bewegung: Migration vom späten 18. Jahrhundert bis zur Gegenwart*. Munich: C. H. Beck.

Bade, Klaus J., and Böhm, Andrea (2000) 'Fleißig, billig, illegal: Der Migrationsexperte Klaus Bade über die wirtschaftliche Bedeutung illegaler Einwanderer', *Die Zeit*, no. 27, 29 June.

Ballard, Roger (1990) 'Migration and Kinship: The Differential Effect of Marriage Rules on the Processes of Punjabi Migration to Britain', in Colin Clarke, Ceri Peach and Steven Vertovec (eds), *South Asians Overseas: Migration and Ethnicity*. Cambridge: Cambridge University Press: 219–49.

Ballard, Roger (2003) 'A Case of Capital-Rich Under-Development: The Paradoxical Consequences of Transnational Entrepreneurship from Mirpur', *Contributions to Indian Sociology* 37(1–2): 25–57.

Barbara, Augustin (1989) *Marriage across Frontiers*. Clevedon and Philadelphia: Multilingual Matters.

Battaglia, Santina (2000) 'Verhandeln über Identität: Kommunikativer Alltag von Menschen binationaler Abstammung', in Ellen Frieden-Blum, Klaudia Jacobs and Brigitte Wießmeier (eds), *Wer ist fremd? Ethnische Herkunft, Familie und Gesellschaft*. Opladen: Leske & Budrich: 183–202.

Bauman, Zygmunt (2009) 'Seeking in Modern Athens an Answer to the Ancient Jerusalem Question,' *Theory, Culture & Society* 26(1): 71–91.

Bauman, Zygmunt (2010) 'Conclusion: The Triple Challenge', in Mark Davis and Keith Tester (eds), *Bauman's Challenge: Sociological Issues for the 21st Century*. Basingstoke and New York: Palgrave Macmillan: 200–5.

Baumann, Gerd (1996) *Contesting Culture: Discourses of Identity in Multi-Ethnic London*. Cambridge: Cambridge University Press.

Baumann, Martin (2002) 'Migrant Settlement, Religion and Phases of Diaspora – Exemplified by Hindu Traditions Stepping on European Shores', *Migration: A European Journal of International Migrations and Ethnic Relations*, nos. 33–5: 93–117.

Beck, Ulrich (1986) *Risikogesellschaft: Auf dem Weg in eine andere Moderne*. Frankfurt am Main: Suhrkamp; Eng. trans. (1992), *Risk Society: Towards a New Modernity*, trans. Mark Ritter. London and Newbury Park, CA: Sage.

Beck, Ulrich (1996) *The Reinvention of Politics: Rethinking Modernity in the Global Social Order*, trans. Mark Ritter. Cambridge: Polity.

Beck, Ulrich (2005) *Power in the Global Age: A New Global Political Economy*, trans. Kathleen Cross. Cambridge: Polity.

Beck, Ulrich (2006) *The Cosmopolitan Vision*, trans. Ciaran Cronin. Cambridge: Polity.

Beck, Ulrich (2010) *A God of One's Own: Religion's Capacity for Peace and Potential for Violence*, trans. Rodney Livingstone. Cambridge: Polity.

Beck, Ulrich (2012) *Twenty Observations on a World in Turmoil*, trans. Ciaran Cronin. Cambridge: Polity.

Beck, Ulrich, and Beck-Gernsheim, Elisabeth (1995) *The Normal Chaos of Love*, trans. Mark Ritter and Jane Wiebel. Cambridge: Polity.

Beck, Ulrich, and Beck-Gernsheim, Elisabeth (2010) 'A Passage to Hope: Migration and the Need for a Cosmopolitan Turn in Family Research', *Journal of Family Theory & Review* 2(4): 401–14.

Beck, Ulrich, and Grande, Edgar (2010) 'Varieties of Second Modernity: The Cosmopolitan Turn in Social and Political Theory and Research', in Ulrich Beck and Edgar Grande (eds), *Varieties of Second Modernity: Extra-European and European Experiences and Perspectives*, *British Journal of Sociology* 61(3): 409–43 [special issue].

Beck, Ulrich, and Poferl, Angelika (eds) (2010) *Große Armut, großer Reichtum: Zur Transnationalisierung sozialer Ungleichheit*. Berlin: Suhrkamp.

Beck, Ulrich, Bonß, Wolfgang, and Lau, Christoph (2003) 'The Theory of Reflexive Modernization: Problematic, Hypotheses and Research Programme', *Theory, Culture & Society* 20(2): 1–33.

Beck, Ulrich, Bonß, Wolfgang, and Lau, Christoph (2005) 'Second Modernity as a Research Agenda: Theoretical and Empirical Explorations in the "Meta-Change" of Modern Society', *British Journal of Sociology* 56(4): 525–57.

Beck, Ulrich, Giddens, Anthony, and Lash, Scott (1994) *Reflexive Modernization: Politics, Tradition and Aesthetics in the Modern Social Order.* Cambridge: Polity.

Beck-Gernsheim, Elisabeth (2006) 'Türkische Bräute und die Migrationsdebatte in Deutschland', *Aus Politik und Zeitgeschichte* 1–2: 32–7.

Beck-Gernsheim, Elisabeth (2007a) 'Transnational Lives, Transnational Marriages: A Review of the Evidence from Migrant Communities in Europe', *Global Networks* 7(3): 271–88.

Beck-Gernsheim, Elisabeth (2007b) *Wir und die Anderen: Kopftuch, Zwangsheirat und andere Mißverständnisse.* Frankfurt am Main: Suhrkamp.

Beck-Gernsheim, Elisabeth (2008) *Die Kinderfrage heute: Über Frauenleben, Geburtenrückgang und Kinderwunsch.* Munich: C. H. Beck.

Beck-Gernsheim, Elisabeth (2009) 'Ferngemeinschaften: Familien in einer sich globalisierenden Welt', in Günter Burkart (ed.), *Zukunft der Familie: Prognosen und Szenarien, Zeitschrift für Familienforschung*, special issue no. 6: 93–110.

Bélanger, Danièle, and Linh, Tran Giang (2011) 'The Impact of Transnational Migration on Gender and Marriage in Sending Communities of Vietnam', *Current Sociology* 59(1): 59–77.

Berger, Peter L. (1963) *Invitation to Sociology: A Humanistic Perspective.* Garden City, NY: Doubleday.

Bethge, Philip (2001) 'Das ist ein Riesengeschäft: Der Präsident der Bundesärztekammer Jörg-Dietrich Hoppe über Leihmütter, Embryonenadoption und die Motive der Babymacher', *Der Spiegel* no. 26: 210–11.

Bielicki, Jan (2006) 'Die Wünsche des Standesamtes', *Süddeutsche Zeitung*, 9 January: 55.

Bijl, R. V., Zorlu, A., van Rijn, A. S., Jennissen, R. P. W., and Blom, M. (2005) *The Integration Monitor, 2005: The Social Integration of Migrants Monitored Over Time: Trend and Cohort Analyses.* The Hague: Centraal Bureau voor de Statistiek; available at: http://english.wodc.nl/onderzoeksdatabase/integratiekaart-monitoring-integratie.aspx.

Blackburn, Nicky (2004) 'I Will Become a Mother at Any Cost', *The Times*, 19 July.

Bledsoe, Caroline H. (2004) 'Reproduction at the Margins: Migration and Legitimacy in the New Europe', *Demographic Research*, Special Collection 3: 87–116.

BMFSFJ (Bundesministerium für Familie, Senioren, Frauen und Jugend) (ed.) (2006) *Familie zwischen Flexibilität und Verlässlichkeit: Perspektiven für eine lebenslaufbezogene Familienpolitik: Siebter Familienbericht*, available

at: www.bmfsfj.de/doku/Publikationen/familienbericht/download/
familienbericht_gesamt.pdf.

Böcker, Anita (1994) 'Chain Migration over Legally Closed Borders: Settled
Migrants as Bridgeheads and Gatekeepers', *Netherlands Journal of the
Social Sciences* 30(2): 87–106.

Bonney, Claire (1993) 'Das Antizipierte-Reaktion-Syndrom – oder wie es
immer anders kam', in Dianne Dicks (ed.), *Amors wilde Pfeile: Liebes- und
Ehegeschichten zwischen den Kulturen*. Munich: C. H. Beck: 105–11.

Borscheid, Peter (1986) 'Romantic Love or Material Interest: Choosing
Partners in Nineteenth-Century Germany', *Journal of Family History*
11(2): 157–68.

Bozic, Ivo (2009) 'Sag einfach "ne" ', *Jungle World* no. 42, 15 October.

Brill, Klaus (2010) 'Kinderland ist abgebrannt', *Süddeutsche Zeitung*, 2
September: 3.

Brown, Gordon (2008) 'Why I Believe Stem Cell Researchers Deserve our
Backing', *The Observer*, 18 May.

Brunold, Georg, Hart, Klaus, and Hörst, R. Kyle (1999) *Fernstenliebe:
Ehen zwischen den Kontinenten: Drei Berichte*. Frankfurt am Main:
Eichborn.

Bukow, Wolf-Dietrich, and Llaryora, Roberto (1988) *Mitbürger aus der
Fremde: Soziogenese ethnischer Minderheiten*. Opladen: Westdeutscher
Verlag.

Burghardt, Peter, et al. (2010) 'Wir brauchen sie: Aus der ganzen Welt
kommen Frauen zu uns, um hier als Mädchen für alles zu arbeiten . . .
Portrait einer weltweiten Industrie, der Nanny-Industrie', *Süddeutsche
Zeitung-Magazin*, 15 October: 42–55.

Cheever, Susan (2003) 'The Nanny Dilemma', in Barbara Ehrenreich and
Arlie Russell Hochschild (eds), *Global Woman: Nannies, Maids, and Sex
Workers in the New Economy*. London: Granta: 31–8.

Clark, Katrina (2006) 'My Father was an Anonymous Sperm Donor',
Washington Post, 17 December.

Conde, Carlos H. (2008) 'Generation Left Behind by Filipino Migrant
Workers', *New York Times*, 23 December.

Connell, R. W. (1995) *Masculinities*. Berkeley: University of California Press.

Constable, Nicole (2003) *Romance on a Global Stage: Pen Pals, Virtual
Ethnography and 'Mail Order' Marriages*. Berkeley: University of
California Press.

Constable, Nicole (2005) 'Introduction: Cross-Border Marriages, Gendered
Mobility, and Global Hypergamy', in Constable (ed.), *Cross-Border Marriages: Gender and Mobility in Transnational Asia*. Philadelphia: University of Pennsylvania Press: 1–16.

Croft, Jane, and Peel, Michael (2010) 'Divorce Capital', *Financial Times*,
5 November.

Darvishpour, Mehrdad (2002) 'Immigrant Women Challenge the Role of
Men: How the Changing Power Relationship within Iranian Families in
Sweden Intensifies Family Conflicts after Immigration', *Journal of Com-
parative Family Studies* 33(2): 271–96.

Deutsche Shell (ed.) (2000) *Jugend 2000*. Shell Jugendstudie, 13. Opladen: Leske & Budrich.

Dicks, Dianne (ed.) (1993) *Amors wilde Pfeile: Liebes- und Ehegeschichten zwischen den Kulturen*. Munich: C. H. Beck.

Dürnberger, Andrea (2011) 'Die Verteilung elterlicher Aufgaben in lesbischen Partnerschaften', in Marina Rupp (ed.), *Partnerschaft und Elternschaft bei gleichgeschlechtlichen Paaren: Verbreitung, Institutionalisierung und Alltagsgestaltung*. Opladen and Farmington Hills, MI: Barbara Budrich: 147–66.

Ehrenreich, Barbara, and Hochschild, Arlie Russell (eds) (2003) *Global Woman: Nannies, Maids, and Sex Workers in the New Economy*. London: Granta.

Elschenbroich, Donata (1988) 'Eine Familie – zwei Kulturen: Deutsch-ausländische Familien', in Deutsches Jugendinstitut (ed.), *Wie geht's der Familie? Ein Handbuch zur Situation der Familien heute*. Munich: Kösel: 363–70.

Esteves, Vasco (1993) 'Be-Rührende Erfahrungen', in Dianne Dicks (ed.), *Amors Wilde Pfeile: Liebes- und Ehegeschichten zwischen den Kulturen*. Munich: C. H. Beck: 183–8.

Ettelson, Jamie, and Ritter, Uwe (1998) 'Nicht ganz koscher? Die Geschichte einer jüdisch-christlich, amerikanisch-deutschen Beziehung', in Micha Brumlik (ed.), *Zuhause, keine Heimat? Junge Juden und ihre Zukunft in Deutschland*. Gerlingen: Bleicher: 76–87.

Fadiman, Anne (1997) *The Spirit Catches You and You Fall Down: A Hmong Child, Her American Doctors, and the Collision of Two Cultures*. New York: Farrar, Straus & Giroux.

Flandrin, Jean-Louis (1984) 'Das Geschlechterleben der Eheleute in der alten Gesellschaft: Von der kirchlichen Lehre zum realen Verhalten', in Philippe Ariès and André Béjin (eds), *Die Masken des Begehrens und die Metamorphosen der Sinnlichkeit: Zur Geschichte der Sexualität im Abendland*. Frankfurt am Main: S. Fischer: 147–64.

Fleischer, Annett (2007) 'Family, Obligations, and Migration: The Role of Kinship in Cameroon', *Demographic Research* 16: 413–40.

Freymeyer, Karin, and Otzelberger, Manfred (2000) *In der Ferne so nah: Lust und Last der Wochenendbeziehungen*. Berlin: Links.

Gamburd, Michele Ruth (2000) *The Kitchen Spoon's Handle: Transnationalism and Sri Lanka's Migrant Housemaids*. Ithaca, NY, and London: Cornell University Press.

Garantiert heiratswillig (1993) Documentary film for ZDF, dir. Elke Wendt-Kummer.

Gentleman, Amelia (2008) 'Foreign Couples Turn to India for Surrogate Mothers', *New York Times*, 4 March.

Giddens, Anthony (1992) *The Transformation of Intimacy: Sexuality, Love and Eroticism in Modern Societies*. Cambridge: Polity.

Gilbert, Elizabeth (2010) *Committed: A Sceptic Makes Peace with Marriage*. London and New York: Bloomsbury.

Goldring, Luin (1997) 'Power and Status in Transnational Spaces', in Ludger Pries (ed.), *Transnationale Migration*. Baden-Baden: Nomos: 179–95.

Google Baby (2009) Israeli documentary film, dir. Zippi Brand Frank.

Gorelik, Lena (2004) *Meine weißen Nächte*. Munich: Schirmer Graf.

Greenawalt, Lindsay (2008) 'Confessions of a Cryokid', internet blog, 15 March.

Gümen, Sedef (2000) 'Soziale Identifikation und Vergleichsprozesse von Frauen', in Leonie Herwartz-Emden (ed.), *Einwandererfamilien: Geschlechterverhältnisse, Erziehung und Akkulturation*. Osnabrück: Universitätsverlag Rasch: 325–50.

Habermas, Jürgen (1998) *The Inclusion of the Other*, trans. Ciaran Cronin and Pablo De Greiff. Cambridge: Polity.

Habermas, Jürgen (2001) *Die Zukunft der menschlichen Natur: Auf dem Weg zu einer liberalen Eugenik?* Frankfurt am Main: Suhrkamp.

Han, Petrus (2003) *Frauen und Migration: Strukturelle Bedingungen, Fakten und soziale Folgen der Frauenmigration*. Stuttgart: Lucius & Lucius.

Hanisch, Carol (1969) 'The Personal is Political', in Shulamith Firestone and Anne Koedt (eds) (1970), *Notes from the Second Year: Women's Liberation*. New York: Radical Feminism.

Hardach-Pinke, Irene (1988) *Interkulturelle Lebenswelten: Deutsch-japanische Ehen in Japan*. Frankfurt am Main and New York: Campus.

Harris, Scott R. (2008) 'What Is Family Diversity? Objective and Interpretive Approaches', *Journal of Family Issues* 29(11): 1407–25.

Hecht-El Minshawi, Béatrice (1990) *'Wir suchen, wovon wir träumen': Studie über deutsch-ausländische Paare*. Frankfurt am Main: Nexus.

Hecht-El Minshawi, Béatrice (1992) *Zwei Welten, eine Liebe: Leben mit Partnern aus anderen Kulturen*. Reinbek bei Hamburg: Rowohlt.

Heine-Wiedenmann, Dagmar, and Ackermann, Lea (1992) *Umfeld und Ausmaß des Menschenhandels mit ausländischen Mädchen und Frauen*. Stuttgart: W. Kohlhammer.

Hellner, Uwe (1995) 'Der schönste Tag im Leben, oder: Wie heirate ich eine Ausländerin?', *Die Tageszeitung*, 13 November: 20.

Herbert, Ulrich (2003) *Geschichte der Ausländerpolitik in Deutschland: Saisonarbeiter, Zwangsarbeiter, Gastarbeiter, Flüchtlinge*. Bonn: Bundeszentrale für Politische Bildung.

Heringer, Hans Jürgen (2007) *Interkulturelle Kommunikation – Grundlagen und Konzepte*. 2nd rev. edn, Tübingen and Basel: Francke.

Hetrodt, Ewald (2007) 'Mutter mit 64: Nur die Eltern sind glücklich', *Frankfurter Allgemeine Zeitung*, 4 December: 58.

Hey, Valerie (1997) *The Company She Keeps: An Ethnography of Girls' Friendship*. Buckingham and Bristol: Open University Press.

Hierländer, Jeannine (2008) 'Medizin-Tourismus: Befruchtende Reisen nach Indien', *Die Presse*, 6 November.

Hillenkamp, Sven (2009) *Das Ende der Liebe: Gefühle im Zeitalter unendlicher Freiheit*. Stuttgart: Klett-Cotta.

Hochschild, Arlie Russell (1975) 'Inside the Clockwork of Male Careers', in Florence Howe (ed.), *Women and the Power to Change*. New York: McGraw-Hill: 47–80.

Hochschild, Arlie Russell (2000) 'Global Care Chains and Emotional Surplus Value', in Will Hutton and Anthony Giddens (eds), *On the Edge: Living with Global Capitalism*. London: Jonathan Cape: 130–46.

Hochschild, Arlie Russell (2003) 'Love and Gold', in Barbara Ehrenreich and Arlie Russell Hochschild (eds), *Global Woman: Nannies, Maids, and Sex Workers in the New Economy*. London: Granta: 15–30.

Hochschild, Arlie Russell (2009) 'Childbirth at the Global Crossroads', *American Prospect*, 5 October.

Hochschild, Arlie Russell, and Machung, Anne (1990) *Der 48-Stunden-Tag: Wege aus dem Dilemma berufstätiger Eltern*. Vienna and Darmstadt: Zsolnay.

Hodson, David, and Thomas, Ann (2009) *When Cupid's Arrow Crosses National Boundaries: A Guide for International Families*. London: International Family Law Group.

Hoffman, Eva (1989) *Lost in Translation*. London: Heinemann.

Hondagneu-Sotelo, Pierrette (1994) *Gendered Transitions: Mexican Experiences of Immigration*. Berkeley: University of California Press.

Hondagneu-Sotelo, Pierrette (2001) *Domestica: Immigrant Workers Caring in the Shadows of Affluence*. Berkeley: University of California Press.

Hondagneu-Sotelo, Pierrette, and Avila, Ernestine (1997) ' "I'M HERE, BUT I'M THERE": The Meanings of Latina Transnational Motherhood', *Gender & Society* 11(5): 548–71.

Honig, Elizabeth Alice (2005) 'Phantom Lives, Narratives of Possibility', in Toby Alice Volkman (ed.), *Cultures of Transnational Adoption*. Durham, NC, and London: Duke University Press.

Illouz, Eva (2012) *Why Love Hurts: A Sociological Explanation*. Cambridge: Polity.

Inhorn, Marcia C. (2003) *Local Babies, Global Science: Gender, Religion and In Vitro Fertilization in Egypt*. New York and London: Routledge.

Inhorn, Marcia C. (2006) 'Making Muslim Babies: IVF and Gamete Donation in Sunni Versus Shi'a Islam', *Culture, Medicine and Psychiatry* 30(4): 427–50.

Jamieson, Lynn (1999) 'Intimacy Transformed? A Critical Look at the "Pure Relationship" ', *Sociology* 33(3): 477–94.

Jensen, An-Magritt (2008) 'Thai Women in the Arctic North', lecture given at the conference *Gender at the Interface of the Global and the Local*, Kunming, China, 4–7 November.

Jeska, Andrea (2008) 'Mein Bauch, dein Kind: Geschäfte mit Leihmüttern', *Brigitte* 25: 120–7.

Jonas, Hans (1985) *Technik, Medizin und Ethik: Zur Praxis des Prinzips Verantwortung*. Frankfurt am Main: Insel.

Joshi, Mary Sissons, and Krishna, Meena (1998) 'English and North American Daughters-in-Law in the Hindu Joint Family', in Rosemary Breger and

Rosanna Hill (eds), *Cross-Cultural Marriage: Identity and Choice*. Oxford and New York: Berg: 171–92.

Kalpagam, U. (2008) ' "America *Varan*" Marriages among Tamil Brahmans: Preferences, Strategies and Outcomes', in Rajni Palriwala and Patricia Uberoi (eds), *Marriage, Migration, and Gender*. Thousand Oaks, CA: Sage: 98–124.

Kant, Immanuel ([1784] 1991) 'Idea for a Universal History with a Cosmopolitan Purpose', in Kant, *Political Writings*, ed. H. S. Reiss, trans. H. B. Nisbet. Cambridge: Cambridge University Press: 41–53.

Kästner, Erich (1990) *Fabian: The Story of a Moralist*, trans. R. S. Livingstone. London: Libris.

Katz, Ilan (1996) *The Construction of Racial Identity in Children of Mixed Parentage: Mixed Metaphors*. London and Bristol, PA: Kingsley.

Kaufmann, Jean-Claude (1994) *Schmutzige Wäsche: Zur ehelichen Konstruktion von Alltag*. Konstanz: Universitätsverlag Konstanz.

Kelek, Necla (2005) *Die fremde Braut: Ein Bericht aus dem Inneren des türkischen Lebens in Deutschland*. Cologne: Kiepenheuer & Witsch.

Khatib-Chahidi, Jane, Hill, Rosanna, and Paton, Renée (1998) 'Chance, Choice and Circumstance: A Study of Women in Cross-Cultural Marriages', in Rosemary Breger and Rosanna Hill (eds), *Cross-Cultural Marriage: Identity and Choice*. Oxford and New York: Berg: 49–66.

Kibria, Nazli (1993) *Family Tightrope: The Changing Lives of Vietnamese Americans*. Princeton, NJ, and Chichester: Princeton University Press.

Kittay, Eva Feder (2008) 'The Global Heart Transplant and Caring across National Boundaries', *Southern Journal of Philosophy* 46(Supplement): 138–65.

Klein, Thomas (2000) 'Binationale Partnerwahl – Theoretische und empirische Analysen zur familialen Integration von Ausländern in der Bundesrepublik', in Sachverständigenkommission 6. Familienbericht (ed.), *Familien ausländischer Herkunft in Deutschland: Empirische Beiträge zur Familienentwicklung und Akkulturation: Materialien zum 6. Familienbericht*, vol. 1. Opladen: Leske & Budrich: 303–46.

Klein, Thomas (2001) 'Intermarriages between Germans and Foreigners in Germany', *Journal of Comparative Family Studies* 32(3): 325–46.

Knecht Oti-Amoako, Andrea (ed.) (1995) *Binationale Familien*, Bulletin no. 58, Interessengemeinschaft Binational.

Kofman, Eleonore (2004) 'Family-Related Migration: A Critical Review of European Studies', *Journal of Ethnic and Migration Studies* 30(2): 243–62.

Kurdek, Lawrence A. (2007) 'The Allocation of Household Labor by Parents in Gay and Lesbian Couples', *Journal of Family Issues* 28(1): 132–48.

Lacayo, Richard (1987) 'Whose Child Is This? Baby M. and the Agonizing Dilemma of Surrogate Motherhood', *Time*, 19 January.

Lamura, Giovanni, Melchiorre, Maria Gabriella, Principi, Andrea, Chiatti, Carlo, Quattrini, Sabrina, and Lucchetti, Maria (2009) *Migrant Work for Elder Care: Trends and Developments in Italy*. Report, IAGG World Congress, Paris, 5–9 July.

Lasch, Christopher (1977) *Haven in a Heartless World: The Family Besieged*. New York: Basic Books.

Lash, Scott, and Urry, John (2002) *Economies of Signs & Space*. Thousand Oaks, CA, and London: Sage.

Lauser, Andrea (2004) 'Ein guter Mann ist harte Arbeit: Eine ethnographische Studie zu philippinischen Heiratsmigrantinnen'. Bielefeld: transcript.

Lazarre, Jane (1996) *Beyond the Whiteness of Whiteness: Memoir of a White Mother of Black Sons*. Durham, NC, and London: Duke University Press.

Lee, Sharon M., and Edmonston, Barry (2005) 'New Marriages, New Families: US Racial and Hispanic Intermarriage', *Population Bulletin* 60(2): 1–36.

Levy, Daniel, and Sznaider, Natan (2010) *Human Rights and Memory*. University Park, PA: Pennsylvania State University Press.

Lewycka, Marina (2005) *A Short History of Tractors in Ukrainian*. London: Viking.

Lievens, John (1999) 'Family-Forming Migration from Turkey and Morocco to Belgium: The Demand for Marriage Partners from the Countries of Origin', *International Migration Review* 33(3): 717–44.

Lu, Melody Chia-wen (2008) 'Commercially Arranged Marriage Migration: Case Studies of Cross-Border Marriages in Taiwan', in Rajni Palriwala and Patricia Uberoi (eds), *Marriage, Migration, and Gender*. Thousand Oaks, CA: Sage: 125–51.

Lucassen, Leo, and Laarman, Charlotte (2009) 'Immigration, Intermarriage and the Changing Face of Europe in the Post War Period', *History of the Family* 14(1): 52–68.

Luhmann, Niklas (1986) *Love as Passion: The Codification of Intimacy*, trans. Jeremy Gaines and Doris L. Jones. Cambridge: Polity.

Lutz, Helma (2007) 'Sprich (nicht) drüber – Fürsorgearbeit von Migrantinnen in deutschen Privathaushalten', *WSI-Mitteilungen*, no. 10: 554–60.

Lyon, Dawn (2006) 'The Organization of Care Work in Italy: Gender and Migrant Labor in the New Economy', *Indiana Journal of Global Legal Studies* 13(1): 207–24.

Madianou, Mirca (2012) 'Migration and the Accentuated Ambivalence of Motherhood: The Role of ICTs in Filipino Transnational Families', *Global Networks* 12(3): 277–95.

Madianou, Mirca, and Miller, Daniel (2011) *Migration and New Media: Transnational Families and Polymedia*. London and New York: Routledge.

Mahmoody, Betty (1987) *Not Without My Daughter*. New York: St Martin's Press.

Maletzke, Gerhard (1996) *Interkulturelle Kommunikation: Zur Interaktion zwischen Menschen verschiedener Kulturen*. Opladen: Westdeutscher Verlag.

Manetsch, Rachel (2008) 'Hürdenlauf jüdische Heirat: Begleittext "Heiraten in Israel" ', *Tachles* 8(39/40), 26 September.

Mann, Thomas ([1924] 1930) *Buddenbrooks: The Decline of a Family*, trans. H. T. Lowe-Porter. London: Martin Secker.

Mayer, Egon (1985) *Love & Tradition: Marriage between Jews and Christians*. New York and London: Plenum Press.

Meier, Marion (2004) 'Das Gericht prüfte und mir blieb nur das Warten', *Süddeutsche Zeitung Magazin*, 7 May: 54.

Merton, Robert K. ([1941] 1976) 'Intermarriage and the Social Structure', in Merton, *Sociological Ambivalence and Other Essays*. New York: Free Press; London: Collier Macmillan: 217–50.

Metz, Johanna (2007) 'Illegale Einwanderer in Deutschland: Die große Scheinheiligkeit', *Das Parlament*, 15 January.

Migration und Bevölkerung, December 2008.

Migration und Bevölkerung, January 2011; available at: www.bpb.de/gesellschaft/migration/dossier-migration/56934/mub-1-2011.

Mitterauer, Michael, and Sieder, Reinhard (1980) *Vom Patriarchat zur Partnerschaft: Zum Strukturwandel der Familie*. Munich: C. H. Beck.

Miyaguchi, Christine (1993) 'Falsch verbunden', in Dianne Dicks (ed.), *Amors wilde Pfeile: Liebes- und Ehegeschichten zwischen den Kulturen*. Munich: C. H. Beck: 172–6.

Montaigne, Michel de (1908) 'Of Moderation', trans. Charles Cotton, available at: www.readbookonline.net/readOnLine/%2022361/.

Moreno, Juan (2010) '"Ich lösche mein Postfach für dich": Der endlose Weg zur richtigen Frau', *Der Spiegel*, 8 November: 79–85.

Morgan, David H. J. (1996) *Family Connections: An Introduction to Family Studies*. Cambridge: Polity.

Munoz, Marie-Claude (1999) 'Epouser au pays, vivre en France', *Revue Européenne de Migrations Internationales* 25(3):101–23.

Nava, Mica (1997) 'Difference and Desire: Vienna, Antifascism and Jews in the Interwar English Imagination', lecture given at the Symposium 'Metropole Wien', Vienna (unpublished manuscript).

Nazario, Sonia (2007) *Enrique's Journey: The Story of a Boy's Dangerous Odyssey to Reunite with his Mother*. New York: Random House.

Niesner, Elvira, Anonuevo, Estrella, Aparicio, Marta, and Sonsiengchai-Fenzl, Petchara (1997) *Ein Traum vom besseren Leben: Migrantinnenerfahrungen, soziale Unterstützung und neue Strategien gegen Frauenhandel*. Opladen: Leske & Budrich.

Nottmeyer, Olga K. (2009) 'Wedding Bells are Ringing: Increasing Rates of Intermarriage in Germany', Migration Information Source, www.migrationinformation.org/Feature/display.cfm?ID=744.

Oksaar, Els (1996) 'Vom Verstehen und Mißverstehen im Kulturkontakt – Babylon in Europa', in Klaus J. Bade (ed.), *Die multikulturelle Herausforderung: Menschen über Grenzen – Grenzen über Menschen*. Munich: C. H. Beck: 206–29.

Ong, Aihwa (2005) *Flexible Staatsbürgerschaften: Die kulturelle Logik von Transnationalität*. Frankfurt am Main: Suhrkamp.

Onishi, Norimitsu (2007) 'Marriage Brokers in Vietnam Cater to S. Korean Bachelors', *International Herald Tribune*, 21 February.

Palriwala, Rajni, and Uberoi, Patricia (2008) 'Exploring the Links: Gender Issues in Marriage and Migration', in Palriwala and Uberoi (eds), *Marriage, Migration, and Gender*. Thousand Oaks, CA: Sage: 23–62.

Pande, Amrita (2010) 'Commercial Surrogacy in India: Manufacturing a Perfect Mother-Worker', *Signs: Journal of Women in Culture and Society* 35(4): 969–92.

Pandey, Heidemarie (1988) *Zwei Kulturen – eine Familie: Das Beispiel deutsch-indischer Eltern und ihrer Kinder*. Frankfurt am Main: Verlag für Interkulturelle Kommunikation.

Parreñas, Rhacel Salazar (2001) *Servants of Globalization: Women, Migration and Domestic Work*. Stanford, CA: Stanford University Press.

Parreñas, Rhacel Salazar (2003) 'The Care Crisis in the Philippines: Children and Transnational Families in the New Global Economy', in Barbara Ehrenreich and Arlie Russell Hochschild (eds), *Global Woman: Nannies, Maids, and Sex Workers in the New Economy*. London: Granta: 39–54.

Parreñas, Rhacel Salazar (2005a) *Children of Global Migration: Transnational Families and Gendered Woes*. Stanford, CA: Stanford University Press.

Parreñas, Rhacel Salazar (2005b) 'Long Distance Intimacy: Class, Gender and Intergenerational Relations between Mothers and Children in Filipino Transnational Families', *Global Networks* 5(4): 317–36.

Peterson, Elin (2007) 'The Invisible Carers: Framing Domestic Work(ers) in Gender Equality Policies in Spain', *European Journal of Women's Studies* 14(3): 265–80.

Pries, Ludger (1996) 'Transnationale Soziale Räume: Theoretisch-empirische Skizze am Beispiel der Arbeitswanderungen Mexico – USA', *Zeitschrift für Soziologie* 25(6): 456–72.

Pyke, Karen (2004) 'Immigrant Families in the US', in Jacqueline Scott, Judith Treas and Martin Richards (eds), *The Blackwell Companion to the Sociology of Families*. Oxford: Blackwell: 253–69.

Refsing, Kirsten (1998) 'Gender Identity and Gender Role Patterns in Cross-Cultural Marriages: The Japanese–Danish Case', in Rosemary Breger and Rosanna Hill (eds), *Cross-Cultural Marriage: Identity and Choice*. Oxford and New York: Berg: 193–208.

Reniers, Georges (2001) 'The Post-Migration Survival of Traditional Marriage Patterns: Consanguineous Marriages among Turks and Moroccans in Belgium', *Journal of Comparative Family Studies* 32(1): 21–45.

Rerrich, Maria S. (1993) 'Gemeinsame Lebensführung: Wie Berufstätige einen Alltag mit ihren Familien herstellen', in Karin Jurczyk and Maria S. Rerrich (eds), *Die Arbeit des Alltags: Beiträge zu einer Soziologie der alltäglichen Lebensführung*. Freiburg am Breisgau: Lambertus: 310–33.

Rerrich, Maria S. (2012) 'Migration macht Schule: Herausforderungen für Care in einer rumänischen Gemeinde', *Mittelweg* 36(October/November): 73–92.

Ritter, Mikkel (2010) 'Welfare-State Nomads: Pakistani Marriage Migrants in the Borderlands of Sweden and Denmark', unpublished manuscript.

Roloff, Juliane (1998) 'Eheschließungen und Ehescheidungen von und mit Ausländern in Deutschland', *Zeitschrift für Bevölkerungswissenschaft* 23(3): 319–34.

Romano, Dugan (1988) *Intercultural Marriage: Promises & Pitfalls*. Yarmouth: Intercultural Press.

Rosenbaum, Heidi (1982) *Formen der Familie: Untersuchungen zum Zusammenhang von Familienverhältnissen, Sozialstruktur und sozialem Wandel in der deutschen Gesellschaft des 19. Jahrhunderts*. Frankfurt am Main: Suhrkamp.

Rosenblatt, Paul C., Karis, Terri A., and Powell, Richard R. (1995) *Multiracial Couples: Black & White Voices*. Thousand Oaks, CA, and London: Sage.

Rupp, Marina (ed.) (2009) *Die Lebenssituation von Kindern in gleichgeschlechtlichen Partnerschaften*. Cologne: Bundesanzeiger.

Said, Edward W. (1978) *Orientalism*. New York: Pantheon.

Sassen, Saskia (2003) 'Global Cities and Survival Circuits', in Barbara Ehrenreich and Arlie Russell Hochschild (eds), *Global Woman: Nannies, Maids, and Sex Workers in the New Economy*. London: Granta: 254–74.

Scheper-Hughes, Nancy (2005) 'The Last Commodity: Post-Human Ethics and the Global Traffic in "Fresh" Organs', in Aihwa Ong and Stephen J. Collier (eds), *Global Assemblages: Technology, Politics and Ethics as Anthropological Problems*. Oxford and Malden, MA: Blackwell: 145–67.

Schneider, Susan Weidman (1989) *Intermarriage: The Challenge of Living with Differences between Christians and Jews*. New York: Free Press.

Schröder, Gerhard (2000) 'Der neue Mensch: Beitrag zur Gentechnik von Bundeskanzler Gerhard Schröder für die Wochenzeitung *Die Woche*', *Die Woche*, 20 December.

Schröder, Gerhard (2001) 'Zur bioethischen Debatte', *Die Zeit*, no. 31, 26 July.

Seibt, Gustav (2011) 'Menschenskinder', *Süddeutsche Zeitung*, 26 May: 3.

Sennett, Richard (1998) *The Corrosion of Character*. New York and London: W. W. Norton.

Shaw, Alison (2001) 'Kinship, Cultural Preference and Immigration: Consanguineous Marriage among British Pakistanis', *Journal of the Royal Anthropological Institute* 7(2): 315–34.

Shaw, Alison (2004) 'Immigrant Families in the UK', in Jacqueline Scott, Judith Treas and Martin Richards (eds), *The Blackwell Companion to the Sociology of Families*. Oxford: Blackwell: 270–85.

Shim, Young-Hee (2008) 'Transnational Marriages in Korea: Trends, Issues, and Adaption Process', *Gender & Society* [South Korea] 7(2): 45–90.

Shim, Young-Hee, and Han, Sang-Jin (2010) 'Family-Oriented Individualization and Second Modernity', *Soziale Welt* 61(3–4): 237–55.

Shorter, Edward (1976) *The Making of the Modern Family*. London: Collins.

Simmel, Georg (1908) 'Exkurs über den Fremden', in *Simmel: Soziologie: Untersuchungen über die Formen der Vergesellschaftung*. Berlin: Duncker & Humblot: 509–12.

Singh, Lea (2009) 'A Creation Myth for the 21st Century', MercatorNet, 9 January, www.mercatornet.com/articles/view/a_creation_myth_for_the _21st_century/.

Sökefeld, Martin (ed.) (2004) 'Jenseits des Paradigmas kultureller Differenz: Neue Perspektiven auf Einwanderer aus der Türkei'. Bielefeld: transcript.

Sollors, Werner (1986) *Beyond Ethnicity: Consent and Descent in American Culture*. Oxford and New York: Oxford University Press.

Sollors, Werner (1997) *Neither Black nor White yet Both: Thematic Explorations of Interracial Literature*. Oxford and New York: Oxford University Press.

Spickard, Paul R. (1989) *Mixed Blood: Intermarriage and Ethnic Identity in Twentieth-Century America*. Madison: University of Wisconsin Press.

Spring, Michelle (1998) *Running for Shelter*. London: Orion.

Stone, Lawrence (1979) *The Family, Sex and Marriage in England, 1500–1800*. New York: Penguin.

Straßburger, Gaby (1999a) ' "Er kann deutsch und kennt sich hier aus": Zur Partnerwahl der zweiten Migrantengeneration türkischer Herkunft', in Gerdien Jonker (ed.), *Kern und Rand: Religiöse Minderheiten aus der Türkei in Deutschland*. Berlin: Das Arabische Buch: 147–67.

Straßburger, Gaby (1999b) 'Eheschließungen der türkischen Bevölkerung in Deutschland', *Migration und Bevölkerung* no. 6(August): 3.

Strauß, Botho (1976) *Trilogie des Wiedersehens*. Munich: Hanser.

Tan, Eugene K. B. (2008) 'A Union of Gender Equality and Pragmatic Patriarchy: International Marriages and Citizenship Laws in Singapore', *Citizenship Studies* 12(1): 73–89.

Thai, Hung Cam (2003) 'Clashing Dreams: Highly Educated Overseas Brides and Low-Wage US Husbands', in Barbara Ehrenreich and Arlie Russell Hochschild (eds), *Global Woman: Nannies, Maids, and Sex Workers in the New Economy*. London: Granta: 230–53.

Thomas, Alexander (ed.) (1996) *Psychologie interkulturellen Handelns*. Göttingen/Bern/Toronto/Seattle: Hogrefe/Verlag für Psychologie.

Thomas, Alexander (1999) 'Kultur als Orientierungssystem und Kulturstandards als Bausteine', *Institut für Migrationsforschung und Interkulturelle Studien IMIS-Beiträge*, no. 10: 91–130.

Tietze, Nikola (2001) *Islamische Identitäten: Formen muslimischer Religiosität junger Männer in Deutschland und Frankreich*. Hamburg: Hamburger Edition.

Treibel, Annette (1999) *Migration in modernen Gesellschaften: Soziale Folgen von Einwanderung, Gastarbeit und Flucht*. 2nd rev. edn, Weinheim and Munich: Juventa.

Treibel, Annette (2004) 'Wandern Frauen anders als Männer? Migrantinnen im Spannungsfeld von Befreiung und Zwang', in Johannes Müller and

Mattias Kiefer (eds), *Grenzenloses 'Recht auf Freizügigkeit'? Weltweite Mobilität zwischen Freiheit und Zwang*. Stuttgart: Kohlhammer: 45–64.

Truscheit, Karin (2007) 'Eizellenspende in Europa: Spanische Gene, deutsche Mutter', *Frankfurter Allgemeine Zeitung*, 4 December.

UNFPA State of the World Population (2006) *A Passage to Hope: Women and International Migration*. New York: United Nations Population Fund.

Van Dülmen, Richard (1990) *Kultur und Alltag in der Frühen Neuzeit*, Vol. 1: *Das Haus und seine Menschen*. Munich: C. H. Beck.

Vertovec, Steven (2004) 'Cheap Calls: The Social Glue of Migrant Transnationalism', *Global Networks* 4(2): 219–24.

Vertovec, Steven (2009) *Transnationalism*. London and New York: Routledge.

Vetter, Stephanie (2001) 'Partnerwahl und Nationalität: Heiratsbeziehungen zwischen Ausländern in der Bundesrepublik Deutschland', in Thomas Klein (ed.), *Partnerwahl und Heiratsmuster: Sozialstrukturelle Voraussetzungen der Liebe*. Opladen: Leske & Budrich: 207–31.

Waldman, Ellen (2006) 'Cultural Priorities Revealed: The Development and Regulation of Assisted Reproduction in the United States and Israel', *Health Matrix: Journal of Law-Medicine* 16: 65–106.

Walt, Vivienne (2008) 'Field of Dreams', *Time*, 30 June: 42–9.

Watzlawick, Paul, Beavin, Janet H., and Jackson, Don D. (1972) *Menschliche Kommunikation: Formen, Störungen, Paradoxien*. Bern, Stuttgart and Vienna: Hans Huber.

Weber, Max ([1922] 1979) *Economy and Society*, trans. Ephraim Fischoff et al. Berkeley: University of California Press.

Weiler, Jan (2003) *Maria, ihm schmeckt's nicht: Geschichten von meiner italienischen Sippe*. Berlin: Ullstein Taschenbuch.

Wießmeier, Brigitte (1993) *Das 'Fremde' als Lebensidee: Eine empirische Untersuchung bikultureller Ehen in Berlin*. Münster and Hamburg: LIT.

Williams, Patricia J. (1997) *Seeing a Colour-Blind Future: The Paradox of Race*. London: Virago.

Withrow, Emily (2007) 'The Market for Human Eggs Goes Global, and Multiplies', *International Herald Tribune*, 30 January.

Zakaria, Rafia (2010) 'The Cheapest Womb: India's Surrogate Mothers', *Ms Magazine* blog, 25 June.

Index